Contemporary Studies in Scripture

An exciting new series from Greg Kofford Books featuring authors whose works engage in rigorous textual analyses of the Bible and other LDS scripture. Written by Latter-day Saints for a Latter-day Saint audience, these books utilize the tools of historical criticism, literature, philosophy, and the sciences to celebrate the richness and complexity found in the standard works. This series will provide readers with new and fascinating ways to read, study, and re-read these sacred texts.

Other titles in the Contemporary Studies in Scripture series:
Authoring the Old Testament: Genesis–Deuteronomy
Re-reading Job: Understanding the Ancient World's Greatest Poem
Search, Ponder, and Pray: A Guide to the Gospels
Beholding the Tree of Life: A Rabbinic Approach to the Book of Mormon
The Vision of All: Twenty-five Lectures on Isaiah in Nephi's Record
Textual Studies of the Doctrine and Covenants: The Plural Marriage Revelation

Gathered in One

Gathered in One

How the Book of Mormon Counters Anti-Semitism in the New Testament

Bradley J. Kramer

Greg Kofford Books
Salt Lake City, 2019

Copyright © 2019 Bradley J. Kramer
Cover design copyright © 2019 Greg Kofford Books, Inc.
Cover design by Loyd Ericson

Published in the USA.

All rights reserved. No part of this volume may be reproduced in any form without written permission from the publisher, Greg Kofford Books. The views expressed herein are the responsibility of the author and do not necessarily represent the position of Greg Kofford Books.

Paperback ISBN: 978-1-58958-709-0
Hardcover ISBN: 978-1-58958-710-6
Also available in ebook.

Greg Kofford Books
P.O. Box 1362
Draper, UT 84020
www.gregkofford.com
facebook.com/gkbooks
twitter.com/gkbooks

Library of Congress Control Number: 2019948722

To Elder Rosenbaum

Contents

Preface, ix
Acknowledgments, xiii
1. Gathered in One, 1
2. A Book Proceeded Forth, 7
3. A Record to Establish the Truth of the First, 39
4. We Did Observe to Keep the Commandments, 67
5. Think Not That I Am Come to Destroy the Law, 91
6. That the Last May Be First and the First May Be Last, 113
7. I Will Gather Them In, 137
Bibliography, 143
Scripture Index, 147
Subject Index, 155

Preface

Few words are as elusive or as explosive as "anti-Semitism."[1] Technically "anti-Semitism" (or, as it is sometime rendered, "antisemitism") is limited to ideas and practices that encourage hostility, prejudice, or discrimination towards Jews as a race or people. Consequently, many of the ideas and practices discussed in this book could be more accurately labeled "anti-Judaic" since they seem to condemn Judaism and its adherents without censuring—or attacking—all Jews regardless of their religious affiliation. However, because several of the sources I quote use the term "anti-Semitism" to encompass both anti-Judaism and anti-Semitism proper and because in practice these two approaches are often intertwined, I have opted to use "anti-Semitic" as the more inclusive and commonly used term. Unfortunately, there is no elegant antonym for "anti-Semitism." Therefore, I have enlisted "pro-Judaic" and "pro-Jewish" for this purpose.

Nonetheless, despite this explanation, some readers may conclude, especially after reading Chapter 2, that by using the word "anti-Semitism" in connection with the New Testament my real goal in writing *Gathered in One* is to build up the Book of Mormon by tearing down the New Testament. This, however, is not so. Even for a non-traditional Christian such as myself, the New Testament is essential, even irreplaceable. The Book of Mormon may testify of Jesus's miraculous birth, but it does not relate the stories that bring that birth to life. The Book of Mormon may also speak generally of Jesus's marvelous earthly ministry, but it lacks many of the particulars that make that ministry marvelous: the parables of the lost sheep and of the prodigal son, the call to render unto Caesar the things that are Caesar's, the invitation to those who are sinless to cast the first stone, the observation that those who live by the sword will perish by

---

1. For an understanding of the issues surrounding this term, see John G. Gager, *The Origins of Anti-Semitism: Attitudes Toward Judaism in Pagan and Christian Antiquity*, 7–10.

the sword. The Book of Mormon may even testify of Jesus's Atonement and resurrection and ratify the reality of these achievements with an appearance by the risen Jesus in the New World after his death in the Old. However, as affirming as this account is, it does not recount the details of these achievements: Jesus's prayers at Gethsemane, his suffering at Golgotha, his burial in a borrowed sepulcher, or his unexpected appearance to Mary in the garden. And without these details, playing quietly in the background as it were, unspoken but not unremembered, the power of this appearance would be greatly diminished. Indeed without the New Testament, Latter-day Saint Christianity—*my* Christianity—would seem meager, anemic, threadbare, hardly Christian at all.

And yet, there are problems with the way the New Testament presents Jews and Judaism, which even traditional Christians find disturbing. Consequently, in my second chapter I rely mainly on the writings of committed Christian scholars, teachers, and ministers as I attempt to show—as gently as I can—how the New Testament encourages an anti-Semitic point of view despite their best efforts to discourage it. To be clear, I do not blame Jesus or his apostles for this situation. Undoubtedly, they had issues with some Jews, contemporaries of theirs, people living and working around them. However, I do not believe they hated all Jews everywhere, nor do I think that they considered Jews inherently evil or corrupt. After all, Jesus and his apostles were Jews themselves—as were their closest neighbors, followers, family members, and friends. Neither do I condemn the original writers of the New Testament. As I see them, they were simply attempting to spread the "good news" of Jesus as best they could during a time when "Christianity" (the term had not yet been coined) was still working out its relationship with what would become mainstream Judaism. These writers did not know how their works would eventually be arranged, nor did they foresee what effect their words would have cumulatively on their readers. Nonetheless, there can be no doubt that many readers of the New Testament, past and present, have found within its pages support for anti-Semitic agendas.

Consequently, in the chapters that follow my second chapter, I attempt to show how the Book of Mormon refutes such agendas: first, by expanding the Christian canon and, second, by adding to it pro-Jewish statements, portrayals, settings, and structure. In this way, the Book of Mormon counters anti-Semitism the same way the New Testament supports it—*literally*, using artistic devices common to novels, short stories, and tales, and it does so *respectfully*, without challenging the New

Testament's text or undermining its religious authority, reliability, or credibility. As a result, the elements in the New Testament that foster anti-Semitic attitudes and behaviors are not deleted or destroyed; they are instead detoxified, their poison either diluted or eliminated entirely by a flood of similar elements from the Book of Mormon, elements that promote a more positive view of Jews, Judaism, and the Mosaic Law. It is my hope, consequently, that this book will bring about a deeper appreciation for the New Testament as well as for the Book of Mormon and will, in the end, foster a closer, more informed, more respectful relationship between Christians and Jews that will help dispel the dark shadow of anti-Semitism that hovers over Christianity still.

My readers may notice that in *Gathered in One* I rely almost entirely on the King James Version of the Bible for my biblical quotations. I do so not because I believe this version is the most accurate, most clear, or most popular translation (especially for modern Jews), but because the Book of Mormon was originally translated into a style very similar to King James English, and therefore the ties between its text and that of the New Testament are most evident when used in connection with this version. When I divert from this practice or when my sources use other versions, I make this plain either in the text or in a footnote. All emphases or italicized words within scriptural quotations are my own.

Acknowledgements

Since the bulk of this book was first drafted at the same time as *Beholding the Tree of Life*, I must thank many of the same people I thanked in that book: President Von R. Nielsen; Rabbis John Friedman and Leah Berkowitz, as well as the other members of the Judea Reform Congregation; Bishop Matthew Nelson, the Chapel Hill 1st Ward, and the Durham Stake Relief Society; Professors Matt Grey and Dana Pike; as well as Jim Maxwell, Artha Lubeck, Anson and M'Liss Dorrance, C.L. Kendell, and Loyd Ericson.

In addition, I want to thank others who contributed to this book: Bishop Michael Kosorok; Rabbis Darryl Crystal, Larry Bach, and John Franken; my patient friends of the Durham Area Jewish History Book Club, who eagerly answered my many questions about them and their faith; my extremely tolerant Institute students, who allowed me to try out many of my ideas on them; and Ryan Webb, who provided me with this unique teaching opportunity. I also must make special mention of Richard D. Rust, Terryl L. Givens, Jason A. Kerr, Abby Parcell, Jason R. Combs, Sarah Street, and Amy-Jill Levine, who, although they contributed significantly to my previous book, reviewed several chapters of this book and made major contributions to it as well. Thank you, my dear friends.

Also, since this book is fundamentally about appreciating religious diversity, I must thank in particular my parents for rearing me in a bireligious home in several multireligious areas. For it was in Cincinnati, Los Altos, and Dayton that I was taught the value of listening before speaking, of thinking before reacting, and of postponing judgment until I understood better why people do what they do, say what they say, and believe what they believe. I am also grateful to my parents for moving me around so much as a child and for teaching me through that experience to be sensitive to people who are new or different or simply shy. My parents felt guilty about these many moves and worried about their effect on me, but in the end, I think the effect was helpful, even healthy.

In addition, I am grateful for the Baptist, Baha'i, Catholic, Jewish, Hindu, Muslim, New Age, Wiccan, and agnostic women and men I have worked with over the years, caring colleagues and friends who forced me, sometimes against my will, to confront my own faith and to engage it in dialogue with theirs. I must also thank my children, my grandchildren, and especially my wife, who went with me to countless Jewish services, musical events, lectures, movies, museums, get-togethers, and parties. For it was through her eyes that I gained my most moving insights into the joys Latter-day Saints have in store for them as they learn more about Judaism and the Jewish people. Thank you, Nance.

Chapter One

Gathered in One

And it shall come to pass that the Jews shall have the words of the Nephites, and the Nephites shall have the words of the Jews; and the Nephites and the Jews shall have the words of the lost tribes of Israel; and the lost tribes of Israel shall have the words of the Nephites and the Jews. And it shall come to pass that my people, which are of the house of Israel, shall be gathered home unto the lands of their possessions; and my word also shall be gathered in one. And I will show unto them that fight against my word and against my people, who are of the house of Israel, that I am God, and that I covenanted with Abraham that I would remember his seed forever. (2 Ne. 29:13–14)

The Book of Mormon is unique. Simply as literature, it stands alone. No book leads up to it, and no book follows it. Although published in an influential time and place in American literature (1830, upstate New York), the Book of Mormon is entirely without a contemporary literary context. Its epic setting, transoceanic sweep, larger-than-life heroes, and universal themes hearken back more to *The Odyssey* and to *Beowulf* than to *Edgar Huntley* and *Rip Van Winkle*.[1] Its intricately arranged poetic expressions, complex forms based on the rhythm of ideas and images, resonate more with the words of the King James Bible than with the works of Bryant, Whittier, or Longfellow. And its overall narrative structure, a tapestry woven together from several sources, each with its own voice and personality, arises no more from Poe or Cooper than it is built upon by Hawthorne or Melville. Put simply, the Book of Mormon is an anomaly, an aberration, a book-length oddity that bursts upon the nineteenth-century American literary scene fully formed, neither reflecting what has come before nor projecting what will come afterwards.

---

1. To read an extended discussion of the literary elements present in the Book of Mormon, see Richard Dilworth Rust, *Feasting on the Word: The Literary Testimony of the Book of Mormon.*

The Book of Mormon is also singular as a volume of scripture. Unlike the Hebrew Scriptures, the Book of Mormon does not present itself as an ancient work written to an ancient audience nor, like the Doctrine and Covenants, does it style itself a modern creation composed for modern readers. Instead it claims to be an *ancient* book written purposefully and prophetically for *modern* readers in a *modern* setting. In this way, for believers, the Book of Mormon is a blend of the timeless and the timely, the eternal and the immediate, the long view and the short. It is a "bridge scripture" that links biblical events with current concerns. Present-day relevance is consequently built into the Book of Mormon; it does not need to be added or imaginatively inserted.

Given the Book of Mormon's unique qualities as literature and as scripture, it is not surprising that it approaches contemporary Christian-Jewish relations in a way markedly dissimilar from anything previously undertaken. Written explicitly and unabashedly for "the convincing of the Jew and Gentile that Jesus is the Christ, the Eternal God" (title page), the Book of Mormon would seem to be just another salvo in the seemingly never-ending war of words between Christians and Jews—a war historically characterized by ignorance, insensitivity, prejudice, and, all too often, violence. However, nothing could be further from the truth. Rather than perpetuating this centuries-old conflict, the Book of Mormon seeks to end it, once and for all, *not* by forcing Jewish readers to capitulate, at last, to supposedly superior Christian logic or authority but instead by using its unique qualities to persuade Christians to cease contending with Jews and join with them in a kind of alliance, a mutually beneficial and deeply respectful relationship where the problems of the past are at last resolved and both parties can finally come together in peace.

Certainly, the Book of Mormon is not the only attempt to end this "war." The Roman Catholic Church, for instance, horrified by the Holocaust and stung by the prospect that it may have played a significant role in setting the stage for this unspeakable tragedy, began soon after World War II to cast aside many of its most anti-Semitically suspect practices and doctrines. In 1958, for example, it removed all references to Jewish "perfidy" and to the "perfidious" Jews from its Good Friday liturgy,[2] and in 1965 it issued an official declaration that deplored "displays of antisemitism directed against Jews at whatever time and by whomever." This declaration, called *Nostra Aetate* or "In Our Times," also addressed some

---

2. Jeremy Cohen, *Christ Killers: The Jews and the Passion from the Bible to the Big Screen*, 171.

of the causes of these displays, stating explicitly that the death of Jesus "cannot be ascribed indiscriminately to all the Jews living at the time nor to the Jews of today" and that "although the church is the new people of God, the Jews should not be represented as rejected by God or accursed, as if this followed from holy scripture."[3] The effect of *Nostra Aetate* was immense. Not only was it followed by additional efforts within the Catholic Church to change the way Jews were portrayed in its preaching, textbooks, and passion plays, but it also led the way for similar declarations from most mainline Protestant churches.[4] For example, in 1972 the Southern Baptist Convention formally adopted a resolution encouraging its members "to combat anti-Semitism in every honorable, Christian way"[5]; in 1994 the Evangelical Lutheran Church in America similarly vowed to oppose "the deadly working of [anti-Semitic] bigotry, both within [their] own circles and in the society around [them]"[6]; and beginning in 1979 the World Council of Churches—a religious body representing three hundred and forty-eight Christian churches, denominations, and fellowships[7]— has repeatedly called upon its member organizations to denounce anti-Semitism, "no matter what its origin, as absolutely irreconcilable with the profession and practice of the Christian faith."[8]

Not all of these declarations have been put into practice as thoroughly as they could, or should, have been.[9] However, because of them and other similar efforts, overt anti-Semitic sentiments by Christians have decreased dramatically, especially in the United States. For example, Amy-Jill Levine, a Jewish New Testament scholar, cites polls indicating that by the end of the twentieth century the number of Americans who blamed the Jews for the death of Jesus went down to between 2 and 8 percent.[10] Rabbi Yechiel Eckstein, the founder of the International Fellowship of Christians and Jews, goes so far as to write that because of *Nostra Aetate* and other such efforts,

---

3. Norman Tanner, ed., *Vatican II: The Essential Texts*, 327.
4. Amy-Jill Levine, *The Misunderstood Jew: The Church and the Scandal of the Jewish Jesus*, 101.
5. Southern Baptist Convention, "Resolution On Anti-Semitism."
6. Church Council of the Evangelical Lutheran Church in America, "Declaration of ELCA to Jewish Community."
7. World Council of Churches, "What is the World Council of Churches?"
8. World Council of Churches, "Ecumenical Considerations on Jewish-Christian Dialogue."
9. Levine, *Misunderstood Jew*, 169–71.
10. Levine, 101.

today, virtually all of the negative, classical stereotypes of Jews, which at one time were pervasive among Christians and central to the church's teachings, have been eliminated from official church doctrine and, increasingly, from practice.[11]

Nonetheless, this does not mean that Christian anti-Semitism has completely disappeared in the United States or elsewhere. As several Jewish scholars are quick to point out, it still lurks on the sides of a deceptively quiet battlefield, poised, ready to pounce in the form of the New Testament. Trude Weiss-Rosmarin, for instance, calls the New Testament a "virtual armory of anti-Jewish statements and utterances" and wonders, in the end, how helpful "the purging of Christian textbooks can be as long as the New Testament, sacred to all of Christianity," retains such statements and utterances.[12] Rabbi Irving Greenberg similarly states that "since the teaching of contempt [for the Jews] goes straight back to the Gospel accounts, . . . it is questionable whether anything less than full confession and direct confrontation with [the New Testament] can overcome it."[13] And Lillian C. Freudmann, after describing in detail how "nearly every book in the New Testament expresses slander and contempt for the Jews," likewise calls for the New Testament to be reevaluated by Christians in such a way as to "reduce and neutralize the pejorative portrayal of Jews" within it.[14]

Here is where the Book of Mormon comes in. Rather than simply denouncing Christian anti-Semitism with official church pronouncements or ecclesiastical resolutions, the Book of Mormon *engages* it at its New Testament source. Both literarily and scripturally, the Book of Mormon counters the New Testament's anti-Semitic suggestions without undermining its religious authority or spiritual reliability. Just as the Gospel of John (as a peer of the synoptic Gospels) adds information to the New Testament relative to Jesus without challenging the accounts of Matthew, Mark, or Luke, so the Book of Mormon (as a peer of the New Testament) adds information to the Christian canon relative to Jews without challenging the New Testament. Coming as they do from a scripture of seemingly equal stature and status, the Book of Mormon's many pro-Jewish statements, portrayals, settings, and structuring elements mix in with their anti-Semitic counterparts in the New Testament, overwhelming them with

---

11. Yechiel Eckstein, *What You Should Know About Jews and Judaism*, 281.
12. Trude Weiss-Rosmarin, *Judaism and Christianity: The Differences*, 95.
13. Irving Greenberg, *For the Sake of Heaven and Earth: The New Encounter between Judaism and Christianity*, 130.
14. Lillian C. Freudmann, *Antisemitism in the New Testament*, xi, 323.

their greater power, broader context, wider sweep, and closer connections to Judaism as it is practiced today. In this way, the Book of Mormon effectively "detoxifies" the New Testament, negating its anti-Jewish negativity, assaulting its supersessionist assaults, and attacking its anti-Mosaic attacks. And it does so respectfully, without altering the New Testament's words, interfering with the New Testament's ability to convey divine meaning, or casting doubt upon the New Testament's overall message of love, forgiveness, and peace. In fact, the Book of Mormon actually expands the New Testament's embrace messianically. By beating its anti-Semitic "swords" into more pro-Jewish "plowshares," the Book of Mormon paves the way for an Isaianic era of peace, a time when Christians are indeed gathered with Jews—as Jews—and both groups figuratively go "up to the mountain of the Lord" as one, to learn of his ways and to "walk in his paths" together (Isa. 2: 3–4).

Chapter Two

A Book Proceeded Forth

And the angel of the Lord said unto me: Thou hast beheld that the book proceeded forth from the mouth of a Jew; and when it proceeded forth from the mouth of a Jew it contained the fulness of the gospel of the Lord, of whom the twelve apostles bear record; and they bear record according to the truth which is in the Lamb of God. Wherefore, these things go forth from the Jews in purity unto the Gentiles, according to the truth which is in God. And after they go forth by the hand of the twelve apostles of the Lamb, from the Jews unto the Gentiles, thou seest the formation of that great and abominable church, which is most abominable above all other churches; for behold, they have taken away from the gospel of the Lamb many parts which are plain and most precious; and also many covenants of the Lord have they taken away. (1 Ne. 13:24–26)

It may shock some Christians to hear the New Testament referred to as a "virtual armory of anti-Jewish statements and utterances."[1] After all, as many followers of Jesus see it, the New Testament not only affirms the Mosaic commandment to love one's neighbor as one's self but expands this injunction to include enemies as well (Matt. 5:44; 22:39; Mark 12:31, 33; Luke 6:27, 35; 10:29–37; Lev. 19:18). Surely, a book that contains such magnanimous sentiments would not advocate hating anyone, much less the people Jesus walked among, talked to, and associated with during his mortal life. Nevertheless, there *are* many anti-Semitic statements, anti-Semitic portrayals, anti-Semitic settings, and anti-Semitic structures within the New Testament, and the problems these elements present are not easily solved, even by committed Christians equipped with time-tested historical, literary, and theological tools.

---

1. Trude Weiss-Rosmarin, *Judaism and Christianity: The Differences*, 95.

Anti-Semitic Statements

For instance, Matthew's infamous blood curse—"His blood be on us, and on our children" (Matt. 27:25)—has been described by at least one Jewish scholar as "the most glaring of New Testament anti-Semitic passages,"[2] and several Christian scholars are inclined to agree. George M. Smiga, Professor of Sacred Scripture at Saint Mary Seminary and a Catholic priest, calls this curse "notorious"[3]; Scot McKnight, Professor of New Testament at Northern Baptist Theological Seminary and an Anglican deacon, denounces it as "an embarrassment to modern Christian sensitivities"[4]; and Raymond E. Brown, professor emeritus at Union Theological Seminary and another Catholic priest, laments that it "has been used to support horrendous antiJudaism."[5] Again, to some Christians, such assessments may seem excessive, even overblown. However, the way this curse is portrayed in the New Testament, extending it to all Jews everywhere throughout time, makes them appear almost understated.

The Problem of the Blood Curse

In chapter 27 of the Gospel of Matthew, Pilate presents Jesus to the Jewish multitude (v. 24). It is Passover, and, according to this Gospel, "at that feast the governor was wont to release unto the people a prisoner" of their choosing (v. 15). Pilate consequently asks those assembled whom he should set free, Barabbas or Jesus, and they, the Jewish multitude, having been persuaded by the "chief priests and elders" (v. 20), choose Barabbas. Pilate then asks this group what should be done with Jesus, and "they *all* say unto him, Let him be crucified" (v. 22). The Roman governor has received his answer. However, he is not satisfied. He protests and asks the Jewish crowd what evil Jesus has done to merit such a death. Again "they cried out the more, saying, Let him be crucified" (v. 23). The increasing specificity and intensity of the crowd's responses seem to exceed what the priests and elders required and suggests that Jesus's death was indeed their true desire. In fact, when Pilate finally acquiesces to the multitude seemingly against his own wishes, "*all the people*" once again demand that Jesus

---

2. Samuel Sandmel, *Anti-Semitism in the New Testament?*, 66.
3. George M. Smiga, *Pain and Polemic: Anti-Judaism in the Gospels*, 86.
4. Scot McKnight, "A Loyal Critic: Matthew's Polemic with Judaism in Theological Perspective," 58.
5. Raymond E. Brown, *An Introduction to the New Testament*, 202n71.

be crucified, adding, "his blood be on *us*, and on *our children*" apparently on their own, without coaching or coercion (vv. 23–25).

Reread and reenacted as it has been for centuries as a traditional part of Good Friday services, this curse, according to the noted Jewish scholar Samuel Sandmel, has been "responsible for oceans of human blood and a ceaseless stream of misery and desolation."[6] The intent of these yearly renditions may have been to encourage increased love for and devotion to the suffering Jesus. However, the result has too often been to incite hatred against the Jews—not just for supposedly causing the death of Jesus long ago but for continually murdering him in their hearts. In this way, this New Testament scene helped to keep the cross of Jesus continually "going on before," but it also enlisted countless Christian "soldiers"—from crusaders to Cossacks, Nazis to next-door neighbors—and marched them as to war, not against sin, intolerance, and pride, but against the Jews. As Levine writes, "From this verse, generations of Christians over hundreds of years concluded that all Jews for all times . . . bore special responsibility for the death of Jesus. The guilt is inherited; it is a stain on Jewish identity; all Jews are 'Christ killers.'"[7]

Although this curse is ostensibly the culminating scene in the trial of Jesus, the innocence of Jesus is never in doubt. What is really being determined is the extent of Jewish guilt, and here the verdict could hardly be more harsh. It is the Jews, after all, who are the "sinners" into whose hands Jesus is being betrayed (Matt. 26:45). It is they who make up the "great multitude" who come "as a thief with swords and staves" to take him (vv. 47, 55). And it is they who lay "hold on Jesus" and lead him "away to Caiaphas the high priest, where the scribes and the elders were assembled" (v. 57). Literally, it is the Jews then, not Jesus, who have been brought before Pilate, charged with blasphemy, and confronted with their own complicity in his death. And now, before all of its readers, the Gospel of Matthew passes judgment on the Jews, not only pronouncing them guilty but, in a sense, inviting its readers to scourge and mock and ultimately execute them, just as these ancient Jews allegedly did Jesus.

---

6. Samuel Sandmel, *A Jewish Understanding of the New Testament,* 164. Rabbi Sandmel, now deceased, was Professor of Bible and Hellenistic literature at Hebrew Union College Jewish Institute of Religion, and the author of many books on Jewish and Bible studies.

7. Amy-Jill Levine, *The Misunderstood Jew: The Church and the Scandal of the Jewish Jesus,* 99.

A Possible Solution

In the spirit of *Nostra Aetate* and other such efforts, several committed Christian scholars have begun, in recent decades, to do just as Rabbi Greenberg suggests and confront the anti-Semitic elements present in the New Testament, beginning with the blood curse. Eugene Fisher, for example, a Catholic official, doubts that this curse was ever uttered. According to him, it is noteworthy that it is found only in Matthew's Gospel and that the author of this Gospel includes a number of additions to the Gospel of Mark that, according to Fisher, were "dictated by the pressure of [the author's times."[8]

Following Father Brown and what he approvingly calls "the common scholarly view,"[9] Fisher sees the Gospel of Matthew as an expansion of the Gospel of Mark, a work composed a decade or so earlier from oral sources sometime in the late 60s or early 70s.[10] This means that the Gospel of Matthew was compiled some "forty to fifty years" after the events it describes,[11] at a time when, according to Fisher, "the survival of the Church depended on Roman tolerance."[12] Then, the teachings of Jesus were beginning to spread throughout the Roman Empire, and some believers were already being persecuted and killed by Roman authorities in certain isolated locales.[13] Consequently, Fisher is not surprised that several of the Matthean additions to Mark served "to improve the image of Pilate," which was already somewhat mitigated in the Gospel of Mark.[14] As he points out, the Gospel of Matthew is the only Gospel that includes the scene where Pilate's wife warns him to have nothing to do with Jesus—"that *just* man"—as well as the scene where Pilate washes his hands and proclaims himself "innocent of the blood of this *just* person" (27:19, 24).[15]

---

8. Eugene J. Fisher, *Faith without Prejudice: Rebuilding Christian Attitudes toward Judaism*, 78. Eugene Fisher was the Director of the Secretariat for Catholic-Jewish Relations of the National Conference of Catholic Bishops from 1977 until 2007.

9. Raymond E. Brown, *An Introduction to the New Testament*, 7.

10. Fisher, *Faith without Prejudice*, 29.

11. For a complete description of the generally accepted scholarly view of the sources and composition of the three Synoptic Gospels, see Bart Ehrman, *The New Testament: A Historical Introduction to the Early Christian Writings*, 84–90.

12. Fisher, *Faith without Prejudice*, 77.

13. Ehrman, *The New Testament*, 430.

14. Fisher, *Faith without Prejudice*, 78.

15. Fisher, 78–79 (bullet points added).

Here, Pilate appears to recognize Jesus's goodness and to distance himself from the man, personally and officially. As Fisher notes, in this way the author of Matthew adds "small but significant phrases" to Mark's account that seem to absolve Pilate of any guilt concerning Jesus's execution.

As an example, Fisher contrasts the two descriptions of the Barabbas scene as they appear in the Gospels of Mark and Matthew:

- Mark 15:15. "So, Pilate, wishing to satisfy the crowd, released to them Barabbas; but Jesus he scourged and delivered to be crucified."
- Matthew 27:26. "Then he (Pilate) released to them Barabbas; but Jesus he scourged and delivered *to them* to be crucified."[16]

As Fisher concludes, the seemingly small addition of "to them" in the last part of this verse in Matthew shifts all responsibility for Jesus's death away from Pilate to the Jews, something Fisher calls historically "doubtful."[17] In summary, rather than "pure history," Fisher sees the blood curse as something the writer of Matthew added in order to appease Roman sensitivity. For him, the historical answer to the question "Who killed Jesus?" is uncertain. As he writes, "while individual Jews may have played a part, it is far from clear whether they played that role because they were Jewish or because they were under the control of the Roman governor."[18]

Marilyn Salmon, an Episcopal priest, concurs with Fisher's assessment and expands upon it. According to her, the entire Barabbas scene is improbable—especially the portrayal of Pilate as weak, indecisive, and merciful. She writes, "There is no extra-biblical evidence that there existed a custom of releasing a prisoner during the Passover feast."[19] On the contrary, "primary sources consistently witness to Pilate's ruthlessness and cruelty toward his subjects." As Salmon explains,

> Pontius Pilate, procurator from 26 to 36 C.E., antagonized Jewish sensibilities by bringing military standards with Roman images into Jerusalem, thus violating the commandment against graven images. Pilate ignored the Jews' request that the standards be removed, threatening to kill the resisters, until the people demonstrated that they were prepared to die rather than allow the presence of Caesar's images. Pilate's confiscation of funds from the Temple

---

16. Fisher, 78.
17. Fisher, 78.
18. Fisher, 73.
19. Marilyn J. Salmon, *Preaching without Contempt: Overcoming Unintended Anti-Judaism*, 133. Marilyn Salmon is an Associate Priest at St. Clement's Episcopal Church in St. Paul, as well as professor of New Testament at United Theological Seminary of the Twin Cities, also in St. Paul.

treasury further infuriated the people; he infiltrated the angry crowd of protestors with disguised troops to kill them. Pilate was removed from his office and recalled to Rome after he ordered an attack on unarmed Samaritans on a pilgrimage.[20]

As to why the Gospel of Matthew is so generous regarding Pilate, Salmon notes that shifting the blame from Pilate to the Jews was something extremely prudent for Christians to do in the late first century CE. As she explains, "in the light of the recent [Jewish] revolt and considering the dominant culture, it is not surprising the Gospel writers downplay Roman involvement and emphasize instead religious motives for Jesus' death."[21]

Salmon's coreligionist John Shelby Spong agrees with her. Although writing with "the passion of a believer," he calls the Barabbas scene a "gospel invention, a literary device created to help exonerate the Roman governor" and to acquit the entire Roman Empire of any guilt with respect to Jesus's death.[22] Spong continues,

> So bitter was [the Roman war against the Jews, 66 to 73 CE] that the Jews . . . became anathema to the Romans for the next few generations. The Christian Church, already alienated from the rigid orthodoxy of Judaism and becoming less Jewish and more gentile during these years, thus attempted to gain for its members the favor of the ruling Roman authorities.

Consequently, "Christians busied themselves with the political task of shifting the blame for Jesus's death from the Romans to the Jerusalem Jews in any way they could."[23] The blood curse therefore was simply one of their more successful efforts to accomplish this task.

John Dominic Crossan, a former Catholic priest, calls the blood curse and the scene that surrounds it something much more serious:

> Knowing, on one hand, what I do about Pilate as an ordinary second-class governor, of his ten-year tenure and his eventual removal, of his attitude toward Jewish religious sensitivities and his tactics toward unarmed but demanding crowds, and on the other hand, of Christian reasons for increasing the responsibility of Jewish and decreasing that of Roman participants in the crucifixion, there can be only one *relatively plausible* conclusion. That reiterated juxtaposition of Jewish demands for Jesus' crucifixion and Roman

---

20. Salmon, 136.
21. Salmon, 145.
22. John Shelby Spong, *Liberating the Gospels: Reading the Bible with Jewish Eyes*, 20, 272. John Shelby Spong was bishop of the Episcopal Diocese Newark, New Jersey before he retired in 2000.
23. Spong, 274.

declarations of Jesus' innocence is not prophecy, and neither is it history. It is Christian propaganda.[24]

Crossan explains that such propaganda can be both "inspired" as well as "innocent"—at least initially. The blood curse and the scenes that surround it had little outside effect as long as "Christians were the marginalized and disenfranchised ones." However, "once the Roman Empire became Christian, that fiction turned lethal" and therefore was rendered indefensible. As Crossan eloquently concludes,

> In the light of later Christian anti-Judaism and eventually of genocidal anti-Semitism, it is no longer possible in retrospect to think of that passion fiction as relatively benign propaganda. However explicable its origins, defensible its invectives, and understandable its motives among Christians fighting for survival, its repetition has now become the longest lie, and, for our own integrity, we Christians must at last name it as such.[25]

Anti-Semitic Portrayals

However, rejecting the blood curse and the scene that surrounds it as ahistorical, although helpful, does not, by itself, solve the larger problem of an anti-Semitic reading of the Gospel of Matthew as a whole. Such a reading is not based on a single statement or on one particular scene. Anti-Semitic rhetoric pervades this Gospel, especially in its portrayal of the Pharisees, the ancestors of rabbinic Jews.[26] According to the Gospel of Matthew, the Pharisees are beneath contempt. They are hypocritical (Matt. 16:3), judgmental (9:11), rule-bound (12:2), scheming (v. 14), stupid (v. 24), sign-seeking (v. 38), superficial (15:1), easily offended (v. 12), spiritually blind (v. 14), corrupt (12:33), petty (23:23), tricky (22:15), prideful (16:6), and murderous (12:14). The rhetoric is relentless and merciless.

---

24. John Dominic Crossan, *Who Killed Jesus?: Exposing the Roots of Anti-Semitism in the Gospel Story of the Death of Jesus*, 152. John Dominic Crossan taught at St. Mary of the Lake Seminary and at Catholic Theological before resigning his priesthood. Afterwards he taught comparative religion at DePaul University from 1969 until 1995.

25. Crossan 152.

26. Sandmel, *A Jewish Understanding of the New Testament*, 26.

The Problem of Matthew

Perhaps, as some Christian scholars have suggested, the original intent here was to pit Jesus's Judaism against Pharisaic Judaism and not to blast away at all Jews in general.[27] However, the number of anti-Pharisaic accusations as well as the power and extent of their insinuations make it difficult for many readers to see them as precision strikes. By the time the blood curse is uttered, near the end of the Gospel of Matthew, corrupt Sadducees, duplicitous scribes, prideful elders, and scheming priests have merged with hypocritical Pharisees to form a single mass of anti-Christian murderers—all Jewish. It is therefore not surprising, given this merging, to hear "all the people" cry out for the blood of Jesus (Matt. 27:25). At this point, *all Jews* have become Christ killers, if not in fact at least by inference. When Jesus is nailed to the cross, "they"—generic Jews, not Pharisees or Sadducees—pass him by, "wagging their heads" and saying, "Thou that destroyest the temple, and buildest it in three days, save thyself" (vv. 39–40). As he hangs there, "some of them," members of this nonspecific group of Jews, hear him cry out "Eli, Eli, lama sabachthani?" "One of them" gives him vinegar to drink but "the rest" taunt him, saying, "Let be, let us see whether Elias will come to save him" (vv. 46–49). Furthermore, when Jesus finally dies and "the graves were opened," it is a Roman centurion who testifies that Jesus is "the Son of God" (vv. 52–54)—compared to what "is commonly reported among *the Jews*" that Jesus's resurrection was fabricated by "his disciples [who] came by night, and stole [his body] away" (28:15).

In other words, it is not Jesus who is ultimately on trial in the Gospel of Matthew. It is the Jews, and their sentence is handed down long before the blood curse is uttered. Several chapters earlier, Jesus, as the supreme judge, foreshadows Matthew's final verdict by pronouncing the scribes and Pharisees guilty of "all righteous blood shed upon the earth" (23:35) and by stating that they will continue to "kill and crucify" prophets and wise men, persecuting them "from city to city" presumably until the end of time (v. 34). In other words, the main message of the Gospel of Matthew then may indeed be, as Sandmel suggests, that Jesus is a "new and greater Moses."[28] However, in presenting this message, this Gospel also portrays the Jews just as clearly and just as powerfully as the new and

---

27. Robert A. Spivey, D. Moody Smith, and C. Clifton Black, *Anatomy of the New Testament*, 111.

28. Sandmel, *Anti-Semitism in the New Testament*, 51.

lesser Egyptians, a people so hard-hearted that they seek to enslave and murder those who attempt to follow Jesus (19:8). Consequently, if the Red Sea or some other catastrophe were to engulf them, so be it. They deserve such treatment. As the Gospel of Matthew presents them, Jews are not meant to be mourned.

A Possible Solution

Recognizing the pervasive problem with anti-Semitism present in the Gospel of Matthew, several modern Christian scholars have broadened their historical approach. Fisher, for instance, very much affirms that the Gospel of Matthew is "the inspired word of God." However, he explains that this Gospel, along with the Gospel of John, has been "historically conditioned"—meaning that "the passions and crises of the times in which [it was] written are reflected in the way their human authors retold the story of Jesus."[29] As Fisher writes, these two Gospels were composed not long after the fall of the Second Temple—Matthew in the 80s and John in the 90s—at a time when the Church had become dominated by Gentile converts and had consequently "begun to lose its original, close identification with Judaism."[30] This situation caused a great deal of tension between Christians and Jews, tension which most certainly included inflammatory accusations as well as reasoned debates—all of which are reflected in these Gospels. Fisher writes,

> These later Gospel writers are relying on long oral traditions for their reconstruction of the story of Jesus, and neither is writing "history" in our modern sense of newspaper reporting. Rather, they are seeking to make the meaning of the Christ-event come alive for the readers of their own time. Jesus' sayings are at times placed into contexts different from those in which they were originally spoken. Sometimes the material is arranged in such a way as to illustrate a theological interpretation applying a statement to a current debate at the time of writing. At other times, key words are added or omitted so that the original saying can be seen as relevant to an issue current in the late first century.[31]

The Gospel of Matthew's portrayal of the Pharisees then, like its presentation of the blood curse, reflects issues the Christian community was dealing with at the time of its writing and was not limited to those Jesus

---

29. Fisher, *Faith without Prejudice*, 56.
30. Fisher, 62.
31. Fisher, 59.

dealt with during his. As Sandmel explains, when Jesus lived it was the Sadducees, not the Pharisees, who were the "party of the Temple and of the court." At that time, the Sadducees were the aristocracy, the nobility, the hereditary elite, the politically powerful, the economically endowed; and therefore they were the people who were not only most susceptible to hypocrisy and corruption but the group in the best position to oppose Jesus institutionally. The Pharisees, on the other hand, were the "party of the synagogue and the Bible."[32] They were the party that taught the "tradition of the elders" (15:2). They were also the party of the people, coming primarily from the middle and lower classes,[33] and the party whose teachings were the closest to Jesus's. As Sandmel notes, Jesus's rendition of the Golden Rule is simply the positive version of Hillel's, a major figure in the Pharisaic tradition,[34] and the Lord's Prayer contains phrases that later appear in the Talmud, a book built upon the same.[35] In addition, Marvin R. Wilson writes that Jesus's teachings "show closest affinity to that of the Pharisees" than any other Jewish sect. As he writes, "It has been estimated that one can find parallels in rabbinic literature to perhaps as much as ninety percent of Jesus teachings."[36] Other well-qualified scholars even go so far as to claim that Jesus was himself a Pharisee or at least "sympathized with or respected the Pharisees."[37]

However, this situation changed radically in 70 CE when Jerusalem was conquered by the Romans and its temple destroyed. With no power base, the Sadducees seem to disappear from history, and Pharisaism, in the form of rabbinic Judaism,[38] eventually triumphs so completely that, as Sandmel explains, it soon became virtually interchangeable with Judaism itself.[39] Such

---

32. Sandmel, *A Jewish Understanding of the New Testament*, 25.

33. Lawrence H. Schiffman, *From Text to Tradition: A History of the Second Temple & Rabbinic Judaism*, 105.

34. Hillel the Elder, according to Jewish tradition, lived a generation before Jesus (110 BCE to 10 CE). He is revered as a sage and a scholar, especially among the Pharisees, as well as credited with founding a comparatively lenient school of Jewish thought, the House of Hillel, which came to dominate rabbinic Judaism and whose teachings figure prominently in both the Mishnah and the Talmud.

35. Sandmel, *A Jewish Understanding of the New Testament*, 150–51.

36. Marvin R. Wilson, *Our Father Abraham: Jewish Roots of the Christian Faith*, 40; Marvin R. Wilson, an evangelical Christian, was professor of Biblical and Theological Studies at Gordon College until he retired in 2018.

37. William Nicholls, *Christian Antisemistism: A History of Hate*, 55.

38. Schiffman, *From Text to Tradition*, 107

39. Sandmel , *A Jewish Understanding of the New Testament*, 26.

a process admittedly took time. However, things were certainly tending in that direction at the time the Gospel of Matthew was written. By that time, Pharisees *were* "the Jews" for many Gentiles, and as the party whose teachings were closest to Jesus's, they presented early Christians with their greatest threat, personally as well as theologically. Differentiating themselves from these rabbinic descendants of the Pharisees soon became a primary concern for these early Christians, and it is for this reason that, as Fisher explains, the Gospel of "Matthew often inserts the Pharisees into scenes in which other evangelists do not." It is also why the Matthean author "constructs some chapters, like the Sermon on the Mount, in such a way as to give the impression that Jesus is arguing with his fellow Pharisees": he is attempting to shore up his community's religious position relative to that of the Jews by placing them in direct conflict with Jesus. As Fisher adds, Matthew's Pharisees are "not the Pharisees of Jesus' time, but those of Matthew's own that the Gospel author is arguing against."[40]

In addition, early Christians wanted to distance themselves from Jews for other reasons. As alluded to earlier, the Jewish rebellion in 70 CE made the Jews extremely unpopular in the Roman Empire. Jews were viewed by many Romans as ungrateful traitors who had fought against a benevolent, civilizing, cultured regime. Is it therefore only natural that the author of the Gospel of Matthew attempted to increase the distance between his people and the despised Jews. As Fisher writes, this author was "struggling for the conversion of the Roman Empire," and therefore he "told the story of Jesus in a way that would most effectively promote this evangelization."[41] Since this is a time of tremendous theological and societal stress for Christians, being a tiny minority, this Gospel's portrayals are not entirely fair or objectively rendered. As a result, according to Fisher, the Gospel of Matthew contains "highly charged language," which gives the Gospel an "almost bitter tone" regarding Jews and Judaism.[42] However, this language may not be as condemnatory as it seems. As Fisher explains, this is the same kind of language used by the ancient Hebrew prophets, and therefore "one cannot conclude to an absolute indictment of Israel in Matthew any more than in Isaiah or Jeremiah." He continues that the author of "Matthew is writing a narrative, not a textbook on doctrine. To confuse emotional language stemming from conflicts in which

---

40. Fisher, *Faith without Prejudice*, 63.
41. Fisher, 57.
42. Fisher, 62, 64.

Matthew was a participant with the absolutism of dogma is to confuse imagery with theology."[43]

Another Possible Solution

Given his assessment of the Gospel of Matthew as a literary presentation, not a history, Fisher also offers another possible solution to the problem of anti-Semitic portrayals in the Gospel of Matthew. Following Irenaeus and other church fathers,[44] he suggests that readers "balance out" this Gospel with the other Gospels in order to separate its divine message from its anti-Semitic presentation. Fisher writes,

> Theologically, it is important to recognize that God inspired not one but four Gospels. . . . It is the New Testament *as a whole* that is inspired and is a source of divine truth for us. We cannot take one passage or one book in isolation from the whole and hope to interpret it correctly.[45]

Such an approach, according to Fisher, helps readers "reconstruct" the original message of the Gospels without the addition of anti-Semitic polemics—especially if they avail themselves of interpretive "tools, such as Gospel parallels, commentaries, and dictionaries of the Bible."[46]

However, for many, reading the Gospels together does *not* balance out the anti-Semitic qualities present in the Gospel of Matthew. In fact, in many ways reading the Gospels as a unit only serves to reinforce them. Certainly, the Gospels of Mark and Luke speak approvingly of the Deuteronomic commandment to love "thy neighbour as thyself" (Mark 12:31, Luke 10:27), and the Gospel of John describes Jesus as commanding his disciples to "love one another" as he has loved them (John 15:12). However, the love these Gospels promote does not seem to extend to Jews. This is particularly true for the Gospel of John. This Gospel, which many have called "the father of antisemitism,"[47] was written at least a decade after the Gospel of Matthew and reflects a world where the Christian community and that of mainstream Judaism are not only quickly separating but are openly antagonistic towards one another. In other words, if the Gospel of Matthew's anti-Semitism is like a pre-invasion artillery barrage,

---

43. Fisher, 64.
44. *Writings of Irenaeus*, trans. Alexander Roberts and W. H. Rambaut, 293–96.
45. Fisher, *Faith without Prejudice*, 57–58.
46. Fisher, 70.
47. Michael J. Cook, *Modern Jews Engage the New Testament: Enhancing Jewish Well-Being in a Christian Environment*, 219.

the Gospel of John's is more like a final assault, a major turning point in Christianity's "war" against the Jews. In this Gospel, the "bitter tone" of Matthew's Gospel has been replaced with outright contempt. All pretense of condemning Jews by disparaging their Pharisaic ancestors is gone. Here it is "the Jews" explicitly who question Jesus (John 2:18), who accuse him of being in league with the devil (8:48), and who instill fear in his followers (7:13; 19:38; 20:19). It is they, not the Pharisees, who repeatedly seek to slay Jesus (5:16, 18; 7:1; 10:31), cry out for his crucifixion, and, in the end, lead him away to be crucified (19:15–16).

Furthermore, "the Jews" in the Gospel of John represent more than simply Jesus's religious adversaries: they are evil incarnate, children of the devil (8:44), the opposite of everything Jesus stands for and teaches. In this Gospel's extremely dualistic world, Jesus is the Light, while the Jews are those who "abide in darkness" (12:46); Jesus comes so that "they which see not might see," but the Jews remain stubbornly blind to his teachings (9:39–40); and Jesus is the Word while they cannot understand his words. They, like Nicodemus, ask, "How can these things be?" but do not comprehend the answers offered them. In John's Gospel, "the Jews" are not able to receive "heavenly things" (3:9–12); they are from beneath while Jesus is from above; they are of this world while Jesus is not (8:23), and they, unlike the enlightened Jesus, love "darkness rather than light, because their deeds are evil" (3:19).

Anti-Mosaic Portrayals and Settings

But what exactly are these evil Jewish deeds? Certainly, the way Jews in the Gospel of John continually attempt to persecute and kill Jesus qualifies as an evil deed (5:16, 18; 7:1, 19; 8:40). However, so does the fact that they observe the Law of Moses. In this Gospel, the Law of Moses is consistently presented not so much as a set of spiritual instructions, a kind of guidebook to goodness, as it is a mass of overly exacting rules that pervert basic decency and counter common sense. For example, when Jesus miraculously heals a man who "had an infirmity thirty and eight years," the Mosaic Law-abiding "Jews" do not rejoice with the man or marvel at the unexpected kindness bestowed upon him from the Lord. Instead they focus on a relatively minor detail—the fact that he "took up his bed" afterwards—and rail against both him and his healing because such a thing is not lawful on the Sabbath (5:8–10). In addition, later on when Jesus causes a blind man to see by putting clay on his eyes, again on the Sabbath, a group of Jews similarly dismisses this miracle, claiming that Jesus "is not of God, because he keepeth not the sabbath day" (9:16). In the Gospel of John, there is no mention of the benefits from setting aside one day a week specifically to worship God, nor is there any hint of the peace brought about by resting weekly from one's menial chores. Instead the Sabbath's sole purpose, apparently, is to promote pettiness, to encourage small-mindedness, and to prevent people from actually helping each other.

The Problem of John, Mark, and Luke

Consistent with this skewed view of the Law of Moses, the Gospel of John goes to great lengths to distance Jesus from it. This Gospel shows Jesus, much like Pilate (18:31), referring to the Mosaic Law as *"your* law" (8:17; 10:34) when speaking to Jews, and *"their* law" (15:25) when speaking about Jews. It similarly calls Mosaic ablutions "the manner of the purifying of *the Jews"* (2:6) and dubs the day before Passover *"the Jews'* preparation day" (19:42), as though these ceremonies and events were completely unconnected to Jesus and his followers. In the Gospel of John, Mosaic festivals too are never something Jesus or his followers are associated with in any meaningful way. Passover is described as "a feast *of the Jews"* or *"the Jews'* Passover" (6:4; 2:13; 11:55), and Sukkot is referred to as *"the Jews'* feast of tabernacles" (7:2). Furthermore, in this Gospel there is no indication that Jesus actually participates in Mosaic festivals, at least religiously. Here, he never ritually eats unleavened bread, drinks the fruit of the vine, partakes of bitter herbs, or lives in a hastily built shelters commemorating the Jews' Exodus from Egypt. Instead Jesus seems to see these festivals only as opportunities for him to do or say something spectacular before a large group of people—driving out the money-changers from the temple, feeding the five thousand, proclaiming himself the bread of life, describing himself as the ultimate source of living water, or announcing his role as the "light of the world" (2:14–16; 6:4–11, 35; 7:37–38; 8:12).

However, the Jews who hear him do not react as one might expect religious celebrants to react. Instead of listening quietly and respectfully to Jesus's words, they question him and harass him (John 6:60–61); instead of showing tolerance, they murmur against him and are offended by him (v. 41); instead of going about their business peacefully, they seek to lay hands on him, take up stones to cast at him, and ultimately kill him (7:44; 8:59; 10:31). And they do this all during some of the holiest days on the Mosaic calendar. Festivals, in other words, like the Sabbath and other Mosaic practices, are consistently portrayed as observances that produce a kind of "anti-spirituality"—a hardened, vicious, even violent state of mind utterly incompatible with what many would call "pure religion" (James 1:27). Little wonder then that in the Gospel of John, the Jews do not cap off their cries for Jesus's crucifixion with "his blood be upon us and our children." Instead they shout, "We have a *law*, and by *our law* he ought to die" (John 19:7). Certainly, according to this Gospel, "the Jews" are culpable for Jesus's death, but so is the Law of Moses. It too is stained everlastingly with his blood.

Compared to the Gospel of John's all-out offensive, the attacks the Gospels of Mark and Luke launch against the Law of Moses are much less ambitious. In Luke, for instance, Jesus is circumcised when he was eight days old, and Mary presents him at the temple to be redeemed, all in accordance with the Law of Moses (Luke 2:21–22). Here too, a "just and devout" Jew takes the baby Jesus in his arms and blesses God for having allowed him to see "the glory of thy people Israel" (vv. 25–32). However, the fact that the Gospels of Mark and Luke contain a few pro-Jewish elements does not mean that they balance out the Gospel of Matthew as Fisher hopes. Far from it. In Mark and Luke, the Pharisees again seem to represent all Jews, and as such they remain confirmed hypocrites (Mark 7:6; Luke 11:44), people who consistently interfere with Jesus's work, seek to slay him at every opportunity (Mark 3:6, Luke 19:47), and are ultimately responsible for his crucifixion (Mark 15:13, Luke 23:21). Furthermore, in the Gospels of Luke and Mark, Mosaic practices are also presented as nonsensical activities that undermine the cause of righteousness. Here, maintaining religious purity is reduced to handwashing before meals (Mark 7:2–4, 7), offering temple sacrifices involves subsidizing thieves (Mark 11:15–17; Luke 19:45–46), and observing the Sabbath is presented not only as an impediment to alleviating suffering (Mark 3:2–3; Luke 6:6–11), as in the Gospel of John, but as a set of rules forbidding such innocent and innocuous activities as rubbing grains of wheat together as one walks through a field (Mark 2:23–24; Luke 6:1–2). In these Gospels, there is no mention of any of spiritual and practical benefits derived from observing the commandments contained in the Law of Moses or from participating in its festivals.

In addition, although the Gospels of Mark and Luke show Jesus presiding over a Passover meal and therefore present him as at least somewhat religiously connected with Mosaic festivals, this "Last Supper" is not the ultimate Seder. It is instead a hollow tradition, a custom utterly emptied of its original biblical significance as well as any connection to contemporary observance. Rather than affirming the Law of Moses, this meal demonstrates instead just how meaningless it is compared to the Gospel of Christ as well as how pointless any tradition is that is based upon this Law. In the Gospels of Mark and Luke, Jesus may indeed celebrate the "feast of unleavened bread" and drink the "fruit of the vine" (Mark 14:1, 25; Luke 22:1, 7, 15–20) in accordance with the Law of Moses, but he never discusses what these foods traditionally symbolize—the bitterness of Israel's captivity, the miracle of their deliverance, the joy they experience as God's special people—or acknowledge their ongoing significance and spirit. In fact, the appearance of bread and wine in this meal seems to serve only as an opportunity for Jesus to "Christianize" them, transforming these traditional Jewish symbols into remembrances of his soon-to-be lifeless body and spilled blood (Mark 14:24; Luke 22:20). In this way, the Gospels of Mark and Luke reinforce the anti-Mosaic position of the Gospel of John as well as the anti-Semitism present in the Gospel of Matthew—by *sacramentalizing* them, by using this Passover setting in order to change a joyous festival of life into a kind of never-ending funeral service where Jesus's death, as well as those who killed him, is continually remembered and the superiority of his way affirmed.

All in all, the Gospels of Mark and Luke may not assail the Jews as relentlessly as the Gospel of Matthew or attack the Law of Moses as fervently as the Gospel of John; however, they by no means renounce or even discontinue these efforts. Their attacks are more like surgical strikes than massive bombardments. Nonetheless, because these attacks are repeated regularly in the form of church rituals and liturgy and are often intensified by the presence of crosses, crucifixes, or other reminders of Jesus's death at the hands of Jews, they have wreaked—and continue to wreak—havoc on Jews by imprinting anti-Semitic ideas in the minds of church-attending Christians. As Freudmann writes, the Gospels "resemble morality plays with fixed and stylized roles assigned to each character. Romans, centurions, and Gentiles, together with Christians themselves, are 'the good guys.' Pharisees, Sadducees, scribes, priests, and teachers of the Law are the villains."[48] Reprising these roles week after week, month after month, year after year, century after century serves to transform them from exaggerations added mainly for dramatic effect into hard and fast facts that are difficult to dislodge. While the Gospels of Mark and Luke may not contain Matthew's blood curse, they help set the stage for

---

48. Freudmann, *Antisemitism in the New Testament*, 225.

such a cry by placing Pilate's trial of Jesus as well as what precedes it at the sacramental center of Christian worship, and they emphasize this by populating this trial with a cast of several thousand murderous, Mosaic-law abiding Jews.

A Possible Solution

Because the other Gospels, in the end, do not balance out the anti-Semitism present in the Gospel of Matthew, several scholars have extended their historical approach to them as well. This effort includes furnishing readers with the "tools" that Fisher recommends in order to better address this issue. The contributors to *The Jewish Annotated New Testament*, as might be expected, pay "special attention to passages that negatively stereotype Jews or groups of Jews," often providing notes that "contextualize them by showing how they are part of the exaggerated language of debate of the first century."[49] However, C. Clifton Black in the more religiously generic *HarperCollins Study Bible* also allows that the Gospel of Mark may have been shaped by the anti-Jewish feeling that existed at the time it was written. Pushing back the date of that composition further than Fisher and Brown, Black suggests that the Gospel of Mark was written during or soon after the first Jewish war with Rome and consequently reflected the anti-Jewish sentiment created by that war.[50] David L. Tiede, another contributor to the *HarperCollins Study Bible*, similarly pushes back the composition of Luke as well, to a time closer to that of Matthew than Mark, sometime between 85 and 95 CE. As he sees it, the Gospel of Luke shows evidence of the tension between Christians and Jews that came later, after the Great Jewish Revolt, when the Church became more Greek and less Jewish. As Tiede writes, the Gospel of Luke "is fundamentally concerned with addressing social and theological issues of crucial importance to the church of the author's own time," especially "the relation of Christian communities to the salvific legacy of Israel, on the one hand, and the political, religious, and social milieu of the Roman-dominated world, on the other." Given

---

49. Amy-Jill Levine and Marc Zvi Brettler, eds., *The Jewish Annotated New Testament*, , xi.

50. Harold W. Attridge, *HarperCollins Study Bible: New Revised Standard Version*, 1722–23. C. Clifton Black is professor of Biblical Theology at Princeton Theological Seminary and an elder in the United Methodist Church.

this situation, he advises his readers that they "would do well to keep these two levels in mind when reading the Gospel [of Luke]"[51]

Such helpful advice regarding the reading of the Gospel of Luke escalates into outright warnings when the contributors of the *HarperCollins Study Bible* turn their attention to the Gospel of John. Here in his preface to John, David K. Rensberger not only provides a much more lengthy introduction to its historical setting but offers a much more specific caution regarding the position of Jews in that Gospel:

> It is now widely recognized that [the apparent hostility between Jesus and "the Jews" in the Gospel According to John] reflects the circumstances not of Jesus himself but of a Christian group some years after his death. The Gospel according to John seems to have been written late in the first century in a specific Christian community that was undergoing a painful separation from the Jewish society to which its members had belonged. Their claim that Jesus was the Messiah, and indeed the Son of God, brought disciplinary action from the synagogue authorities. . . . For some, the punishment only emboldened their confession of belief. Others apparently sought to remain within the synagogue as secret Christians. . . .
>
> It is important to remember, then, that when John speaks of "the Jews," it does not refer to the Jewish people as a whole. . . . Generally, however, the ultimate referent seems to be the synagogue authorities of a particular time and place who were inimical to the Christian movement, although another option might be those Jewish believers whose faith, or their courage in expressing it, fell short in the writer's view. Most probably, the hostile debates between "the Jews" and Jesus in John indicate the intensity of the conflict between the synagogue authorities and the Jewish Christian community in which the Gospel was written.[52]

Anti-Supersessionist Epistles

In addition to advising Christians to avail themselves of study bibles and other helpful interpretive tools, Fisher also advocates using Paul's Epistles to counter the many anti-Semitic elements present in the Gospels.[53] These letters are central to his "balanced" approach and present the most promising "inside the Bible" solution to this problem.

---

51. *HarperCollins Study Bible*, 1759. David L. Tiede is a retired professor of New Testament and a one-time associate pastor at Trinity Lutheran Church in Minneapolis.

52. *HarperCollins Study Bible*, 1814–15. David K. Rensberger is a professor of New Testament at the Interdenominational Theological Center in Atlanta.

53. Fisher, *Faith without Prejudice*, 58.

Several of Paul's letters are known to have been written before the Jewish war.[54] Consequently, they are not so "historically conditioned," as Fisher puts it, and tend to present Jews and Judaism in much more positive ways. For one, Paul, in these Epistles, says little about Pharisaism, and, when he does, he presents it as something positive, even admirable. In the Letter to the Philippians, for instance, Paul proudly proclaims himself to be "of the stock of Israel, of the tribe of Benjamin, an Hebrew of the Hebrews" and describes himself as a Pharisee, blameless concerning the "the righteousness which is in the law" (Phil. 3:5–6). Secondly, although some people of Jewish background certainly opposed Paul, he does not resort to calling "the Jews" names, accusing them of rampant hypocrisy, or describing them in satanic, stereotypic terms. As Krister Stendahl, writes, "When Paul speaks about Jews, he really speaks about Jews, and not simply the fantasy Jews who stand as a symbol or as the prime example of a timeless legalism."[55] Thirdly, and most importantly, Paul in his letters does not seem concerned about who killed Jesus. For the most part, he instead focuses on why Jesus died and on what that death accomplished. For instance, Paul frequently comments on the people Jesus died for—the "ungodly" (Rom. 5:6), the sinners (v. 8), and the "weak brother" (1 Cor. 8:11)—as well as the purpose his death served—to make intercession for these people (Rom. 8:34), to redeem them from sin (1 Cor. 15:3), and to cause them to rise again (2 Cor. 5:15). Only in one passage does he appear to blame the Jews for Jesus's death (1 Thess. 2:14–15), and that passage is generally thought to have been written by someone else.[56]

The Problem of Augustine

For these and other reasons, the Pauline Epistles are often seen as crucial to the Christian effort to negotiate the New Testament's anti-Semitic

---

54. The undisputed letters of Paul (1st Thessalonians, Galatians, 1st and 2nd Corinthians, Philippians, Philemon, and Romans) were written between 49 CE and sometime before 64 CE, when Paul allegedly died. For more information, see Ehrman, *New Testament*, 286–88, 302, 360.

55. Krister Stendahl, *Paul among Jews and Gentiles*, 36–37. Krister Stendahl, now deceased, was at one time the Church of Sweden Bishop of Stockholm as well as dean of Harvard's Divinity School.

56. Sidney G. Hall III, *Christian Anti-Semitism and Paul's Theology*, 164n20. Sidney G. Hall III is a writer, pastor, and activist. He has been the senior minister of Trinity United Methodist Church in Austin, Texas, since 1988.

rhetoric, particularly as it pertains to supersessionism. Supersessionism is the doctrine that the Jews have been so disobedient for so long, failing to follow their own law as well as murdering its originator (Jesus), that their ancient connection to God has been revoked and replaced by a new covenant with Christian Gentiles. In this way supersessionism reinforces the blood curse by associating it with divine punishment, a punishment which Gentiles are encouraged to join in on. Augustine (an influential refiner of supersessionism) frequently taught that Jews are guilty of malice, evil, perversity, spite, envy, arrogance, and murder. All of them, not just a few specific Jewish priests or leaders in Jerusalem, were deemed by him to be responsible for Jesus's death and were consequently deserving of punishment.[57] However, as several scholars make clear, Augustine did not call for all Jews everywhere to be executed. Instead he proposed that they should be severely limited in their economic, political, and social opportunities. As he viewed them, Jews, like Cain, murdered a righteous innocent, and so, like Cain, they should be condemned to wander the earth as fugitives and vagabonds (Gen. 4:14), witnessing by their woeful state both the severity of their crime as well as the ultimate triumph of Jesus.[58] For Augustine, Jews are object lessons, in other words, living examples of the misery that comes to those who reject Jesus and his church.

A Promising Solution

For the most part, ancient and early medieval Christians followed Augustine's policy and used Paul's writings to defend it. According to John G. Gager, his Epistles were historically read as confirming "both the rejection of the old Israel and the abrogation of the ritual commandments."[59] However, since the Holocaust, several Christian scholars have reexamined Paul's Epistles and have found them to be more of a refutation of supersessionism than an affirmation of it. As Fisher writes, a closer look at Paul's Epistle to the Romans shows clearly

---

57. Paula Fredriksen, *Augustine and the Jews: A Christian Defense of Jews and Judaism*, 305–6.

58. Paul Johnson, *A History of the Jews*, 165; Augustine, *City of God*, 18.46; Fredriksen, *Augustine and the Jews*, 270, 319.

59. John G. Gager, *The Origins of Anti-Semitism: Attitudes Toward Judaism in Pagan and Christian Antiquity*, 191. John G. Gager was professor of Religion at Princeton University until he retired in 2006.

that it is not possible for Christians to teach that Judaism was deprived of its own special election because of Christ's coming. [In chapters 9–11,] Paul faces the question squarely: "I ask, then: Has God rejected his people?" (Rom. 11:1). And he answers the question with equal candor: "Of course not! I myself am an Israelite, descended from Abraham, of the tribe of Benjamin. No, God has not rejected his people whom he chose so long ago" (11:2).[60]

Consistent with Fisher's position, Sidney G. Hall III writes that "Christians have largely ignored [Romans 11] for many centuries." However, if they will read this chapter carefully they will see that "any form of salvific condemnation toward the people of Israel is simply out of the question for Paul." Hall explains, "[Paul's] metaphor of the olive tree in Romans 11 suggests that some gentile Christians already adhered to a rejection and replacement theology toward Judaism." However, Paul warns them against becoming proud and reminds them that they, as wild branches, have been grafted into the covenantal olive tree. Therefore, if they do boast, they should remember it is not they that support the root, but it is the root that supports them (11:17–18).[61]

Several Christian scholars have also used Romans 11 to formulate a "dual covenant" approach in direct opposition to supersessionism. According to these scholars, Paul primarily preached to Gentiles, not to Jews. Consequently, the harsh words in his Epistles against the Law and its efficaciousness were not directed at Jews but to Judaizing Christians, people who would require converted Gentiles to observe Mosaic practices as an expression of their new covenantal relationship with God. As Hall summarizes this approach, to these scholars "Paul's gospel is one in which the Gentiles are grafted into covenant relationship with God," much like the Jews. However, this covenant is not the same as the Jews, nor does it require them to be ousted from it:

> In this relationship Christians and Jews participate together in the righteousness of God. Law is upheld; Christ is upheld. Separate people have separate paths, but out of God's faithfulness both Jews and Gentiles are brought together in one promise.[62]

Such an approach, however, may not be clearly supported by the Gospels or the other books in the New Testament. In fact, according to Hall the Pauline letters may be "the only New Testament sources that move directly

---

60. Fisher, *Faith without Prejudice*, 84.
61. Hall, *Christian Anti-Semitism and Paul's Theology*, 59. Hall is here quoting the New Revised Standard Version.
62. Hall, 61.

toward a theology including the Jewish people and still upholding the integrity of proclaiming Jesus as the Christ."[63] Nevertheless, for him Paul's letters are enough. Hall concludes,

> Christians must recognize a Paul who entreats the church to embrace a theology that is distinctively Christian yet universally inclusive of the Jewish people and people of other faiths. It is difficult to know what impact inclusive theology could have in today's divided and groaning world. Even a small measure of victory makes a difference.[64]

Supersessionist Structure

Once called "new-perspective scholarship," this no-longer-new, anti-supersessionist view of Paul's Epistles as put forth not just by Hall but by such Christian luminaries as Krister Stendahl, E. P. Sanders, James D. G. Dunn, and N. T. Wright has gained wide acceptance among academics,[65] and such an approach could work for nonacademics as well—*if* they could read the Pauline Epistles by themselves, without the larger context of the other books in the New Testament. However, the presence and placement of the book of Acts makes such a reading nearly impossible.

The Problem of Acts

Literarily speaking, The Acts of the Apostles governs almost everything about the New Testament. According to Brevard S. Childs, Acts functions as a connector, a "bridge" between the Gospels and the "apostolic witness of the Pauline and Catholic epistles."[66] However, by this Childs does not envision a narrow structure that merely allows sporadic "traffic" between two very different and very distant literary units. He sees Acts as filling in the gulf that separates these units, eliminating it entirely, reworking the "geography" of the New Testament so fundamentally as to bring together all of its various parts into a single, coherent, unified work. As Childs

---

63. Hall, 64.
64. Hall, 154.
65. Pamela Eisenbaum, *Paul Was Not a Christian: The Original Message of a Misunderstood Apostle*, 60–62.
66. Brevard S. Childs, *The New Testament as Canon: An Introduction*, 153. Brevard S. Childs, now deceased, was an ordained Evangelical minister of the Wisconsin Synod of the Evangelical and Reformed Church as well as professor of Old Testament at Yale University.

explains, not only does the inclusion of Acts in the New Testament provide a "historical link" between the Gospels and the Epistles, but it has "the canonical effect of rendering the material in a way commensurate with the larger, more general canonical pattern and of strengthening the unity of the whole."[67] Unfortunately, the canonical pattern Acts promotes condemns Jews on account of their ongoing wickedness, and the unity it creates confirms Gentiles spiritual superiority and presents them as the rejected Jews' replacements as God's covenant people.

A Pattern of Jewish Wickedness

Such a link with regards to the Gospels is not difficult to see. Just as the Gospels of Matthew, Mark, Luke, and John show Jesus preaching to multitudes, healing the sick, and raising the dead, so Acts presents Jesus's apostles similarly preaching to multitudes, healing the sick, and raising the dead. As Kyle Keefer states, one of the main themes of the book of Acts is that "the historical life of Jesus continued to have historical effects,"[68] and these "acts" clearly support such a theme, especially in relation to the Gospel of Luke. Written by the same author as Luke, Acts contains events that are organized geographically like Luke but in reverse—starting off its ministerial story not in Galilee with Jesus's water baptism and then moving gradually through Samaria and Judea to Jerusalem, but with the apostles "baptism of fire" in Jerusalem and then progressing step-by-step back through Judea and Samaria beyond Galilee "unto the uttermost part of the earth" (Acts 1:18). In this way, Acts unites with Luke in a chiasm, a structure that transforms it (as well as the other Gospels by implication) from independent narrative units into the first part of a much larger story.

And, just as Acts reaches backward to the Gospel of Luke, so it also projects forward to the Pauline Epistles, providing these letters with a similar framework into which they can fit. By showing Paul traveling to Thessalonica, Corinth, Philippi, and the other cities mentioned in his letters, Acts offers important information as to whom he met in these cities, how he was received, what prompted him to leave, as well as how he managed to be there in the first place. In this way, Acts not only helps explain why he wrote his Epistles and when, but it determines, in many ways, how these letters are perceived and understood.

---

67. Childs, 238, 240.
68. Kyle Keefer, *The New Testament as Literature: A Very Short Introduction*, 43. Kyle Keefer is a professor of New Testament at Converse College.

And that is the problem. As Rosemary Ruether writes,

> The idea that the religious authority of "apostate Israel" has "always" killed the prophets, and, therefore, culminates its own heritage of apostasy by killing the great messianic prophet [Jesus], totally governs the entire story line of the Gospels. . . . In Acts the same dogmatic thesis governs [its] story line, so that the rejection of the gospel by the "Jews" and their constant efforts to kill God's messengers result in the turn from the mission to the Jews to that of the Gentiles.[69]

In other words, because of its connection to the Gospels, Acts presents Paul's going "to the Gentiles" (18:6) as not just one man's impulsive abandonment of the few Jews living and working around him but as God's rejection of all Jews everywhere—the culmination of a New Testament-wide examination of Jewish faults and failings. Indeed, divided as its ministerial account is into four distinct geographic locales—Jerusalem, Judea, Samaria, and the larger Gentile world—Acts appears much like a formal court proceeding, with witnesses being called up in an orderly fashion, one by one, site by site, specifically so that they can reinforce many of the anti-Semitic elements present in the Gospels.

Peter, for instance, first takes the stand, as it were, on Pentecost, in Jerusalem, in the same place where Jesus, according to the synoptic Gospels, observed Passover with his disciples. There, he and the other apostles come together "with one accord in one place" (Acts 2:10), much as they did a few weeks earlier with Jesus in an upper room (Luke 22:12). And they approach Pentecost much as Jesus did Passover, not as required by the Law of Moses (with meal offerings brought to the temple in gratitude for the wheat harvest [Ex. 23:14–19; 34:22; Num. 28:26]) nor according to Jewish tradition (with scriptural readings in commemoration of the Lord's giving of the Torah to Israel on Sinai[70]), but simply as a convenient occasion in which to speak to a large group. Just as Passover is presented in the synoptic Gospels, Pentecost in Acts is a hollow holy day, an empty tradition, a religious observance with a hole in it so great that only Christianity can fill it. And it does so in dramatic fashion. Immediately after the apostles are gathered together, "there came a sound from heaven as of a rushing mighty wind, and it *filled* all the house where they were sitting," and, being "*filled* with the Holy Ghost," they "began to

---

69. Rosemary Ruether, *Faith and Fratricide: The Theological Roots of Anti-Semitism*, 89. Rosemary Ruether, a Catholic theologian, is professor of Religion and Feminist Theology at Claremont School of Theology.

70. George Robinson, *Essential Judaism: A Complete Guide to Beliefs, Customs, and Rituals*, 127–28.

speak with other tongues, as the Spirit gave them utterance" (Acts 2:2–4). Pentecost, in other words, is presented in Acts as something merely to be fulfilled by the apostles, just as Passover is presented in the Gospels of Matthew, Mark, and Luke as something merely to be fulfilled by Jesus. It has been replaced, supplanted, superseded by a more supposedly vibrant Christian ritual, a holiday often celebrated with special vestments, special choir robes, and special flowers, not in commemoration of the arrival of Israel at Sinai and the birth of the Jewish people but of the coming of the Holy Spirit and the commencement of the Christian Church. In this way, the setting at the start of Acts recalls a similar setting at the end of the Gospels and reinforces its anti-Mosaic implications.

Similarly, what Peter says in Jerusalem recalls the Matthean blood curse and reinforces its anti-Semitic implications. Here, in Acts, a "multitude" of Jews comes together before the apostles, much as one did before Pilate in the Gospel of Matthew (Acts 2:6; Matt. 27:20). In Acts, however, Matthew's somewhat vague "all the people" becomes "devout men, [Jews] out of every nation under heaven . . . Parthians, and Medes, and Elamites, and the dwellers in Mesopotamia, and in Judæa, and Cappadocia, in Pontus, and Asia, Phrygia, and Pamphylia, in Egypt, and in the parts of Libya about Cyrene, and strangers of Rome, Jews and proselytes, Cretes and Arabians" (Acts 2:5, 9–11). In this way, the inclusiveness of this group of Jews is more explicit than the one Pilate speaks to, as is their guilt. Here, Peter testifies plainly that it was the "men of Israel"—not the Romans—who took Jesus and with their "wicked hands" crucified their "Lord and Christ" (2:22–23, 36). And Peter repeats this charge twice: once in a formal, legal setting before Annas, Caiaphas, and "all the people of Israel" (4:10), and again at the temple before a large group of Jews that had assembled around him after he had healed a lame man. He tells them:

> Ye men of Israel, why marvel ye at this [miracle]? Or why look ye so earnestly on us, as though by our own power or holiness we had made this man to walk? The God of Abraham, and of Isaac, and of Jacob, the God of our fathers, hath glorified his Son Jesus; whom ye delivered up, and *denied him in the presence of Pilate*, when he was determined to let him go. But ye denied the Holy One and the Just, and *desired a murderer* to be granted unto you; And *killed the Prince of life*, whom God hath raised from the dead; whereof we are witnesses. (Acts 3:12–15)

In this way, Peter affirms both the blood curse as well as the circumstances under which it was accepted.

Stephen too, sometime later in Jerusalem, testifies that the Jews are responsible for the blood of Jesus. However, in doing so, he presents this act not as an isolated incident but as one in a series of incidents where Jews respond to prophets by killing them. In this way, the book of Acts intensifies the Gospels' portrayal of Jews as the sworn enemies of all that is good and right and true (Luke 11:48–49). Like Peter, Stephen is called before a formal council, and there, although charged with disparaging the temple and maligning the Law of Moses, he does not so much defend himself as prosecute his own case against the Jews. He begins with Abraham but quickly moves to incidents from the lives of the twelve patriarchs, the enslaved children of Israel, the wandering children of Israel, and finally the pre-exilic Jews—all in order to show how Jews, throughout their history, have shown themselves to be "stiffnecked and uncircumcised in heart and ears" and to "always resist the Holy Ghost" (Acts 7:51). Stephen subsequently sums up his case by asking his Jewish listeners, "Which of the prophets have not your fathers persecuted?" and it is then, at the end of his speech, that he accuses them of murdering Jesus, "the Just One" of whom these prophets testified (v. 52). To this accusation, the Jews present do not respond verbally. However, their actions appear to justify his accusation. After his summation, they are "cut to the heart" and gnash "on him with their teeth" (v. 54). Stephen does not seem concerned and instead looks up into heaven and declares that he sees Jesus "on the right hand of God." This is too much for this already incensed Jewish crowd. They cry out with a loud voice, stop up their ears, run upon him, cast him out of the city, and stone him to death—just as Stephen accused Jews of continually doing to the prophets of old (vv. 57–59). In this way, the book of Acts confirms the Gospels' anti-Semitic portrayal of Jews, much as it recalls and reinforces their anti-Semitic statements and anti-Mosaic settings.

The Unity of Gentile Spiritual Superiority

Once again, here, in Acts, it is the Jews who are on trial, not Jesus or his apostles, and once again it is the Jews who are found guilty on all charges. Nonetheless, Jewish culpability with regards to Jesus's death and that of the prophets is not the only issue considered in Acts' "court." Who is righteous enough to replace the Jews in God's covenant once they have been convicted is also addressed—and answered. Consistently, the book of Acts portrays Gentiles as spiritually superior to Jews and positions them as the people most likely to succeed them as God's covenant people.

Following Stephen's death, another apostle, Philip, leaves Judea and, following Jesus's instructions, goes down "to the city of Samaria" to preach to the inhabitants (Acts 8:5). Here, the Samaritans represent an intermediate step between the Jews and the Gentiles. As a group whose religious traditions connect with those of the Jews but do not align with them completely, they present not only a contrast to the wickedness of the Jews but offer hints as to the righteousness of the Gentiles. Here, there is no talk of Samaritan guilt with respect to Jesus's blood or any accusation of unfaithfulness on to God's prophets (although there certainly could have been [see Ezra 4]). Instead they are presented as "Good Samaritans," people who, "with one accord," give "heed unto those things which Philip spake" and are consequently baptized in great numbers, "both men and women" (Acts 8:6, 12). Even Simon, a powerful sorcerer who had long "bewitched the people of Samaria" (v. 9), "believed also: and when he was baptized, he continued with Philip" (v. 13).

Such portrayals of Samaritans recall the generally positive way Gentiles are presented in the Gospel of Matthew, especially in contrast with Jews. In this Gospel non-Jewish wise men "from the east" recognize the signs of Jesus's messianic birth when the vast majority of Jews do not (Matt. 2:1); a "woman of Canaan," despite being called a "dog" and having to content herself with spiritual "crumbs," finds her spiritual master (15:24–28) while the children of Israel are described as the "lost sheep of the house of Israel" and require Jesus's disciples to be sent out to them (10:6). Even non-Jewish devils, demons possessing Gentile men from Gergesenes, recognize Jesus as the Son of God (8:29) while Jesus's Jewish disciples are still wondering "what manner of man is this?" (v. 27). Throughout the Gospel of Matthew, Jesus frequently notes this contrast and comments on it. Early on, he is so impressed with a Roman centurion's request that he heal his servant with just a word that he claims he has "not found so great faith, no, not in Israel." (v. 10). And later, Jesus similarly exclaims that the Gentiles cities of Tyre and Sidon are more religiously sensitive than that the Jewish towns of Chorazin and Bethsaida (11:21) and claims that the long dead "men of Nineveh," non-Jewish Assyrians who repented after Jonah's warning, will one day rise up to condemn unrepentant Jews (12:41).

Given these precedents as well as those in the other Gospels,[71] it comes as no surprise that Paul is generally welcomed by Gentiles as the apostles' message moves beyond Samaria into the larger Gentile world (Acts 14:21–27;

---

71. This is particularly true of the Gospel of Luke, which includes this pro-Gentile material in Matthew and adds to it a pro-Gentile vision, more pro-Gentile

15:2–3; 16:12–15, 30–34; 17:1–4, 12) or that "the Jews" take "counsel to kill him" in Damascus (9:20, 23), contradict and blaspheme him in Antioch (13:45), make "their minds evil" against him in Iconium (14:2), set "all the city on an uproar" against him in Thessalonica (17:5), and stir up "the people" against him in Berea (v. 13). As Sandmel writes, "In Acts, 'the Jews' are villains and their villainy could not be worse."[72] Little wonder then that when Paul finally shakes his raiment against the blaspheming Jews in Corinth as a witness against them, he seems to be doing so against all Jews everywhere. As Acts has repeatedly shown, it is not just the Jews in Jerusalem and Judea who are "stiffnecked" persecutors of God's prophets; Jews throughout the eastern Mediterranean similarly oppose his "chosen vessels" (9:15). Consequently, their blood too, it seems, is very much upon their own heads, and God, like Paul, has left them to go unto the much more spiritually receptive and accommodating Gentiles (18:6).

The fact then that Paul's letters were written exclusively to Gentiles appears consistent with the way Acts is structured. After all, the narrative movement in Acts is not limited to places, as it moves step-by-step away from Jerusalem into the world; it also concerns people. In other words, just as the apostles forsake Jerusalem in order to go "unto the uttermost part of the earth," so they also abandon the Jews as they go forth to "teach all nations" (Acts 1:8; Matt. 28:19). As Sandmel writes, "Consistent with the view that the church was from the start destined to be Gentile, Acts sets forth in a progressive, indeed logical way, the circumstances of [the church's] transition from a Jewish to the Gentile character,"[73] and the fact that Paul's letters are written exclusively to Gentile congregations only seems to confirm this transition. In other words, Krister Stendahl, E. P. Sanders, and other like-minded scholars may claim that "Christians have been misreading Paul for centuries" and state, again and again, that his letters in no way promote supersessionism.[74] However, given that many Christians read Paul's letters through what John Gager calls "the lens of Acts," such supersessionist misreadings cannot help but continue.[75]

---

examples, and even a pro-Gentile description of the audience of his Sermon on the Plain (Luke 2:28–32; 4:24–28; 6:17).

72. Sandmel, *Anti-Semitism in the New Testament*, 100.
73. Sandmel, 86.
74. Eisenbaum, *Paul Was Not a Christian*, 61.
75. John G. Gager, *Reinventing Paul*, 74–75.

The Ultimate Solution, the Ultimate Problem

Without Paul's letters to counter the vast array of anti-Semitic elements present in the New Testament, Christian scholars and ministers ultimately have few defenses against them. Some, like Reverend Salmon, relabel the two divisions of the Christian Bible using the less categorical "Newer" and "Older" Testaments instead in order to avoid the impression that "the New supersedes the Old."[76] Others, like Michael L. Brown, dissect the New Testament in excruciating detail in order to pull each scene out of the general presentational flow and pick off each charge individually, one by one, in insolation.[77] However, in the end, all such efforts are, for many readers, unsuccessful. Overwhelmed as they are by the sheer volume and force of the New Testament's anti-Semitic rhetoric, they are too often swept away in its current and are carried quietly out to sea, as it were, without realizing it. Their only recourse is to stand firm, dig in, and anchor themselves against this tide regardless of what the text says. As Levine writes, ultimately "the only resolution to the question of New Testament anti-Judaism cannot come from historians. The elimination of anti-Jewish readings must come from the theologians, from those members of the church who conclude that anti-Judaism is wrong and who insist on Christian sensitivity to the issue."[78]

However, such resolve, especially if taken to the extreme, comes dangerously close to denying the spiritual utility and authority of the New Testament itself. Bishop Spong, for instance, in his book *Liberating the Gospels* ardently affirms that he believes in the reality of Jesus and in the "scripturality" of the New Testament. However, his efforts to read the Bible "with Jewish eyes" have so modified his belief that to some it may not seem like belief at all. As he writes, a great deal of the events in the Gospels are simply "untenable," primarily because they represent literary, not historical, efforts to portray Christianity as superior to Judaism. Specifically, Spong asserts that there were "no literal shepherds, no angels, no guiding star, no magi, and no flight into Egypt," no temptation in the Wilderness, no Sermon on the Mount, "no literal raising of Lazarus from the dead,"

---

76. Salmon, *Preaching without Contempt*, 41.

77. Michael L. Brown, *Answering Jewish Objections to Jesus, Volume One: General and Historical Objections*, 145–77. Michael L. Brown, a very active proponent of Messianic Judaism, has taught Old Testament at Trinity Evangelical Divinity School and Jewish apologetics at Fuller Theological Seminary.

78. Levine, *Misunderstood Jew*, 116.

"no miraculous feeding of the multitudes," and "no literal triumphal entry of Jesus into Jerusalem." Spong also doubts that several major figures in the Gospels even existed—in particular Judas Iscariot, who he writes was expressly "created by early Christians in order to shift the blame for Jesus' death from the Romans to the Jews." He further offers the possibility that "though the crucifixion of Jesus was real, most of the narrative events of Holy Week, including the Last Supper and the words from the cross, were creations of an interpretive liturgical process and not literal acts that Jesus ever did or literal words that Jesus ever spoke."[79]

As Spong understands him, Jesus represents in the most powerful terms possible a God of "wasteful love, embracing love, inclusive love," a being who steps across racial and cultural divides in an effort to enfold all humanity in that love.[80] To him, Jesus is indeed historical. However, Jesus's impact on the Jews of the first century was "so deep, so real, and so profound" that they simply did not have the words to describe it. They therefore resorted to "traditional legends" in order to "acknowledge the inbreaking presence of God," and in so doing "reinterpreted their familiar Jewish liturgical festivals so that this Jesus became the content of those celebrations."[81] In other words, the writers of the Gospels were using a kind of Jewish "metalanguage," which, though powerful and true in its own way, was necessarily dependent upon the culture and conditions in which it was used. It was never meant to be interpreted literally. However, as Spong sees it, the later Gentile culture, which took over the New Testament did not understand this and therefore received from the Gospels an extremely anti-Semitic message. The challenge then, according to Spong, is for modern readers to look beyond the literal and culturally dependent interpretation of the Gospels and see their true, more modern meaning—a meaning that he sees as not only countering anti-Semitism but as eliminating racism, chauvinism, and homophobia, as well as undermining anti-abortion positions and those supporting "necessary welfare reform."[82]

Other Christian scholars do not go as far as Spong does, either politically or theologically. Fisher, for instance, believes that much of what is recorded in the Gospels is indeed historical and that, to some degree, it does represent actual events. However, even Fisher feels that the New

---

79. Spong, *Liberating the Gospels*, 322–23.
80. Spong, 332.
81. Spong, 326–27.
82. Spong, 329–30.

A Book Proceeded Forth

Testament, especially the Gospels, requires a great deal of education in order to be interpreted correctly. Fisher writes,

> The passion accounts should never be read from the pulpit or in the classroom without an adequate catechesis and preparation. Classes in the period before Holy Week should include sound historical and theological background for both teacher and student. . . . Children and adults alike should approach the passion accounts only with a good awareness of the complex political events surrounding the events and with an understanding of the historical context of the Gospel authors.[83]

Fisher further advises his readers to avoid certain New Testament passages, such as the Parable of the Marriage Feast in Matthew (22:1–15), entirely "if there is no time for preparation, or if the children are too young to understand the *full* background necessary for understanding a biblical passage." [84]

Salmon too advises extreme care in presenting certain passages from the New Testament, In her book *Preaching without Contempt,* she offers a multitude of tips—complete with examples—as to how Christian ministers can reframe, modify, discount, and avoid problematic passages all together. These include:

- Highlighting points of agreement to lessen the conflict with the Pharisees[85]
- Using versions of the New Testament, such as the *Contemporary English Version*, that substitute "our people," "the crowd," or "the public" for John's "the Jews"[86]
- Presenting a traditionally anti-Judaic story, such as Nicodemus's visit, "imaginatively through a person whom the writer casts in an unfavorable light"[87]
- Changing the lectionary so that passages that are often seen as anti-Semitic (particularly from John) are read in an extended way and thoroughly explained[88]

Norman A. Beck, a professor of biblical theology and classical languages at Texas Lutheran University, similarly calls for the New Testament's "most viciously defamatory particles" to be reduced to small print and

---

83. Fisher, *Faith without Prejudice,* 80.
84. Fisher, 71.
85. Salmon, *Preaching without Contempt*, 96–99.
86. Salmon, 119–21.
87. Salmon, 121–26.
88. Salmon, 128–29.

appeals for the parts that are "less virulent" to be written around, using "circumlocution and translation according to the sense of the text in order to reduce pejorative statements about the Jews, Jewish religion, and the Pharisees." In addition, he, like Fisher, urges ministers to be more selective in their choice of lectionary texts.[89]

In the end, however, none of these solutions is completely satisfying to all readers, and each gives rise to additional questions and problems. For instance, even if Christians agree that the New Testament should be "reprocessed" somehow, who should lead this effort? Catholic scholars? Episcopal clergy? Evangelical preachers? Secular college professors? Jewish leaders? A blend? It is not clear. In addition, what does such a project say about the New Testament itself? If authorities must be consulted to determine this sacred volume's true meaning, how valuable is it to ordinary readers? If they cannot hear the word of God through the New Testament's words directly, personally, without an intermediary or interpreter, is it really scripture at all or is it simply a platform from which humans can launch their own ideas regardless of what the text says?

These are just a few of the difficult questions faithful Christians must face as they attempt to rid themselves of anti-Semitic attitudes and doctrines—and they are also questions that the Book of Mormon addresses.

---

89. Norman A. Beck, *Mature Christianity in the 21st Century: The Recognition and Repudiation of the Anti-Jewish Polemic in the New Testament*, 324. Norman A. Beck is professor of Biblical Theology and Classical Languages at Texas Lutheran University, as well as a pastor in the Evangelical Lutheran Church in America.

Chapter Three

A Record to Establish the Truth of the First

And after it had come forth unto them I beheld other books, which came forth by the power of the Lamb, from the Gentiles unto them, unto the convincing of the Gentiles and the remnant of the seed of my brethren, and also the Jews who were scattered upon all the face of the earth, that the records of the prophets and of the twelve apostles of the Lamb are true. And the angel spake unto me, saying: These last records, which thou hast seen among the Gentiles, shall establish the truth of the first, which are of the twelve apostles of the Lamb, and shall make known the plain and precious things which have been taken away from them. (1 Ne. 13:39–40)

As stated in Chapter 1, the Book of Mormon, like *Nostra Aetate* and other similar efforts, counters the anti-Semitism present in the New Testament with statements condemning Christian persecution of the Jews as well as doctrines that promote such behavior. However, unlike *Nostra Aetate*, the Book of Mormon does not do so simply as an official church declaration or as a matter of ecclesiastical policy but as scripture—*Christian* scripture—that reinforces its pro-Judaic statements literally, employing many of the same mechanisms as the New Testament but for the opposite effect. In this way, the Book of Mormon confronts the New Testament on its own turf and on its own terms and does so respectfully, even reverentially, modifying how the New Testament is understood without altering its words or undermining its authority.

Countering Anti-Semitic Statements

For instance, in the Book of Mormon both 2 Nephi 29:5 and 3 Nephi 29:8 clearly condemn the Christian "war" against the Jews. However, they do so not as communiques from fellow humans—"Christian solders," as it were—but as orders from God, the Supreme Commander:

> O ye Gentiles, have ye remembered the Jews, mine ancient covenant people? Nay; but ye have cursed them, and have hated them, and have not sought to recover them. But behold, I will return all these things upon your own heads; for I the Lord have not forgotten my people. (1 Ne. 29:5)

> Yea, and ye need not any longer hiss, nor spurn, nor make game of the Jews, nor any of the remnant of the house of Israel; for behold, the Lord remembereth his covenant unto them, and he will do unto them according to that which he hath sworn. (3 Ne. 29:8)

In the former, it is God Himself who condemns Christians for persecuting Jews, and in the latter, it is Mormon, one of God's prophets, who commands these same Gentile Christians to cease oppressing them. Notice that these statements do not comment upon any particular passage in the New Testament, nor do they challenge the veracity of any specific New Testament event. However, given their source and their clarity of expression, they make it very difficult for Christians to interpret the New Testament anti-Semitically.

And that is the point. Again, the Book of Mormon does not change the New Testament's words or call into question what might be called their "scripturality"—that is, their ability to convey divine messages to their readers directly, without an intermediary—but, for believers, it alters how the New Testament's words are understood. In many ways, the Book of Mormon functions in relation to the New Testament much as the Gospel of Matthew functions in relation to the Gospels of Mark, Luke, and John. According to Brevard Childs, "The theological implications of the canonical shaping [of the New Testament] are highly significant. The unity of the one Gospel lies within its fourfold witness."[1] In other words, the Gospels work together, despite their differences, to provide Christians with a more complete and more religiously accurate picture of Jesus and his teachings. Similarly, the Book of Mormon joins with the New Testament in order to clarify its message with respect to Jews. In this way, the Book of Mormon "balances out" the New Testament just as Fisher hoped the other Gospels would balance out Matthew, by adding pro-Judaic material to the Christian canon without undermining or displacing the New Testament.

In addition to supplying statements condemning anti-Semitic ideas and behavior, prophets in the Book of Mormon also offer other state-

---

1. Brevard S. Childs, *The New Testament as Canon: An Introduction*, 156.

ments that promote a positive view of Jews. Nephi, for instance, claims to have "charity for the Jew" (2 Ne. 33:8), and Jacob praises those who "still wait for the coming of the Messiah" (6:13). Nonetheless, despite the power of these statements, statements by themselves cannot turn the tide of anti-Semitism in the New Testament. The sheer number and variety of the literary elements in the New Testament that support such a reading are just too numerous and too compelling to be repelled by statements alone. Anti-Semitic portrayals, settings, and structures wash over them, like so much surf over a sandbar, eroding them, engulfing them, effectively drowning them under their cumulative mass. Something else is needed to reverse this flow, something more pervasive, more persuasive, something that affects believing readers deeply, altering their "gut reaction" to the New Testament as a whole.

Fortunately, explicit scriptural statements are not the only or even the most effective way the Book of Mormon works against an anti-Semitic reading of the New Testament. Just as wave after wave of different literary elements come together in the New Testament to encourage an anti-Semitic understanding of its words, so too does a continual stream of similar elements in the Book of Mormon unite to sweep away such an understanding. In particular, the many hopeful portrayals of Jews in the Book of Mormon counter and eventually overwhelm their nearly hopeless depiction in the Gospels. Simply by adding these portrayals to the Christian canon and by placing them in larger contexts, the Book of Mormon effectively affirms the overall goodness of Jews, confirms their ongoing place in God's covenant, and does so despite charges of Christ-killing and the addition of believing Gentiles into that covenant.

Redeeming "the Jews"

As discussed in Chapter 2, the Gospel of John is often viewed as the most anti-Semitic of the canonized Gospels chiefly because of the way it uses the term "the Jews," pitting it against everything Jesus does and stands for. In this Gospel, it is "the Jews" who "abide in darkness" (John 12:46) while Jesus shines as the "true Light" (1:9); it is "the Jews" who are the wicked "masters of Israel" (3:10) while Jesus is the righteous servant of all (13:14–16); it is "the Jews" who are blind to all things spiritual (9:39–41) while Jesus invites all to "come and see" (1:39, 46); and it is "the Jews" who are children of the devil while Jesus is the Son of God (8:16, 44). In short, the Gospel of John presents "the Jews" as so thoroughly and consistently insensitive to all things good and true and right that it is unthinkable that they could continue as God's covenant people. Jesus may have come unto the Jews as "his own," but in this Gospel it seems clear that it is the Gentiles—those who "were born, not of blood . . . but of God"—to whom his power is given (1:11–13).

The Book of Mormon, however, counters such supersessionist ideas, first by supplying descriptions of Jews that show them to be continuously connected to God, both by covenant and by deep feeling. For example, in addition to referring to the Jews early on as the Lord's "ancient covenant people" (2 Ne. 29:4–5), the Book of Mormon, as if to emphasize the ongoing nature of this relationship, later on drops the word *ancient* and describes them simply as the "covenant people of the Lord" (Morm. 3:21). Furthermore, Book of Mormon prophets as temporally diverse as Nephi's brother Jacob, Nephi himself, and Moroni claim that despite being scattered "upon all the face of the earth," the Jews will one day be "armed with righteousness and with the power of God in great glory" (1 Ne. 14:14), that they will be delivered from their enemies (2 Ne. 6:17), and that pure people everywhere will seek "the welfare of the ancient and long dispersed covenant people of the Lord" (Morm. 8:15).

Secondly, the Book of Mormon depicts many, if not most, Jews as being inherently sensitive to spiritual matters, especially in relation to the scriptures. According to the Book of Mormon, Jews are responsible for completing the scriptures, both the Greek scriptures as well as the Hebrew (1 Ne. 13:23), and for sending these sacred books forth "in purity unto the Gentiles," a people who, incidentally, waste no time in corrupting these books after they have received them (vv. 25–26). The Book of Mormon also describes Jews as being so naturally adept at perceiving what is truly going on in the scriptures that it claims that "there is none other people that understand the things which were spoken unto the Jews like unto them" (2 Ne. 25:5).

Thirdly, the Book of Mormon shows that sins like those the Gospel of John attributes to the Jews of Jesus's time—even if they were true—do not merit divine rejection. After all, the Book of Mormon begins just before the Babylonian Captivity, at a time when the sins of the Jews in general were so severe "there came many prophets, prophesying unto the people that they must repent, or the great city Jerusalem must be destroyed" (1 Ne. 1:4). According to Jeremiah, one of the most prominent of those prophets, many of the Jews at that time were vain (Jer. 2:5), treacherous (3:10), foolish, drunken, ignorant, (4:22), adulterous (5:7), deceitful

(5:27), and covetous (6:13). He claims that they oppressed "the stranger, the fatherless, and the widow"; that they spilled "innocent blood"; that they walked "after other gods" (7:6); and, perhaps most tellingly, that they "[had] eyes, and [saw] not" (5:21). In other words, like the Jews in the Gospel of John, these pre-Captivity Jews were not only extremely wicked, but they were spiritually blind as well, and as a result, Jeremiah, much like Jesus, used parables, not parables of words alone but visual parables—wearing yokes and breaking jugs—so that his people might somehow overcome their ocular affliction and "*see* . . . the word of the Lord" (2:31).

Lehi too, Nephi's father and the first prophet in the Book of Mormon, similarly focuses on the John-like blindness of these pre-Captivity Jews, and he does so for similar reasons. However, unlike Jeremiah, he uses not visual aids but visions to highlight his contemporaries' situation. He prays, for instance, "in behalf of his people" and receives a transcendent experience where he "*saw* and heard much" (1 Ne. 1:5–6). He is so overwhelmed by "the things which he had *seen*" that he returns home to rest, but he receives no reprieve (v. 7). He is again "carried away in a *vision*," much like Ezekiel's, in which "he *saw* the heavens open, and he thought he *saw* God sitting upon his throne" (v. 8). Lehi then "*saw* One descending out of the midst of heaven" who gives him a book to read that proclaims to Jerusalem that God has "*seen* thine abominations!" and that many of its inhabitants "should perish by the sword, and many should be carried away captive into Babylon" (v. 13). In this way, Lehi's ability to see and understand spiritual matters stands in stark contrast with that of his fellow Jerusalemites. They, unlike Lehi, did not perceive the danger and instead mocked him and plotted to kill him. However, Lehi is warned of their murderous plot by another vision where their scheme is shown to him, and he takes his family and departs into the wilderness to safety (2:2).

Given Lehi's very visual description of his experience, it is not surprising then that Nephi and Jacob, decades after their father's experience, would use similar terms to describe the wickedness of pre-Captivity Jews—and employ the past tense to distinguish between them and Jews who lived during and after the time that they wrote.[2] According to both Nephi and Jacob, the works of these pre-Captivity Jews "*were* works of *darkness*, and their doings *were* doings of abominations" (2 Ne. 25:2); they

---

2. For more information on how the Book of Mormon differentiates between pre-captivity Jews and post-captivity Jews, condemning the former while lauding the latter, see Bradley J. Kramer, *Beholding the Tree of Life: A Rabbinic Approach to the Book of Mormon*, 89–90.

"*were* a stiffnecked people; and they *despised* the words of plainness, and *killed* the prophets, and *sought* for things that they *could* not understand." Unlike later Jews, who understand the things that are written to them, these pre-Captivity Jews, like the Jews in the Gospel of John, are depicted as being totally blind to spiritual matters, an affliction that "*came* by looking beyond the mark" (Jacob 4:14). Indeed, the sins of these Jews were so extreme that they were cast out of their God-given homeland and sent, like Eve and Adam, into a lone and dreary world where their sorrow was multiplied and their ground cursed (Gen. 3:16–17). So completely had they disobeyed "all [of God's] commandments and his statutes" (Deut. 28:15) that the curses Moses pronounced upon them in Deuteronomy 28 were realized, and they were "removed into all the kingdoms of the earth," became "oppressed and spoiled," and were transformed into "an astonishment, a proverb, and a byword, among all nations" (vv. 25, 29, 37).

Nevertheless, despite the severity of the sins of these pre-Captivity Jews, Jews in general were not cast out of God's covenant. Jeremiah, the same prophet who catalogued their many sins also prophesied of a time, after their dispersion, when God would renew his covenant with them and would put his "law in their inward parts, and write it in their hearts" (Jer. 31:31, 33). Jeremiah further quotes God as promising to "gather the remnant of my flock out of all countries whither I have driven them" (23:3), to call them "from the north country, and . . . from the coasts of the earth," (31:8), and to "bring them again unto [Jerusalem]" (32:37). This general return of Israel is also emphasized in the Book of Mormon. Nephi, for instance, quotes Isaiah saying that God will yet "set up an ensign for the nations, and shall assemble the outcasts of Israel, and gather together the dispersed of Judah from the four corners of the earth" (2 Ne. 21:12). He also quotes a revelation by the non-biblical prophet Zenos, which has God affirming his commitment to the Jews: "I remember the isles of the sea; yea, and all the people who are of the house of Israel, will I gather in . . . from the four quarters of the earth" (19:16).[3] Indeed, it is not an exaggeration to say that the restoration of Israel, whatever that "restoration" entails, is one of the major themes of the Book of Mormon. Certainly, this theme is not unique to the Book of Mormon. However, the Book of Mormon's emphasis on it, particularly in connection with the

---

3. According to the Book of Mormon, Zenos, Zenoch, and Neum were ancient Israelite prophets whose writings were preserved in the brass plates Nephi acquired from Laban. These writings, however, are not part of the standard Hebrew scriptures, nor are they known outside of this canon.

Gospel of John, is—and this emphasis revolutionizes how the Gospel of John is interpreted.

Again, according to most scholars it seems clear that the Jews living during Jesus's earthly ministry were nowhere near as evil as the Gospel of John portrays them. The spiritual blindness this Gospel attributes to them is a theological exaggeration (possibly based on the Johannine community's experience with Jews living around them at the time[4]) and was created to set off the light and clarity of sight that Jesus brought. However, even if some Jews were as evil as the Gospel of John describes them, this does not mean that all Jews everywhere were rejected by God. After all, their First Temple ancestors performed "works of darkness" and were blind to matters of the spirit, and yet they were not kicked out of God's covenant. Why then would the possibility that some Second Temple Jews may have committed similar sins cause all Jews to be expelled from that same covenant? It makes no sense, especially since the Book of Mormon so frequently affirms the Jews' ongoing connection to God, presents them as being spiritually sensitive to the scriptures, and confirms that "the Lord will set his hand again the second time to restore *his people*," the Jews (25:15–17).

Challenging "Pharisaism"

In addition to contesting the way Jews are portrayed in the Gospel of John, the Book of Mormon also challenges the way they are portrayed in the Gospels of Mark, Matthew, and Luke. These synoptic Gospels similarly promote supersessionist ideas by describing Jews in condemnatory terms. However, these Gospels do so not directly, by blaming "the Jews" explicitly. Instead, they do so implicitly, through the Pharisees. Such a portrayal is neither fair nor historically accurate. As discussed in Chapter 2, the Pharisees in general were not nearly as evil as these Gospels portray them, and those few who might have been do not represent all Jews then or later. However, the fact that they are portrayed in consistently negative terms without being balanced by more positive presentations of other Jewish groups serves to taint all Jews by implication. In other words, in the synoptic Gospels Jews by any other name—be they elders, chief priests, scribes, Sadducees, Herodians, Zealots, or even "the multitude" (Matt. 16:21; 22:23; 26:47; 27:20)—smell just as rotten. Like the Gospels, the Book of Mormon also describes several subgroups of Jews. However, it

---

4. Bart Ehrman, *The New Testament: A Historical Introduction to the Early Christian Writings*, 172.

presents them in much more appealing terms. In this way, the Book of Mormon undermines the seeming universality of "Pharisaism" and tips the overall canonical assessment of Jews away from a supersessionist position to one that is more favorable.

It may sound strange to some readers to call the people described in the Book of Mormon Jews. However, that is exactly what they are. Certainly, Lehi and his family are descendants of Jacob's son Joseph (1 Ne. 5:14) and therefore not Jews in the sense that they came from the tribe of Judah. However, they are very much Jews in a more general, political, and cultural sense. Nephi, Laman, Lemuel, Sam, and others of the first generation grew up in the Kingdom of Judah, in Jerusalem. They consequently "know concerning the regions round about" (2 Ne. 25:6) and have a thorough understanding of "the learning of the Jews" (1 Ne. 1:2) as well as of the "manner of prophesying among the Jews" (2 Ne. 25:1). In this way, as Nephi states, it is clear that all of Lehi's progeny are indeed "descendants of the Jews" (30:4).[5] He and other Book of Mormon writers may therefore occasionally use the term "Jews" to distinguish themselves from the people "from whence [they] came" (33:8), but the Lehites are still Jews, a "remnant of the house of Israel" (1 Ne. 13:33–34; 19:24).

This term "Jew" is particularly applicable to Nephi and his brother Sam. In addition to being ethnic Jews, these two sons of Lehi and Sariah are, in a broadly biblical way, religious Jews as well. Following the example of Moses and Aaron (Ex. 7:6, 10, 20), they attempt to "go and do the things which the Lord hath commanded" (1 Ne. 3:7). They therefore eagerly embark on whatever assigned task their prophet-father gives them—be it leaving their home in Jerusalem, living in tents in the wilderness, or returning to Jerusalem for the plates of brass, a metallic book containing "the five books of Moses" (5:11). After all, having such a book is vital to all observant Jews because, as Nephi so Jewishly puts it, he and his people "could not keep the commandments of the Lord according to the law of Moses, save they should have the law" (4:15). Nephi's oldest brothers, however, are not nearly so observant—or obedient—and yet their behavior connects them with other Jews. Like the pre-Captivity Jews they leave behind, Laman and Lemuel mock their father and "murmur in many things against [him]." They call him a "visionary man" and complain about leaving "the land of their inheritance, and their gold, and their silver, and their precious things to perish in the wilderness"—all because

---

5. The Doctrine and Covenants similarly states that "the Lamanites are a remnant" of the Jews (D&C 19:27).

of what they call "the foolish imaginations" of their father's (2:11). Nephi even states that Laman and Lemuel "were like unto the Jews who were at Jerusalem, who sought to take away the life of my father" (v. 13)—a similarity these two brothers affirm by plotting to kill their father (16:37) and by attempting to kill Nephi as well (7:16; 17:48; 2 Ne. 5:2). Like these pre-Captivity Jews, Laman and Lemuel simply do not "believe that Jerusalem, that great city, could be destroyed" (1 Ne. 2:13). They therefore rebel against those who say otherwise and frequently seek to rejoin like-minded Jews back in Jerusalem (7:7; 16:36).

In this way, the Book of Mormon, right from the beginning, sets up two subgroups of Jews: one extremely "good," the other extremely "bad." Nonetheless, despite their different behaviors, both factions remain connected to God. Soon after Lehi's family reaches the promised land, Lehi dies, and the simmering divisions within his family boil over. From this feud two distinct peoples emerge. Nephi and Sam, along with Zoram, their younger brothers Jacob and Joseph, and their families, leave the main group and "journey in the wilderness for the space of many days" (2 Ne. 5:7). There, in a land to the north, they become *Nephites*—Jews who, like their namesake Nephi, "observe to keep the judgments, and the statutes, and the commandments of the Lord in all things, according to the law of Moses" (v. 10). In fact, so Mosaically observant are these Nephites that their laws are later described as "exceedingly strict." They are said to not only keep the Sabbath day holy, but they "profaned not; neither did they blaspheme" (Jarom 1:5).

Laman and Lemuel, on the other hand, as well as their families remain in the place where their parents first landed and become *Lamanites*, "an idle people, full of mischief and subtlety" (2 Ne. 5:24). These Lamanites grow to be "exceedingly more numerous" than the Nephites, possibly by joining with other peoples already living in the Americas, and their behavior also becomes exceedingly more wicked than the Nephites as well. In contrast with the Nephites, these Lamanites are described in terms that are almost caricatures of Mosaic evil. They are said to be a people who "loved murder and would drink the blood of beasts" (Jarom 1:6); they are called spiritually "dark, and loathsome," "a filthy people, full of idleness and all manner of abominations" (1 Ne. 12:23); they are described as being a "wild, and ferocious, and a blood-thirsty people, full of idolatry and filthiness; feeding upon beasts of prey" and eating "nothing save it was raw meat" (Enos 1:20). Just as the Pharisaic Jews are portrayed in the Gospels as opposing everything Jesus stands for, these Lamanite Jews are presented in the Book of Mormon as similarly resisting everything the Nephite Jews stand for, and as a result, they, again like the Gospels' Pharisees in relation to Jesus, continually seek to destroy the Nephites and frequently come against them in battle. In fact, so deep is their hatred for the Nephites, that, in the end, when the Lamanites finally destroy the Nephites (the Nephites having become even more wicked than the Lamanites), they sacrifice captured Nephite women and children to idols and leave the "flesh, and bones, and blood" of their victims unburied upon the ground, "to molder upon the land, and to crumble and to return to their mother earth" (Morm. 4:14, 21; 6:15).

And yet, the point of laying out the sins of this wicked subgroup of Jews in the Book of Mormon seems not so much to revel in their moral turpitude, as the Gospels appear to do with respect to the Pharisees, as it is to reveal the strength of God's commitment to them. Laman and Lemuel, for instance, despite their frequent rebellions are not left behind or otherwise sent away by their father. They are instead frankly forgiven and even coaxed along towards better behavior. Lehi, the same man who prophesied destruction for the inhabitants of Jerusalem because of their sins, implores Laman and Lemuel, despite their sins, to be faithful and steadfast. He even names rivers and valleys after them and expresses confidence in their ability to continually flow figuratively "into the fountain of all righteousness" and be "immovable in keeping the commandments of the Lord" (1 Ne. 2:9–10). The Lord too, like Lehi, pleads with Laman and Lemuel, sending them an angel to encourage them when their commitment to his cause flags (3:29) and later commanding Nephi to stretch forth his hand to shock them, all so "that they may know that [Jehovah is] the Lord their God" (17:53). To be sure, Laman and Lemuel are often warned and chastised, but throughout the journey to the Promised Land they remain valuable members of their father's family as well as of God's kingdom.

The same is true of Laman and Lemuel's descendants. Despite all the carnage, death, and destruction the Lamanites cause, these Jews are never severed from God nor are they removed from their covenantal relationship with Him. Certainly, these descendants are eventually "scattered before the Gentiles," apparently as punishment for their evil deeds (1 Ne. 13:14); however, their connection to divinity remains intact. As the Book of Mormon makes clear, the descendants of the Lamanites are to be protected from annihilation and are assured that they will receive a portion of the Americas as their promised inheritance (vv. 30–31). They constitute a few of the Israelite "isles of the sea," spoken of by Isaiah, and as such are to be sought after by God and gathered in with "all the people who are of the house of Israel . . . from the four quarters of the earth" (19:16).

Such optimism in God's covenantal constancy with respect to all Israelites is affirmed literally by how these Jews are portrayed in the Book of Mormon. Certainly, the Lamanites start off and end up extremely wicked. However, in the middle of the book, the Lamanites demonstrate a remarkable ability to change, and this ability seems to justify their continued inclusion in God's good graces. In the book of Mosiah, King Mosiah's repentant sons ask if they can go among the Lamanites as missionaries. Their father eagerly grants them their request and predicts that "many shall believe on their words" (Mosiah 28:7). However, other Nephites "laughed [them] to scorn" and mocked them, using phrases eerily similar to those used in the New Testament to describe Pharisees (Matt. 7:23; 9:4; 15:2; 23:28–38; Acts 7:51–51):

> Do ye suppose that ye can bring the Lamanites to the knowledge of the truth? Do ye suppose that ye can convince the Lamanites of the incorrectness of the traditions of their fathers, as stiffnecked a people as they are; whose hearts delight in the shedding of blood; whose days have been spent in the grossest iniquity; whose ways have been the ways of a transgressor from the beginning? (Alma 26:24)

Nonetheless, despite such a pessimistic reaction, Ammon, Aaron, Omner, and Himni make their way among the Lamanites, and after overcoming some initial misunderstandings, are heartily embraced, even to the point of being given royal protection so that "they might go forth and preach the word according to their desires" (Alma 23:1–3) without opposition or obstruction. Consequently, these sons of Mosiah travel from city to city, "establishing churches, and consecrating priests and teachers throughout the land among the Lamanites," and they are so successful that Mormon asserts that they did bring thousands of Lamanites "to the knowledge of the Lord, yea, thousands were brought to believe in the traditions of the Nephites" (vv. 4–5). In fact, one large subgroup of Lamanites sees the error of their murderous ways so vividly that they vow to never again take up arms, and as token of their commitment, they bury their swords "deep in the earth, that they may be kept bright, as a testimony that [they] have never used them" since their conversion (24:16). Their resolve is later put to a grisly test when other Lamanites, riled up by Nephite dissenters, come against these new converts expressly to slaughter them. However, rather than fighting back and breaking their oath, the Anti-Nephi-Lehies, as they are later called, prostrate themselves before their fellow Lamanites.

As a result, these Lamanites were not met with any resistance and "did slay a thousand and five of them" until at last they did forbear and they themselves "repented of the things which they had done" (vv. 22–24). In fact, so completely did the converted Lamanites "observe strictly to keep the commandments of God, according to the law of Moses" (Hel. 13:1) that their righteousness is said to "exceed that of the Nephites" (6:1), and they began sending them prophets instead of vice versa.

The magnificent Samuel the Lamanite, for instance, in a remarkable turnabout, mounts a wall surrounding the Nephite capital and chastises the inhabitants for sins usually attributed to Lamanites: "envyings, strifes, malice, persecutions, and murders, and all manner of iniquities" (Hel. 13:22). He also accuses them of casting out, mocking, and attempting to slay prophets of God (vv. 22–24)—accusations that these Nephite Jews quickly justify by throwing rocks and shooting arrows at Samuel. Nevertheless, "the Spirit of the Lord was with [Samuel,] insomuch that they could not hit him with their stones neither with their arrows" (16:2). The role reversal is consequently clear, as is its point: "evil" Lamanite Jews can repent just as "good" Nephite Jews can turn wicked. In this way, the Book of Mormon refutes out of hand the Synoptics' suggestion that the spiritual state of Jews, as Pharisees, cannot change. Neither they nor the Lamanites are so inherently murderous and stiffnecked that they cannot repent.

The portrayal of the Nephites in the Book of Mormon makes a similar point. Unlike the Lamanites, these Jews are not so much prone to murder as they are inclined towards hypocrisy, the second of the supposedly great Pharisaic sins according to the Synoptic Gospels. Amulek, for instance, sounds almost Jesus-like in his denunciation of the Nephite "lawyers and hypocrites" living in the city of Ammonihah (Alma 9:1). They constitute, like the Gospels' Pharisees, "a wicked and perverse generation"; they are a people who persist in laying "traps and snares to catch the holy ones of God," that "by their cunning devices . . . they might find witness against them, . . . that they might be slain or cast into prison" (10:13, 17). And yet, although these Ammonihahites do eventually imprison Amulek and Alma (14:17), even they are not beyond hope or redemption. To be sure, many of the worst of these Nephites are killed when an earthquake destroys the building in which they are gathered (vv. 23–27). However, many others believe the words of these prophets "and began to repent, and to search the scriptures" (v. 1)—including Zeezrom, "the foremost to accuse Amulek and Alma" (10:31).

Much as Matthew's chief priests offer Judas thirty pieces of silver to betray Jesus (Matt. 26:14–15), Zeezrom attempts to give Amulek "six onties of silver" (roughly one and a half months of Zeezrom's salary) if he would "deny the existence of a Supreme Being" (Alma 11:22). When this approach fails, Zeezrom, like Luke's Pharisees, cunningly resorts to legalistic word-twisting in order to "take hold of his words" (Luke 20:20). However, when Amulek withstands him, Zeezrom begins to tremble "under a consciousness of his guilt" (Alma 11:46; 12:1) and pleads for the release of Amulek and Alma (14:7). In other words, Zeezrom repents, and after he is "scorched with a burning heat" because of his sins, he is healed, spiritually and physically. He then joins Alma and preaches to his fellow Nephites (15:3–12). In the end, not only is Zeezrom's hypocrisy, like that of his fellow Ammonihahites, redeemable, but he very much remains connected to God and involved in his work.

Similarly, Amulek and Alma, a few chapters later, encounter another subgroup of Nephite Jews who, despite being almost the embodiment of the kind of "vain repetitions" Jesus condemns (Matt. 6:7), are similarly confirmed as members of God's covenant. These Zoramites, as they are called, mount a "holy stand" in the center of their synagogue and, one at a time, recite "the selfsame prayer unto God," week after week, each time returning afterwards "to their homes, never speaking of their God again until they had assembled themselves together again to the holy stand" (Alma 31:13, 23). They, like the hypocritical scribes and Pharisees of Matthew's Gospel, exalt themselves and figuratively "shut up the kingdom of heaven against men" (Matt. 23:13) by casting out "the poor class of people" from their synagogues (Alma 31:18; 32:2). To Alma, these Zoramites, like the Ammonihahites, are clearly "a wicked and a perverse people." He can see that their hearts are "set upon gold, and upon silver, and upon all manner of fine goods" (31:24) and not at all inclined towards God or His children. He therefore offers, in contrast to their hypocritical prayer, a sincere prayer on their behalf and afterwards delivers a series of homilies, with Amulek, that more or less mirror many of Jesus's words in the Sermon on the Mount. Like Jesus, Alma begins his first speech on a high place, on the "hill Onidah" (32:4), and then, echoing the Beatitudes, pronounces the outcasts blessed for being "lowly in heart" (v. 8), a seed-thought that blossoms into a short but profound discourse on the beatific qualities of humility. His next sermon centers directly on the subject of sincere prayer, the main point of which is that prayer need not be public to be effective. In fact, according to Alma, private prayer is often preferred since it is less subject to the temptations of hypocrisy. He then concludes his sermon with a list of places and situations where one should pray privately, the point of which is to encourage his hearers to continue in prayer in all places and at all times, especially, as Jesus similarly counseled, "in your closets, and your secret places" (34:19–26).

However, even sincere, private prayers by themselves are not enough to dispel all charges of hypocrisy. According to Alma, such prayers must be followed by actions or they too are vain. As he says,

> After ye have done all these things, if ye turn away the needy, and the naked, and visit not the sick and afflicted, and impart of your substance, if ye have, to those who stand in need—I say unto you, if ye do not any of these things, behold, your prayer is vain, and availeth you nothing, and ye are as hypocrites who do deny the faith. (Alma 34:28)

In the end, although the "more popular part of the Zoramites" was not convinced or humbled by the words of Alma and Amulek (Alma 35:3), the point here is that many *were* repentant and *did* accept prophetic counsel (v. 6). In other words, hypocrisy alone, even hypocrisy as bad as that attributed to the Pharisees in the Synoptic Gospels, is not enough to cast a people out of God's covenant. There is still hope. Even if some Pharisees were as hypocritical as the Gospels contend (and if they were like most people, there must have been a few who were), they, like these Zoramites, can change.

The Book of Mormon seems to reinforce this hopeful assessment by showing how later Nephite Jews responded positively to the actual Sermon on the Mount. Here in the New World, just as he did in the Old, Jesus enjoins these Jews not to sound a trumpet before them when they offer alms "as will hypocrites do" (3 Ne. 13:2). They too are told not to pray "standing in the synagogues and in the corners of the streets" (v. 5) and not to fast with a sad countenance. In other words, Jesus's condemnation of hypocrisy is just as relevant and meaningful to the Nephites as it was to the Pharisees. However, the Nephite Jews actually heed Jesus's council and change their ways. Soon after Jesus ascends again to heaven, his New World disciples form a church "in all the lands round about" and minister unto the people. And all of the people here, repent of their respective sins so much so that all were "converted unto the Lord . . . both Nephites and Lamanites, and there were no contentions and disputations among them, and every man did deal justly one with another" (4 Ne. 1:1–2). In the end, then, neither widespread murderous intent nor individual hypocrisy disqualifies Jews from membership in God's covenant. Despite what the Synoptics may imply, for any Jews guilty of these sins there is always hope of repentance and change—just like everyone else.

Acquitting "All the Jewish People" of Killing Jesus

In addition to confirming the Jews' ongoing place in God's covenant despite occasional disobedience, sinfulness, and hypocrisy, the Book of Mormon refutes other reasons Christians have traditionally considered Jews rejected by God. The most cited reason is, of course, the Matthean claim that "all the [Jewish] people" called for Jesus's crucifixion and that his blood has therefore stained them and their descendants forever (Matt. 27:25). This the Book of Mormon repudiates out of hand simply by virtue of its subject matter: a group of Jews living so far away from the events described in the Gospels that they clearly could not have been involved in Jesus's death in any way whatsoever. However, as effective as this point may be by itself, the Book of Mormon bolsters it by including supportive statements and analogous portrayals that similarly limit Jewish involvement and guilt with respect to Jesus's death.

Regarding these supportive statements, it should be noted first of all that none of the prophets in the Book of Mormon, living somewhere across the ocean, far off in the ancient Americas, is acquainted with the Judean political, religious, or military situation during the first century of the Common Era. They therefore are incapable of addressing any specific issues relevant to this area during this time. Secondly, how Jesus died appears to be only minimally relevant to the main messianic message these prophets attempt to convey—namely, that Jesus died for humanity's sins, was resurrected, and will one day usher in an extended era of peace, prosperity, equality, and righteousness. For instance, the Book of Mormon prophets most often describe Jesus's death using passive voice constructions, which leave unspecified those who were responsible for his death. Nephi, for one, recounts his vision of Jesus's death saying only that Jesus "was lifted up upon the cross and slain for the sins of the world" (1 Ne. 11:33). Abinadi similarly prophecies that Jesus will be "led, crucified, and slain" without mentioning who will do the leading, crucifying, and slaying (Mosiah 15:7). Samuel the Lamanite too states that Jesus will "suffer many things and shall be slain for his people" (Hel. 13:6). And even Jesus himself, soon after his death and resurrection in Jerusalem, descends from the heavens in Bountiful and commands the Nephite multitude to feel his wounds, so that they may know that he has "been slain for the sins of the world" (3 Ne. 11:14).

Furthermore, during the rare times when the prophets in the Book of Mormon do attempt to identify Jesus's killers, they do so using vague terms, such as "the world" or "wicked men" (1 Ne. 19:7–10), or they employ phrases that while they may appear at first to indict all Jews everywhere actually absolve the vast majority of Jews of any involvement whatsoever in Jesus's death. Jacob's "they at Jerusalem" (2 Ne. 10:5), for example, may seem to some readers unfamiliar with Jewish history to prophesy that the Jews in general will crucify Jesus. These readers link this phrase with "the Jews" in verse 3 and see it as both affirming and intensifying Jewish culpability. To them, the statement that "there is none other nation on earth that would crucify their God" seems to damn all Jews everywhere. However, only a relatively small percentage of the world's Jews in the first century lived in Jerusalem and the area around it. During the time of Jesus, most Jews were still residing in Babylon or were scattered throughout the eastern Mediterranean, in cities such as Alexandria, Antioch, and Ephesus. These "diaspora" Jews were the descendants of the vast number of Jews who did not return to their ancient homeland after the Persians defeated the Babylonians and instead took advantage of the new opportunities afforded them by their conquerors to spread themselves throughout the region. Indeed, David Klinghoffer, a Jewish historian and essayist, estimates that during Jesus's time there were about a million Jews living in "Jewish Palestine" while five million Jews were dispersed around the Mediterranean and throughout the Middle East.[6] Other scholars, such as Samuel Sandmel, think that this 5 to 1 ratio could have been even higher—possibly even 10 to 1.[7] And Jerusalem was only one city in this "Jewish Palestine." As a result, "they at Jerusalem" instead of prophetically spreading the responsibility of Jesus's death to all Jews everywhere actually limits it to a small segment of the overall Jewish population. Rather than serving as a synonym of "the Jews," this phrase in fact functions as an appositive, the last element in a grammatical sequence that shrinks the number of Jews connected to Jesus's death geographically, place by place, from all Jews everywhere to "those who are the more wicked part of the world" to just those Jews living in Jerusalem during the early first century.[8]

But were all Jews living in 1st century Jerusalem responsible for Jesus's death? Not according to the Book of Mormon. Just as the subject of 2

---

6. David Klinghoffer, *Why the Jews Rejected Jesus: The Turning Point in Western History*, 44.

7. Samuel Sandmel, *A Jewish Understanding of the New Testament*, 19–20.

8. Nephi and Mormon use similar phraseology to limit Jewish involvement in Jesus's death to a small number of Jews living at a specific place and time (1 Ne. 19:13; 2 Ne. 25:10–13; 4 Ne. 1:31).

Nephi 10:5 prophetically reduces the number of Jews who will be involved in Jesus's death to a small fraction of the Jews living during the first third of the first century CE, its predicate softens what that involvement will be. Here, "they shall crucify him" of verse 3 becomes "they . . . will stiffen their necks against him, that he be crucified." In other words, not only will a small number of Jews contribute to Jesus's death sometime in the future but their contribution will also be small—possibly consisting only of an unwillingness to speak up against it or a reluctance to challenge publicly those pushing it. Furthermore, as the introductory phrase of 2 Nephi 10:5 points out, whatever these people will (or will not) do will occur not because of an informed, deep-seated, conscious conviction but "because of priestcrafts and iniquities." In other words, many of these first-century Jerusalemites will be manipulated, psychologically or physically, by corrupt priests and leaders. Consequently, it is these Jewish priests and leaders who bear most of the non-Roman responsibility for Jesus's death, not the general Jewish populace.

In this way, instead of reinforcing the traditional Christian charge that all Jews are to blame for Jesus's death, 2 Nephi 10:3–5 actually refutes it and does so purposefully. Jacob, speaking five centuries before Jesus, may not have known many of details of the great post-Captivity Jewish dispersion, but he was certainly well-versed as to its extent. Not only was his family led by God to a distant continent, far across the sea, long before Jesus's birth, but he sees in Isaiah's use of the term "isles" (Isa. 51:5) a reference to other groups of Jews in similar situations. As a result, he concludes that "the Lord God has led away [others] from time to time from the house of Israel, [out of Jerusalem] according to his will and pleasure" (2 Ne. 10:21–22). Furthermore, Jacob also cites Zenos's prophecy, which describes how *many* Israelite "branches" were broken off from the main trunk and were taken to the "nethermost parts of [God's] vineyard" (Jacob 5:14). Most of these were placed in poor spots of land. However, all of them flourished for a time and brought forth "much fruit," meaning people, far away from their homeland in Jerusalem—and they did so long before Jesus was born, grew up and died (vv. 20–23).

However, 2 Nephi 10 is not the only section in the Book of Mormon that counters the notion that Jews as a whole were guilty of Jesus's death. The entire last half of the book of Mosiah also addresses this issue—not directly, by providing its readers with a clear statements of Jewish innocence, but analogically, by presenting them with a similar death in a similar society where the people in general are not held responsible. In these chapters, readers of the Book of Mormon are introduced to the Zeniffites, a group of Nephite Jews who, like the first-century inhabitants of Jerusalem, represent a small part of the larger Jewish population around them. They, like the Jerusalemites of Jesus's time, have ancestors who left the main group of Jews in that region in order to reclaim the "land of their fathers" (Mosiah 7:9). And their ancestors, again like those of Jesus's Jerusalemites, soon fell under the sway of a corrupt leader—not a Maccabean king or a Herodian successor, but King Noah, a ruler who, like these Judean kings, burdened his people with grievous taxes, installed his cronies as temple priests, and built "many elegant and spacious buildings" (11:1–8).

Like the first-century Jerusalemites, the Zeniffites were also visited by a prophet who, in addition to testifying of Jesus, sounds very much like him. Like Jesus, Abinadi comes unexpectedly, not as an impressive figure or as a military hero but as a man much like any other at that time. Like Jesus, he pronounces woes "unto this generation." And, like Jesus, he predicts their imminent demise and destruction (Mosiah 12:2–8; Matt. 23:33–39). In addition, Abinadi prophesies "concerning the coming of the Messiah" and quotes Isaiah 53, explaining that "God himself shall come down among the children of men," that he shall "go forth in mighty power upon the face of the earth," and that he shall be "led, crucified, and slain" all in order to take upon himself the iniquity of his people, (Mosiah 13:33–34; 15:7–9). These prophecies find fulfillment both in Abinadi's life as well as in Jesus's. Much like Jesus, Abinidi is arrested and called before a council of his political and religious leaders, where he is questioned as to his messianic beliefs, mocked, and sentenced to be scourged and executed in an extremely gruesome manner.

However, unlike Jesus, Abinadi does not go like a lamb, silently, to the slaughter (Matt. 27:12). Just before he is burned at the stake, he pronounces a curse upon his killers:

> And it will come to pass that ye shall be afflicted with all manner of diseases because of your iniquities. Yea, and ye shall be smitten on every hand, and shall be driven and scattered to and fro, even as a wild flock is driven by wild and ferocious beasts. And in that day ye shall be hunted, and ye shall be taken by the hand of your enemies, and then ye shall suffer, as I suffer, the pains of death by fire. (Mosiah 17:16–18)

In many ways, Abinadi's curse is similar to the punishment Christians have traditionally thought God pronounced upon the Jews for killing Jesus. However, in Abinadi's case only those leaders directly involved in his death are punished in this way. King Noah, the person who actually sentenced Abinadi, suffers death by fire in direct fulfillment of Abinadi's word (Mosiah 19:20), and the priests, those who advised King Noah and goaded him on, are similarly hunted down and executed by the Lamanites (Alma 25:8–12). However, the general Zeniffite population is not affected. To be sure, they are later conquered by the Lamanites, afflicted with high taxes, and finally forced to abandon their lands and return, at great cost, to the main body of Nephites. However, these difficulties arise from their sins in general, their pride and greed and selfishness, and not as a result of their involvement in Abinadi's death (Mosiah 21:5–15). In addition, the main group of Nephites in Zarahemla and elsewhere in the Americas are completely unaffected by Abinadi's death and therefore appear to bear no responsibility whatsoever for it. In other words, although all of the Zeniffites may have to some degree participated in Abinadi's death since he was executed in their land, only their king and his priests, through their deaths, are shown to be blameworthy. The people themselves are innocent, as are their children and the Nephite nation in general.

In this way, by analogy, the Book of Mormon renders a verdict as to who was responsible for Jesus's death. Ruling decision-makers, mostly Roman, are clearly guilty, as are to some degree their advisors, those who pressed for his death. However, the general population of Jerusalem was not. And neither were the vast majority of Jews who lived outside of Jerusalem. Some Jewish leaders at that time were most likely involved in Jesus's death in some way or other and therefore bear some guilt, but given the methods used to execute him, even they cannot, strictly speaking, be called Christ-killers. Since only Romans crucified people, that term can only be applied to Romans—not to Jews then and certainly not now.

Rejecting Anti-Jewish Covenantal Rejectionism

Another reason sometimes cited in support of supersessionism is that the Jews needed to be expelled from God's covenant in order to make room for Gentiles. Although this idea is not supported in any overt way in the Gospels, they often hint at it. For example, the Gospel of Matthew shows Jesus, soon after his arrival in Jerusalem, relating a parable about "a certain householder" who let out his vineyard to "husbandmen" and then "went into a far country" (Matt. 21:33). These husbandmen, however, do not tend this vineyard honorably and later kill the householder's servants when he sends them to receive his crop. Thinking that the husbandmen will respect his heir, the householder subsequently sends his son to them.

Nonetheless, the husbandmen cast the son out of the vineyard and slay him in order to "seize on his inheritance" (v. 38). At this point in the story, the Gospel of Matthew shows Jesus asking those around him what the householder should do to the husbandmen, and they respond: "He will miserably destroy those wicked men, and will let out his vineyard unto other husbandmen" (v. 41). Jesus agrees with what has been said and adds, pointedly, "Therefore say I unto you, The kingdom of God shall be taken from you, and given to a *nation* bringing forth the fruits thereof" (v. 43). At this point, the Gospel of Matthew states that "when the chief priests and Pharisees had heard his parables, they perceived that he spake of them" and "sought to lay hands on him" (vv. 45–46). In other words, the antagonists in this parable may indeed be limited to these Jewish leaders. However, Jesus does not confirm this limitation, nor is his statement that a "nation" will replace the wicked husbandmen consistent with it. Here, membership in the Kingdom of God seems to be an either/or situation: only with the ouster of the Jews can Gentiles be included. Indeed, the fact that in just a few chapters "all the [Jewish] people" will call for Jesus's blood to be on them and on their children (27:25) suggests that this parable applies to all Jews everywhere and illustrates how their wickedness has caused them to be removed from God's covenantal "vineyard" and replaced by Gentiles.

The clearest statement in support of this kind of Jewish rejectionism, however, comes in chapter 11 of Paul's letter to the Romans. Here, in the same chapter where Paul affirms that God has *not* cast off all Jews from God's covenant (v. 2), he confirms that the Jews in general have nonetheless fallen from God's grace and that "through their fall salvation is come unto the Gentiles" (v. 11). This is an odd thought, linking Jewish misfortune with Gentile opportunity. However, it is not necessarily rejectionist. Isaiah too calls scattered Israel a "light to the Gentiles" and similarly claims that it will bring "salvation unto the end of the earth" (Isa. 49:6). But Paul is not finished. In subsequent verses, he likens his non-Jewish co-religionists to branches from "a wild olive tree" that have been grafted into God's covenant and advises them to "boast not against the [natural Jewish] branches" but say instead that these branches "were broken off, *that* I might be grafted in" (Rom. 11:17–19). In other words, this thought *is* rejectionist. It may not happen all at once, but eventually all non-Christian Jews will be removed from God's covenant in order to make way for Christian Gentiles. According to Paul, there are a limited number of spots in that covenant. Therefore, if Gentiles are added to it, Jews must of necessity be subtracted from it. It is simple zero-sum math. For one to increase, the other must decrease. As a result, although the purpose of Romans 11 may indeed be to connect Gentile Christians with Jews, here in these verses, this connection seems to function more as a cautionary tale than as an invitation for mutual respect. As Paul sums up his message to his Gentile readers, "Be not highminded, but fear: For if God spared not the natural [Jewish] branches, take heed lest he also spare not thee. Behold therefore the goodness and severity of God: on them which fell, severity; but toward thee, goodness, if thou continue in his goodness: otherwise thou also shalt be cut off." (vv. 20–23).

Given the pro-Jewish elements in this chapter, many scholars are inclined to reject any possible rejectionist interpretation of these verses. They point out that the Greek word translated as "broken off" (Rom. 11:17) can also mean "bent" or that the wild branches were "grafted in *among*" the other branches, not "in their place" (v. 17).[9] Such interpretations are both plausible and attractive. Nonetheless, a certain amount of interpretative ambiguity remains—particularly since the New Revised Standard, the New International, and several other popular versions of the Bible state that the natural Israelite branches were "broken off" and affirm that the wild Gentile branches were indeed "grafted in their place." The Book of Mormon, however, helps clear up this ambiguity by providing an expanded version of Paul's arboreal metaphor as well as by including portrayals of near-Gentiles that show how Gentiles can in fact come into God's covenant without displacing Jews. In this way, the Book of Mormon erodes the scriptural foundation on top of which Christian supersessionism is built—and again does so indirectly, literally, without undermining one of Christianity's most revered texts.

Allegory of the Olive Tree

Paul's likening of God's covenant to an olive tree in Romans 11 is brief and somewhat undeveloped. Not so in the Book of Mormon. In the Book of Mormon, this simple metaphor blossoms into a complex and somewhat lengthy allegory covering the entire life-cycle of God's covenant. In Jacob 5, the non-biblical prophet Zenos likens the house of Israel explicitly to a "tame olive-tree," which prospered and grew but eventually "waxed old, and began to decay" (v. 3). God, "the master of the vineyard," consequently decided to "prune it, and dig about it, and nourish it," hoping "that perhaps it may shoot forth young and tender branches" (v. 4). And

---

9. Amy-Jill Levine and Marc Zvi Brettler, eds., *Jewish Annotated New Testament*, 277, footnotes for Romans 11:17–24.

indeed the covenantal tree began to do so. However, at the same time, the main top of the tree started to wither (v. 6), and therefore the master, now identified as the "Lord of the vineyard," resolved to pluck off some of its "main branches" and graft into it "branches of the wild olive-tree" in order to strengthen it (vv. 7, 9). In other words, Zenos, at least in the beginning, sounds very much like Paul. Here, many of the Jews (the tame olive branches) have gone spiritually astray (withered), and as a result, several have been removed and replaced by repentant Gentiles (the wild olive branches). However, Zenos goes on, effectively adding another chapter to Paul's account. According to him, not all of the natural branches that were cut off from the tree were removed from the master's care. Several of its "young and tender branches" were instead taken by his servants and transplanted elsewhere within the orchard under the Lord's direction. This scattering was not done haphazardly or with destructive intent. On the contrary, it was carried out carefully so that the Lord of the vineyard could "preserve the [good] fruit" of the natural tree (v. 8). In other words, not all of the various Jewish exiles were, according to the Book of Mormon, punishments for wicked behavior. Some Jews, like Lehi's family, were led away from their home as a reward for their righteousness and therefore were not only protected from the calamities that plagued the House of Israel in general but their righteousness was preserved so that all Israel might one day benefit from it.

By itself, this single bit of additional information significantly undercuts any supersessionist interpretation of Paul's metaphor. However, the Book of Mormon goes on, weakening such an interpretation further by confirming that Jews do not need to be cut off from God's covenant in order to make room in it for Gentiles. After describing how the branches from "the wild olive tree" were grafted into the tame tree and, for a time, produced good fruit, Zenos recounts how these branches soon began to "overrun" its roots and created such a problem that the Lord of the vineyard ordered all of the scattered natural branches to be grafted back into the tame tree and commanded that those wild branches "whose fruit is most bitter" be plucked off (Jacob 5:37, 52, 57). In other words, as the Book of Mormon shows, there is no limit to the "slots" in God's covenant, nor is there any inherent conflict between Israelites and non-Israelites within it. Both can coexist within God's covenant at the same time. The only reason people would be cut off from that covenant would be that they produce "bad fruit." Again, this does not mean that Romans 11:17–19 is necessarily wrong. According to the Book of Mormon, Paul's portrayal of the covenantal inclusion of Gentiles is basically correct. However, it is limited in scope; it does not include the rest of the story; it does not show how both Israelites and non-Israelites can be brought "together again," how they can unitedly "bring forth the natural fruit," and how, in this way, "they may be one" (Jacob 5:68).

In this way, by adding additional information to Paul's metaphor and by developing it, the Book of Mormon changes how this metaphor is understood without altering Paul's words or challenging their authority. Similarly, the Book of Mormon also changes how Romans 11:17–19 is interpreted. As mentioned previously, Stendahl writes that Paul wrote Romans "for the very specific and limited purpose of defending the rights of Gentile converts to be full and genuine heirs to the promises of God to Israel."[10] Zenos's allegory does not dispute this. However, it also supports the idea that despite the inclusion of Gentiles into God's covenant, Jews remain heirs to those same promises and maintain their special place in God's heart. From the start, Zenos's allegory shows God as someone emotionally tied to his ancient covenant people. When the tree begins to decay, he, as "master of the vineyard," says, "I will prune it, and dig about it, and nourish it" because "it *grieveth* me that I should lose this tree" (Jacob 5:4, 7). When his pruning does not improve matters as he had hoped, the master repeats this sentiment, using the same words with the same feeling (vv. 13, 32). In fact, God is so emotionally connected to Israel that he later cries out in agony, "What could I have done more in my vineyard? Have I slackened mine hand, that I have not nourished it?" God's pain is palpable, and he once again exclaims that "it grieveth me that I should hew down all the trees of my vineyard" (v. 47).

In many ways, Zenos's allegory is also a gloss on Exodus 19:5, where God states that Israel "shall be a peculiar treasure unto me above all people." In this allegory, God not only mourns for Israel but exults in it as well. He says that he works with the tree representing Israel so that he may "glory in the fruit of [his] vineyard" and have "joy again" in its fruit (Jacob 5:54, 60). He also blesses the laborers who work in his vineyard, twice promising them that they too "shall have joy with [him] because of the fruit of [his] vineyard" (vv. 71, 75). It is clear in this allegory that Israel indeed has a treasured place in God's heart—and that it cannot be displaced by Gentiles. In the Book of Mormon repentant Gentiles are "numbered *among*" or "numbered *with*" the Jews. Nephi, for example, records a con-

---

10. Krister Stendahl, *Paul among Jews and Gentiles*, 2.

versation with an angel where he is told that Gentiles who "shall hearken unto the Lamb of God . . . shall be numbered *among* the seed of thy father; yea, they shall be numbered *among* the house of Israel" (1 Ne. 14:1–2). And during his post-resurrection visit to the inhabitants of the New World, Jesus also reiterates this inclusivist position multiple times:

> But if the Gentiles will repent and return unto me, saith the Father, behold they shall be numbered *among* my people, O house of Israel. (3 Ne. 16:13)

> For thus it behooveth the Father that [certain mighty works] should come forth from the Gentiles, that he may show forth his power unto the Gentiles, for this cause that the Gentiles, if they will not harden their hearts, that they may repent and come unto me and be baptized in my name and know of the true points of my doctrine, that they may be numbered *among* my people, O house of Israel. . . .
>
> But if [the Gentiles] will repent and hearken unto my words, and harden not their hearts, I will establish my church among them, and they shall come in unto the covenant and be numbered *among* this the remnant of Jacob, unto whom I have given this land for their inheritance (21:6, 22)

In fact, so pervasive is this idea in the Book of Mormon that Mormon repeats it, again, explicitly for his future non-Jewish readers and lays out what exactly they need to do in order to join with the Jews in God's covenant:

> Turn, all ye Gentiles, from your wicked ways; and repent of your evil doings, of your lyings and deceivings, and of your whoredoms, and of your secret abominations, and your idolatries, and of your murders, and your priestcrafts, and your envyings, and your strifes, and from all your wickedness and abominations, and come unto me, and be baptized in my name, that ye may receive a remission of your sins, and be filled with the Holy Ghost, *that ye may be numbered with my people* who are of the house of Israel. (3 Ne. 30:2)

Mulekites

Although some Latter-day Saint scholars see evidence in the Book of Mormon that Lehi and his family encountered indigenous peoples when they arrived in the Americas,[11] Gentiles, as such, do not appear in the main narrative of the Book of Mormon. Consequently, there are no true examples of non-Israelites being numbered with Israelites in this text. Nonetheless, the Mulekites, a group of what could be called *near-Gentiles*, come close. Like the Lehites, they "came out from Jerusalem" but later, "at the time that Zedekiah, king of Judah, was carried away captive into Babylon" (Omni

---

11. John L. Sorenson, *An Ancient American Setting for the Book of Mormon*, 84

1:15). Like the Lehites, they were led by a man, Mulek, a hitherto unknown son of King Zedekiah (Hel. 6:10), across the ocean to the Americas. And, like the Lehites, they prospered in this new land and soon became "exceedingly numerous." However, unlike the Lehites, the Mulekites lost much of their Israelite heritage. As the Book of Mormon states, because they failed to bring with them any scriptural records from Jerusalem, the Mulekites were afflicted by "many wars and serious contentions," so much so that by the time the Nephites "discovered" them, they had begun to deny "the being of their Creator" and had allowed their language to become so "corrupted" that neither the Nephite king nor his people could understand them (Omni 1:17). In other words, although the Mulekites had some claim on a Israelite identity, they were not Jews in any meaningful way. Like pagan Gentiles, they knew nothing of the Hebrew God, the Hebrew Scriptures, or even Hebrew. Consequently, they had to be taught these things afresh.

It is therefore significant that when the Nephites migrated north and essentially took over the Mulekite kingdom, the Mulekites did not resist or rebel. Instead, they greeted the Nephites with "great rejoicing" (Omni 1:14) and handed over to them not only their faith, their language, and their land, but their sovereignty over these things as well. As the Book of Mormon states, the Mulekites and the Nephites "did unite together; and Mosiah [the Nephite king] was appointed to be their king" (v. 19). In fact, the Mulekites joined with the Nephites so thoroughly that although they were essentially "adoptees" into Nephite culture and society, they quickly became almost indistinguishable from natural-born Nephites. The name "Mulekite" does not even appear in the Book of Mormon. Instead, its authors early on use phrases such as "the people of Zarahemla" or "those who came with [Mulek] into the wilderness" (Omni 1:21; Mosiah 25:2) to *describe* the Mulekites without *labeling* them as a separate people. Furthermore, as the Book of Mormon progresses, even these descriptions disappear. By the end of 4 Nephi, when Jacobites, Josephites, and other "ites" again emerge after having been subsumed into a larger, more inclusive society for over two hundred years, the Mulekites are neither mentioned nor alluded to (4 Ne. 36–38). In other words, the Mulekites were indeed "numbered with" the Nephites (Mosiah 25:13) much as Gentiles are to be "numbered with" the Jews (3 Ne. 30:2)—totally, completely, without displacing or replacing them. Unlike Paul's tree in Romans, here in the Book of Mormon no natural Israelite branches were removed in order to make room for these wilder, less Israelite branches. On the contrary, there seems to be plenty of land for both Nephites and Mulekites to reside together, comfortably, agreeably, even amicably, side by side.

This is not to say such a unity was easy to accomplish or that it happened all at once. Much as Mormon admonishes modern Gentiles to repent of their lying, whoring, idolatry, and other evils in order to be joined with the House of Israel (3 Ne. 30:2), these near-Gentiles also had to purge themselves of similar "evil doings." Earlier in their history, long before they were discovered by the Nephites, the Mulekites met and intermingled with the Jaredites, a much older *pre-Israelite* people whose history is summarized in the Book of Mormon by the last Jaredite prophet, Ether. These Jaredites, like the Lehites and the Mulekites, also left the Near East for the Americas, but they did so centuries earlier, around the time of the Tower of Babel. Consequently, they knew nothing of Abraham, Moses, David, or any of the other biblical figures that came after them. They had prophets, to be sure, but since the Hebrew Scriptures had yet to be written, they lacked exposure to almost all of the laws, stories, covenants, and promises these scriptures contain. As a result, the Jaredites were even more Gentile-like than the Mulekites, and their society was consequently rife with distinctly non-Israelite wickedness and war. In fact, so prevalent were conflicts among the Jaredites that their civilization eventually destroyed itself—but not before passing on many of their worst qualities to the Mulekites.

According to Hugh Nibley, this Jaredite influence can be seen both in the names as well as in the ideas that suddenly appeared among the Nephites soon after the Mulekites joined them. He writes:

> That the Mulekite-Jaredite background represented a definite cultural tradition among the Nephites and was consciously cultivated is, I believe, very clearly shown in the behavior of men with Jaredite names. Five out of the six whose names are definitely Jaredite betray strong anti-Nephite leanings. . . . Morianton sought to lead a great body of people back into the wilderness; Coriantumr was a notorious apostate and subversive; Korihor rebelled against the church and state and tried to inaugurate a mass uprising; Nehor actually succeeded in setting up a rival system of religion and government in opposition to the Nephite rulers, and was only stopped when he was executed for murdering a righteous judge; King Noah, perhaps of mixed Mulekite descent, horrified the Nephites by introducing the ways of the old Jaredite kings—oppressive taxation, whoredoms, and abominations, "elegant and

spacious buildings," the pursuit of his opponents into the wilderness, priestly colleges and ritual hierodules, and all the rest.[12]

In other words, the Book of Mormon not only lays out what Gentiles need to do in order to be "numbered with the Jews," but it provides examples of the problems—and solutions—that such a union involves. Here in the Book of Mormon, the strife caused by Morianton's rebellion is subdued by Moroni (Alma 50:25–36), the murders that were central to Coriantumr's coup are stopped by Moronihah (Hel. 1:15–33), the lies and deceptions put forth by Korihor are exposed by Alma the Younger (Alma 30:6–60), the priestcraft inherent in Nehor's appeal is adjudicated by that same Alma (1:1–15), and the idolatry and whoredoms and exploitation promoted by Noah and his priests are roundly condemned by Abinadi and resisted by Gideon (Mosiah 12:1–8, 25–37; 19:4–24). In this way, the portrayal of the Mulekites, further fleshes out Zenos's allegory, adding muscle and sinew to its somewhat skeletal anti-supersessionist stance; as a result, it further strengthens the Book of Mormon's already strong covenantally inclusivist position. Certainly, there will be challenges as Jews and non-Jews come together in God's covenant. However, as the Book of Mormon shows, unity can eventually be achieved.

As a result, Paul's arboreal metaphor in Romans 11 in contrast seems incomplete and almost sketchy. It appears to present just one small part of the much longer story of how Jews and Gentiles relate to God and to each other. For believers in the Book of Mormon, Zenos's allegory as well as the story of the Mulekites make it so that Romans 11 can no longer be used to justify a rejectionist approach towards Jews. As Jacob states, addressing Jews in much the same way and along the same lines as Paul did Gentiles in Romans 11:17–19:

> How merciful is our God unto us, for he remembereth the house of Israel, both roots and branches; and he stretches forth his hands unto them all the day long . . . [and] as many as will not harden their hearts shall be saved in the kingdom of God. (Jacob 6:4)

---

12. Hugh Nibley, *Lehi in the Desert; World of the Jaredites; There Were Jaredites*, 245–46.

Chapter Four

We Did Observe to Keep the Commandments

And we did observe to keep the judgments, and the statutes, and the commandments of the Lord in all things, according to the law of Moses. And the Lord was with us; and we did prosper exceedingly; for we did sow seed, and we did reap again in abundance. And we began to raise flocks, and herds, and animals of every kind. (2 Ne. 5:10–11)

Just as the New Testament's portrayal of Jews literally condemns them as murderous hypocrites, so its portrayal of the Law of Moses seems to convict it as spiritually injurious. In the Gospel of Matthew, for instance, the laws of religious purity are reduced to compulsive handwashing (Matt. 15:2), the laws of religious dress become abused status symbols (23:5), and the laws of Sabbath observance are portrayed as absurd prohibitions against doing good one day out of every seven (12:10). In this way, the Gospels attack Mosaic practices just as they do their practitioners—by presenting them in unsympathetic, unrealistic, and unfair terms. And, just as the Book of Mormon counters the New Testament's deleterious depiction of Jews, so it similarly refutes this condemnatory portrayal—respectfully, not by changing or challenging the text of the New Testament but by adding to the Christian canon portrayals of Mosaic laws functioning positively, even practically, in the lives of spiritually commendable people as well as by integrating Mosaic festivals vitally and vibrantly into the story it tells.

Portraying Mosaic Observance Positively

"Wo, wo, unto Jerusalem, for I have seen thine abominations!" This sentence from the first chapter of the Book of Mormon could easily have come from the twenty-third chapter of Matthew. Just as Jesus censures the Jerusalemites of his day, so Lehi rebukes those of his (1 Ne. 1:13; Matt.

23:13–16, 36–38). However, unlike the Gospel of Matthew, the Book of Mormon does not link abominable behavior to Mosaic obedience. Never is there any suggestion that this Law involves "heavy burdens . . . grievous to be born" or includes loads laid forcibly "on men's shoulders" by hypocrites (23:4). On the contrary, the Book of Mormon consistently links Mosaic obedience to blessings, not burdens, and often shows admirable people observing the Law of Moses admirably and effectively.

Righteous Lehi

Lehi's own experience is a case in point. Here is a Jew so righteous that, like Paul, he receives a vision from God, and yet, unlike Paul, he does not portray the Law of Moses as a tedious, overbearing "schoolmaster" (Gal. 3:24) or imply that it gets in the way of his righteousness. Instead, Lehi consistently expresses his righteousness in terms consistent with the Law. Soon after escaping from Jerusalem, Lehi builds a Mosaic "altar of stones" and makes a Mosaic offering unto the Lord in gratitude (1 Ne. 2:7).[1] Three chapters later, he again offers Mosaic "sacrifice and burnt offerings," not once but twice—the first time in appreciation to the Lord for the safe return of his sons after obtaining the brass plates (5:9) and the second time because the Lord "did soften the heart of Ishmael" and caused him to bring his family to join Lehi's in the wilderness (7:5, 22). In each of these instances, there is no hint of hypocrisy or evil intent; rather, Lehi is unquestionably sincere and selfless. In fact, his actions and experiences mirror those of Moses in multiple ways. Like Moses, Lehi prays unto the Lord, not for himself, but "with all his heart, in behalf of his people" (1:5; Num. 21:7). Like Moses, he fears "exceedingly" when he sees a miraculous fire before him and hears the voice of the Lord (1 Ne. 1:6; Ex. 3:6). Like Moses, he is mocked and threatened when he attempts to share what he has seen but forges ahead anyway despite threats to his life (1 Ne. 1:19–20; Ex. 2:15; 5:20–23). And, like Moses, when he is finally commanded to do so, Lehi dutifully leads his family to safety, despite their complaints, while leaving behind much and forgoing whatever status and position he had in

---

1. Although Deuteronomy 12:5–14 would seem to forbid Lehi from offerings sacrifices in any other place besides the Temple in Jerusalem, the fact that Moses, the "author" of Deuteronomy, had commanded Israel to offer sacrifices on an "altar of stones" immediately after crossing the Jordan (Deut. 27:1–7) seems to mitigate this prohibition. After all, both actions seem to represent a renewed commitment to obey the Lord under very similar circumstances.

his community (1 Ne. 2:1–6, 11; Ex. 13:17–20; 16:2–3). There is nothing duplicitous, deceptive, self-serving, hypocritical, or conniving about Lehi. He is simply a good man attempting to do good things in a good way. Consequently, the fact that Lehi acts like Moses and employs ancient Mosaic practices to thank God for his blessings, such as they are, connects those practices to his goodness. In other words, here, at the beginning of the Book of Mormon, Mosaic practices are presented as both natural and commendable. Unlike the way Pharisees are portrayed in the New Testament, Lehi has nothing to gain socially or economically by observing them. He is simply showing his deep devotion to God the best way he knows how—through the Law of Moses.

Nephites and Lamanites

This positive view of the Law continues with Lehi's family. Soon after Lehi and his family arrive at their promised land in the Western Hemisphere, they split up into two groups: the "good" Nephites and the "bad" Lamanites. However, in this dichotomy, it is the Nephites, not the Lamanites, who are described in Mosaic terms. The Nephites "observe to keep the judgments, and the statutes, and the commandments of the Lord in all things, according to the law of Moses" (2 Ne. 5:10), while the Lamanites become "an idle people, full of mischief and subtlety" (v. 24). In other words, it is the non-Mosaic Lamanites who resemble devious New Testament Pharisees, not the pro-Mosaic Nephites. In fact, the Nephites follow the Law of Moses so assiduously that soon after they separate from the Lamanites, they construct a temple "after the manner of the temple of Solomon" (v. 16),[2] so that they may more completely keep the Mosaic Law—again, with no hint of criticism or negativity in how this very Mosaic activity is presented. Throughout the Book of Mormon, Mosaic temples are portrayed favorably, serving as appropriate places for priests, kings, prophets, and even the resurrected Jesus to teach their people the ways of righteousness (Jacob 1:17; Mosiah 1:18; 3 Ne. 11:1). The only regret voiced by Nephi and his people concerning their first temple is that they could not honor it more, that it was "not built of so many

---

2. Although Josiah's reforms (2 Kgs. 22–23) would seem to preclude the construction of other temples besides Solomon's in Jerusalem, the fact that Lehi had received a vision in which he was shown that Jerusalem and its temple had been destroyed prior to the construction of this temple may have helped justify it (2 Ne. 1:4).

precious things; for they were not to be found upon the land, wherefore, it could not be built like unto Solomon's temple" (2 Ne. 5:16).

Within the narrative of the Book of Mormon, such a regret regarding their inability to properly adorn their temple is more than understandable. Far from being meaningless or inconsequential as the Gospels cast it, here the Law of Moses brings tangible blessings. Continuing as they began, the Nephites are later said to have kept "the law of Moses and the sabbath day holy unto the Lord" for hundreds of years (Jarom 1:5). As a result, they are described as not only being protected from Lamanite attacks because of their obedience, but as prospering, multiplying rapidly, and spreading out widely "upon the face of the land." They are also portrayed as being "exceedingly rich in gold, and in silver, and in precious things, and in fine workmanship of wood, in buildings, and in machinery, and also in iron and copper, and brass and steel"—again, precisely because their leaders were "mighty men in the faith of the Lord," exhorting "with all longsuffering the people to diligence; teaching the law of Moses" (1:7–8, 11).

Prosperity and Blessings

Such a causal link between obedience to the Mosaic commandments and material blessings is bolstered by Nephi's observation that because his people observed the Law of Moses they "did prosper exceedingly" (2 Ne. 5:10–11). In fact, so frequently is this connection made in the Book of Mormon that it becomes one of the book's most prominent themes—almost a motto. Long before Nephi arrives in the Promised Land, he is told by the Lord that "inasmuch as ye shall keep my commandments, ye shall prosper" (1 Ne. 2:20). This promise is then repeated by Lehi (2 Ne. 1:9, 20; 4:4), Jarom (Jarom 1:9), Amaron (Omni 1:6), King Benjamin (Mosiah 1:7; 2:22, 31), Alma (Alma 9:13; 36:1, 30; 37:13; 38:1), and Mormon (48:15). It is also expanded upon, provided with more specific promises of protection and divine support. Lehi, for example, tells his people that obedience to the Mosaic commandments will ensure that none will "molest them" in their new land, that no one will "take away the land of their inheritance," and that they "shall dwell safely forever" (2 Ne. 1:9).

Granted, not all of the blessings derived from obedience to the Law of Moses are material. Many are spiritual or intellectual. However, it is an undisputed fact, according to the Book of Mormon, that blessings arise as a direct result of obedience to the Mosaic laws just as cursings come from disobedience to these same laws. In contrast with the Nephites, the Lamanites reject the Ten Commandments, flout the kosher laws, and openly violate several other Mosaic injunctions. Jarom, for instance, writes that the Lamanites "loved murder and would drink the blood of beasts" (Jarom 1:6); Enos describes them as a "wild, and ferocious, and a blood-thirsty people," a people "full of idolatry and filthiness; feeding upon beasts of prey" (Enos 1:20); and Mormon claims that they "were a lazy and an idolatrous people," a people "desirous to bring [the Nephites] into bondage, that they might glut themselves with the labors of [other people's] hands" (Mosiah 9:12). Consequently, as a result of their rejection of the Law of Moses, the Lamanites frequently fail to enjoy any measure of divine protection or favor. Time and time again, they come against the Nephites in battle. However, because they know "nothing concerning the Lord, nor the strength of the Lord" and depend instead "upon their own strength" (10:11), they are just as often soundly defeated. Only later, after the Nephites stray from the Mosaic laws and the Lamanites begin to "observe strictly to keep the commandments of God, according to the law of Moses" (Hel. 13:10) do the Lamanites prosper, sending to the Nephites not warriors to attack them but prophets to warn the now-wicked Nephites and enjoin them to follow the Lamanites' example and "observe to keep [God's] commandments and his statutes and his judgments according to the law of Moses" (15:5).

Portraying Mosaic Holy Days as Spiritually Vital and Vibrant

Nonetheless, as persuasive as these portrayals are, they are not enough, by themselves, to counter all of the anti-Mosaic arguments put forth by the Gospels, where not only are those who attempt to keep the Law of Moses generally depicted as people bereft of any inner sincerity or innate devotion, but the Mosaic holy days themselves are often presented as events devoid of any real religious function or spiritual significance. Furthermore, because the Gospels' presentation of these holy days contains no hint of the traditions Jews today commonly associate with them, it seems to suggest that Jewish practices, as they have developed over time, are similarly pointless and religiously ineffective. In the Gospel of John, for instance, the drama of Jesus standing and crying out, "If any man thirst, let him come unto me, and drink" (John 7:37) completely overwhelms the fact that this event occurred during Sukkot. Here, there is little connection between what Jesus says and how this festival is biblically or traditionally observed. No one throws a week-long banquet (Deut. 16:13–14), rejoices with the "boughs of goodly trees" before the Lord (Lev. 23:40), constructs a temporary shelter in remembrance of their dependence upon God (v. 42), or uses that shelter to entertain strangers. As a result, to many readers, what this Gospel calls "the Jews' feast of tabernacles" (John 7:2) looks no more like modern Sukkot than its murderous "Jews" do the Jewish people of today (v. 1). Far from a time full of worship and celebration, Sukkot in this Gospel has been completely gutted, hollowed out, emptied of anything resembling traditional Jewish worship. It seems to serve only one purpose: as an excuse to bring large numbers of people together so that they can see Jesus and hear his words.

This anti-Mosaic slant is particularly pronounced—and effective—with regards to Passover. Like Sukkot, this festival is referred to as "*the Jews' Passover*" in the Gospel of John (2:13; 11:55), a Gospel that further distances it from Jesus by never actually showing him celebrating this festival or discussing any of its elements. The synoptic Gospels, on the other hand, show Jesus eating a Passover meal and quote him commenting on two of its most distinctive elements: the bread and the wine. However, in none of these Gospels is any of the Mosaic meanings of these elements presented or discussed as stipulated by the Law (Ex. 12:25–27). Instead, the Gospels of Matthew, Mark, and Luke present the paschal bread and wine as meaningless remnants of a long forgotten religious tradition, an observance that can be easily repurposed into memorials of Jesus's soon-to-be-dead body and spilt blood. In addition, the fact that none of these Gospels mentions, however obliquely, the other foods and practices commonly associated with Passover today, although perhaps historically accurate, similarly undermines the utility—and ongoing validity—of medieval and modern Judaism. In these Gospels, no one dips greens in salt, samples *charoset*, constructs a "Hillel sandwich," or sets out a special goblet for Elijah. The wise, wicked, simple, and silent sons are not discussed nor are the four questions asked. As a result, readers of the Gospels who are acquainted with these practices may see in this Seder a reminder of how Judaism has added to the biblical commandments over the years and view those additions, as well as the faith that developed them, as spiritually suspect. After all, if Jesus challenged the Pharisees, asking them "Why do ye also transgress the commandment of God by your tradition?" (Matt. 15:3), what would he say to those who follow the later traditions of the Talmudic rabbis, the Pharisees' religious descendants?

Mosaic Festivals in the Book of Mormon

The Gospels' case against observing the Law of Moses may seem formidable, possibly even irrefutable. However, the Book of Mormon, like a good defense attorney confronts these literary arguments head-on, directly, on their own terms, by supplying several well-developed examples of Mosaic festivals that demonstrate just how spiritually full these festivals can indeed be—alone, by themselves, without Christian adaptation or interpretation. Again, notice that although the Book of Mormon clearly challenges any supersessionist interpretation of the New Testament based on the way Mosaic festivals are portrayed in the Gospels, it leaves entirely untouched the scriptural authority and spiritual reliability of the New Testament itself. Just as the Book of Mormon did through its portrayals of Jews, it's portrayal of their Law similarly modifies the way it is understood by contributing additional material to the Christian canon *without* criticizing or in any way altering the New Testament's text. Simply by supplying more witnesses, the Book of Mormon opens Christian readers up to a larger scriptural context where the events in the New Testament are not all the evidence they must consider before reaching any final interpretive verdict.

Nonetheless, as commendable as such a strategy may seem to some, to others it may appear untenable. After all, the Book of Mormon does not actually use the Hebrew names of these festivals nor does it employ any of their various English equivalents. Neither does it describe, in obvious terms, their observance. It would appear, therefore, that any rebuttal of Mosaic supersessionism based on the Book of Mormon's treatment of Sukkot, Pesach, or Shavuot is simply not possible. Nonetheless, such an approach does not require that the actual names of these festivals be used or that all of the activities associated with them be detailed in a definitive, step-by-step manner. All that is necessary is that the Book of Mormon *suggest* their traditional observance and *show* that observance affecting its central figures in vital and vibrant ways. And on this score the Book of Mormon excels. So integrated are the activities and purposes of several Mosaic festivals in the Book of Mormon's story that they make it very difficult to disregard them and dismiss their influence without destroying the overall structure and message of the Book of Mormon as a whole. John S. Thompson, for example, sees Jacob's sermon early on in the Book of Mormon as connecting closely with "the Israelite autumn festivals, which in turn links much of the imagery in the Isaiah portions of speech to ritual and enthronement themes."[3] Similarly, John W. Welch and Terrence L. Szink write that King Benjamin's final address is so intertwined around these same Mosaic holy days as to "highlight the importance of this public occasion as a significant religious event."[4] In other words, just as the Gospels' portrayal of the feasts of Tabernacles, Passover, and Pentecost detaches these festivals from their original biblical and traditional purposes and essentially empties them of any lasting practical or religious significance, so the presentation of these same festivals in the Book of Mormon retains those purposes and fills them full of ongoing relevance and meaning. And the Book of Mormon, as a scripture written to modern readers, does so primarily by integrating that relevance and meaning into its plot in a way that is recognizable to these readers, especially if they are acquainted with Jews and Judaism.

Ten Days of Repentance

For instance, although the Book of Mormon does not mention Rosh Hashanah by name, the observances and ideas traditionally associated with this festival resonate remarkably with the initial context and impetus of Book of Mormon. The Book of Mormon begins, after all, at "the *commencement* of the first year of the reign of Zedekiah" (1 Ne. 1:4)—a phrase consistent with Rosh Hashanah, or "head" of the year. This holy day, although occurring during the seventh month of the Jewish calendar, nonetheless celebrates the start of a new year, much as college commencement services officially begin post-graduate life sometimes months after such a life has already begun. However, unlike college commencements and secular New Year's celebrations, this "Jewish New Year," as Rosh Hashanah is sometimes called, is not a period of celebration and revelry. Instead Rosh Hashanah initiates a period of intense self-examination called *Aseret Y'may T'Shuvah*, or the "Ten Days of Repentance."

During these days, observant Jews prepare for Yom Kippur, or the Day of Atonement, by making themselves right before God, a process that not only requires that they ask God for forgiveness but demands that they review their behavior during the past year, identify any harm they may have inflicted upon others, and actively seek to remedy that harm. As Rabbi George Robinson writes: "Traditionally, Jews will ask their friends, family, and colleagues to for-

---

3. John S. Thompson, "Isaiah 50–51, the Israelite Autumn Festivals, and the Covenant Speech of Jacob in 2 Nephi 6–10," 124.

4. John W. Welch and Terrence L. Szink, "King Benjamin's Speech in the Context of Ancient Israelite Festivals."

give them for transgressions they may have committed in the previous year. God may pardon our transgressions against the Eternal, but only a person who has been sinned against may forgive one who traduced her."[5] Consequently, Rosh Hashanah, for many Jews, is a day where they are alerted to the reality of their need to repent. In services, a shofar, or ram's horn, is sounded several times in order to rouse them from their moral slumber and wake them to the need to improve in their lives. The sermons delivered on this day similarly stress the necessity of repentance. As Rabbi Hayim Halevy Donin writes, "The Sabbath which falls during this ten-day period is known as Shabbat Teshuvah, or the Sabbath of Repentance,"[6] and it is devoted to this subject. Indeed, as Rabbi Robinson explains, "even before it became the custom for a rabbi to sermonize regularly, this Shabbat was marked by a sermon, often given by a leader of the Jewish community, exhorting Jews to repent."[7]

It is therefore consistent with this ten-day period of intense self-scrutiny that there came at the beginning of the Book of Mormon many prophets to Jerusalem, "prophesying unto the people that they must repent" (1 Ne. 1:4). It is also consistent with this period that Lehi would then go forth and pray "unto the Lord . . . in behalf of his people" (v. 5). According to Rabbi Wayne Dosick, in addition to the sermons, the prayers during this time similarly "revolve around evaluation of conduct and behavior in the year just ended, repentance for mistakes, and transgressions, and seeking forgiveness from fellow human beings and from God."[8] Rabbi Robinson writes: "*Selikhot* prayers [penitential prayers] are read before the morning service and *Avinu Malkeinu* (Our Father, Our King) is recited after the *Amidah*."[9] One such *selikhah* from the *Amidah* reads:

> Forgive us, our Father, for we have sinned,
> Pardon us, our King, for we have transgressed,
> For Thou art a pardoner and forgiver.
> Blessed art Thou, Lord, Gracious One who forgives abundantly.[10]

---

5. George Robinson, *Essential Judaism: A Complete Guide to Beliefs, Customs, and Rituals*, 95–96.

6. Hayim Halevy Donin, To *Be a Jew: A Guide to Jewish Observance in Contemporary Life*, 246.

7. Robinson, *Essential Judaism*, 96.

8. Wayne Dosick, *Living Judaism: The Complete Guide to Jewish Belief, Tradition, and Practice*, 130.

9. Robinson, *Essential Judaism*, 96.

10. Hayim Halevy Donin, *To Pray as a Jew: A Guide to the Prayer Book and the Synagogue Service*, 84.

Like most Jewish prayers, these prayers are expressed in the first-person plural and as such unite the supplicant with all Israel. Though individual sins are of paramount importance, individual Jews do not often ask for forgiveness for these alone; they plead instead for forgiveness for all of Israel's sins. As Rabbi Donin writes, such prayers, like Lehi's for "*his* people" (1 Ne. 1:5), very much affirm the very Jewish "principle of mutual responsibility and concern."[11]

In addition to the fact that Lehi prays for his people, what happens to him afterwards similarly resonates with Jewish traditions associated with the period between Rosh Hashanah and Yom Kippur. As he prays, Lehi experiences a vision so powerful that "he did quake and tremble exceedingly" (1 Ne. 1:6). He is overcome and returns to his home to rest. He receives none, however, and instead is carried away in another vision in which he sees God "sitting upon his throne, surrounded with numberless concourses of angels," all singing praises unto Him (v. 8). During this vision, one of the angels descends from this heavenly court and gives Lehi a book to read (v. 11). The words he reads are full of condemnation and chastisement, as well as predictions that Jerusalem "should be destroyed" and that many of the inhabitants "should perish by the sword, and . . . be carried away captive into Babylon" (v. 13).

This view of God and his relation to the city of Jerusalem is identical to the way Jews traditionally picture God and his relation to them on Rosh Hashanah. According to Rabbi Dosick, Jews visualize God at this time as a king "sitting on the Throne of Judgment, on the Day of Judgment, writing the fate of each individual for the coming year in the Book of Life."[12] The idea is that during this ten-day period the Book of Life is open and will not be closed until after Yom Kippur. In other words, the judgments written down in this book can yet be altered. Sincere repentance can change God's mind and modify one's future. As a result, during this time prayers such as these dominate synagogue services:

> Remember us unto life, O King who delightest in life, and inscribe us in the Book of Life so that we may live worthily for Thy sake, O Lord of life. . . .
>
> O inscribe all the children of Thy covenant for a happy life. . . .
>
> In the book of life, blessing, peace and ample sustenance, may we, together with all Thy people, the house of Israel, be remembered and inscribed before Thee for a happy life and for peace. Blessed art Thou, O Lord, who establishest peace.[13]

---

11. Donin, *To Pray as a Jew*, 7.
12. Dosick, *Living Judaism*, 132.
13. *Sabbath and Festival Prayer Book*, 20, 24–25.

In keeping with these prayers, the traditional greeting for Rosh Hashanah is *L'shanah tovah tikatevu*, or "May you be inscribed (in God's Book of Life) for a good year."[14] Much like the people of Nineveh in the book of Jonah (the biblical book traditionally read on Yom Kippur[15]), traditional observant Jews hope that they can elude destruction and death by repenting, honestly and sincerely. Lehi too has the same hope for his people. After he has experienced his terrible vision of Jerusalem's demise, he exclaims:

> Great and marvelous are thy works, O Lord God Almighty! Thy throne is high in the heavens, and thy power, and goodness, and mercy are over all the inhabitants of the earth; and, because thou art merciful, thou wilt not suffer those who come unto thee that they shall perish! (1 Ne. 1:14)

Such an enthusiastic reaction does not make sense unless the fate of Jerusalem has not yet been sealed. The Book of Life must still be open. There is still a chance that what is written in it can yet be altered. Otherwise, Lehi's praise of God's mercy and his description of God as merciful is senseless, even cruel. In this way, the Book of Mormon not only connects with Rosh Hashanah, but this connection helps explain what is going on in it.

Yom Kippur

Given the linkages to Rosh Hashanah in the Book of Mormon, it is natural to expect some connection to Yom Kippur to follow. After all, Yom Kippur is the culminating fast at the end of the Ten Days of Repentance, the day when all this intense self-reflection and penance finally bear fruit. However, there is none—no reference to priests or to blood, no mention of the Holy of Holies or the Ark of the Covenant, and no suggestion of the rituals modern Jews have come to associate with this day: the blowing of the shofar, the priestly blessing, or the symbolic casting off of lint and crumbs (representing past sins) into a flowing body of water. It is almost as if Yom Kippur does not exist. And for these pre-Captivity Jerusalemites this may have been the case. Unrepentant to the last, they cannot access the divine forgiveness that Yom Kippur epitomizes. For them, the Book of Life has indeed been closed, and their fate sealed. Lehi, like the Azazel scapegoat, may have been driven out of their midst into the wilderness, but he does not carry with him their sins. These pre-Captivity Jews remain stained by

---

14. Dosick, *Living Judaism,* 134, 137.
15. Dosick, 136–37.

greed, tarnished by idolatry, and rendered unclean by robbery, adultery, and murder. Consequently, Jerusalem will soon be attacked by the Babylonians, its temple burned, and its inhabitants will be either killed or taken captive. But this is not so for Lehi. He has come before the Lord as Yom Kippur requires, he has attempted to right his relationship with God by first correcting his connection with his neighbors, and he has pled for them to repent. As a result, he will be saved from destruction while they will not (1 Ne. 1:14). And so his story continues, as does its connection to Mosaic festivals.

Sukkot

Very soon after fleeing Jerusalem, Lehi is described as dwelling in a tent (1 Ne. 2:15). Not only is he initially said to have "pitched his tent in a valley by the side of a river of water" (v. 6), but his tent quickly becomes the center of activity for the family. It is where Nephi goes after he speaks to the Lord and where he receives an assignment to procure the brass plates (3:1–4). It is where he and his brothers return after they have completed this assignment (4:38) and where the joy of their mother and father is said to be full (5:7). It is also where Nephi and his brothers receive another assignment, this time to retrieve Ishmael and his family from Jerusalem (7:2), and it is where they must bring them (v. 5). Such an emphasis on Lehi's tent may mystify some readers. However, to anyone steeped in Jewish tradition, this emphasis resonates remarkably with Sukkot, especially given the Mosaic events that precede it. Sukkot, after all, occurs five days after Yom Kippur, and dwelling in temporary shelters, such as tents, is central to how it is celebrated. As Rabbi Donin explains, the name Sukkot, also spelled *Succot* or *Succoth*, "refers to the temporary dwelling places used by the children of Israel in the desert during the forty-year period of wandering following the exodus from Egypt."[16] During this festival, traditionally observant Jews construct makeshift huts or booths and live in them for a week, as commanded in Leviticus:

> Ye shall dwell in booths seven days; all that are Israelites born shall dwell in booths: That your generations may know that I made the children of Israel to dwell in booths, when I brought them out of the land of Egypt: I [am] the Lord your God. (Lev. 23:42–43)

However, not only are the repeated references to Lehi's tent consistent with Sukkot, but Lehi's actions while dwelling within it are also conso-

---

16. Donin, To *Be a Jew*, 250.

nant with one of the central purposes of this festival: to reenact Israel's wanderings in the wilderness. Here, much like Moses in that wilderness, Lehi gives thanks to God for his family's deliverance (1 Ne. 2:7; 5:9; Ex. 15:1–19), blesses his children (1 Ne. 2:9–10; Deut. 33:1–25), speaks to them "with power" (1 Ne. 2:14; Ex. 4:1–12), and reviews the story of how the ancient children of Israel "were also led out of captivity" (1 Ne. 5:15; Deut. 11:1–5). Indeed, Lehi fills the role of Moses so well that he almost seems like a reincarnation of Judaism's ancient lawgiver. Like Moses, Lehi is well acquainted with the "learning of the Jews and language of the Egyptians" (1 Ne. 1:2; Ex. 2:6–12). Like Moses, he foretells woes that will come upon his Egypt-favoring people and is mocked by them for doing so (1 Ne. 1:19; Ex. 5:1–2; 11:4–6). Like Moses, he is led, as it were, by a pillar of fire (1 Ne. 1:6; Ex. 13:21–22) out of a wicked land, where his life too was threatened, and takes his people "three days in the wilderness" (1 Ne. 2:6; Ex. 3:18, 5:3, 8:27). And finally, like Moses, when he has escaped to safety in the wilderness he builds "an altar of stones, and [makes] an offering unto the Lord, and [gives] thanks" (1 Ne. 2:7; Ex. 17:15). Furthermore, some members of Lehi's family seem to join in on the act. Not only do Laman and Lemuel "murmur" against Lehi and his heir apparent, Nephi, just as the children of Israel did against Moses, but they do so in the same way and for the same reasons. Almost immediately after leaving Jerusalem, they complain that they are being led "to perish in the wilderness" (1 Ne. 2:11; Ex. 14:11); they desire instead "to return unto the land" from which they came (1 Ne. 7:7; Num. 14:3); and they claim that it is "a hard thing" that their leaders have required of them (1 Ne. 3:5; Ex. 5:21). As a result, Laman and Lemuel, again like Moses's wandering Israelites, are called "stiffnecked," (1 Ne. 2:11; Ex. 32:9) and are described as people who do not know "the dealings of that God who had created them" (1 Ne. 2:12; Ex. 6:3).

One of the main purposes of reenacting the Exodus during Sukkot, according to Rabbi Donin, is to identify with and learn from this experience, particularly the need to trust God and rely on his protection.[17] And this lesson is not lost on Nephi. For example, when Nephi sees his brothers' behavior, he blames it immediately on a Pharaoh-like "hardness of their hearts" (1 Ne. 2:18; Ex. 16:7–8). Furthermore, when it looks like he and his brothers may not be able to complete a task their father had given them inside his tent, Nephi points out the similarity of their situation

---

17. Donin, 250.

with that of children of Israel and looks to Moses's dividing of the Red Sea for inspiration. As he says to his brothers:

> Therefore let us go up; let us be strong like unto Moses; for he truly spake unto the waters of the Red Sea and they divided hither and thither, and our fathers came through, out of captivity, on dry ground, and the armies of Pharaoh did follow and were drowned in the waters of the Red Sea. Now behold ye know that this is true; and ye also know that an angel hath spoken unto you; wherefore can ye doubt? Let us go up; the Lord is able to deliver us, even as our fathers, and to destroy Laban, even as the Egyptians. (1 Ne. 4:2–30)

In this way, the Exodus story dominates this section of the Book of Mormon just as it controls Sukkot, and it does so in practical, realistic, positive terms.

Another purpose of celebrating Sukkot, according to Rabbi Robinson, is to understand one's dependence upon God and to give thanks to God for His blessings. As Robinson writes, Sukkot demonstrates how reliant Israel remains on "the will of God in a hostile world."[18] This point was certainly evident during their wanderings in the wilderness—when manna, quail, and water were produced miraculously—and it continues to be manifest in the fruit harvest, an event that coincides with Sukkot and whose success is very much dependent upon the providence of God. This is another reason why the structures customarily made on this holiday are fairly flimsy, requiring only three walls and a roof that is constructed so that "the stars may be visible through it on a clear night."[19] These structures represent the tents the ancient Israelites dwelt in, but they also present their inhabitants with an image of just how fragile human existence is and how dependent they are upon God. According to Robinson, these booths, or *sukkot,* serve as vivid object lessons, teaching that God alone supplies "true shelter."[20] Expressing thanks to God for His protection and providence consequently is an important aspect of Sukkot. Along these lines, Sukkot is also known as *Chag Ha'asif* or the Festival of the Ingathering,[21] and, as a harvest festival, it is a time for thanking God for his bounty. According to Rabbi Donin, Sukkot is a time "when the spirit of thankfulness and gratefulness to the Lord for providing for people's needs is more naturally forthcoming."[22] Robinson even goes so far as to describe Sukkot as "a sort

---

18. Robinson, *Essential Judaism,* 105.
19. Donin, To *Be a Jew,* 253.
20. Robinson, *Essential Judaism,* 105.
21. Dosick, *Living Judaism,* 147.
22. Donin, To *Be a Jew,* 250.

of Jewish equivalent of the American Thanksgiving,"[23] as it is also a time "to offer an offering made by fire unto the Lord" as an expression of thanks (Lev. 23:33–37).

This thankful purpose is also emphasized while Lehi dwells in a tent. Having left behind "his house, and the land of his inheritance, and his gold, and his silver, and his precious things" (1 Ne. 2:4), Lehi is in a very vulnerable position. Furthermore, he is living in the wilderness and does not know where he is going or what he is supposed to do. Indeed, one might wonder what exactly Lehi has to be thankful for. Nevertheless, consistent with Sukkot, his time in his tent is marked by sacrificial offerings and expressions of gratitude to God. As Leviticus instructs:

> Seven days ye shall offer an offering made by fire unto the Lord: on the eighth day shall be an holy convocation unto you; and ye shall offer an offering made by fire unto the Lord: it [is] a solemn assembly; [and] ye shall do no servile work [therein]. These [are] the feasts of the Lord, which ye shall proclaim [to be] holy convocations, to offer an offering made by fire unto the Lord, a burnt offering, and a meat offering, a sacrifice, and drink offerings, every thing upon his day: Beside the sabbaths of the LORD, and beside your gifts, and beside all your vows, and beside all your freewill offerings, which ye give unto the Lord. (Lev. 23:36–38)

Lehi is therefore not so much rejoicing in the abundant blessings present in his immediate circumstances as he is celebrating a Mosaic holy day that emphasizes how generous God is (or will be) even in the most difficult of circumstances. Little wonder then that Lehi not only offers an offering of thanks when he first reaches the valley of Lemuel (1 Ne. 2:7), but he does so again when his sons return with the plates of brass (5:9), as well as later when Ishmael and his family join him (7:22). Sukkot is a time of giving thanks for all of God's blessings no matter how small or seemingly insignificant.

Furthermore, Sukkot is not meant to be celebrated alone or with one's own immediate family. It is a time of sharing one's blessings with friends, neighbors, even strangers, and, in this way, Lehi's time in his tent is both consistent with the biblical description of Sukkot, as well as with several later non-biblical customs associated with this festival. Lehi's sudden interest in inviting Ishmael and his family to join them, for instance, as well as Ishmael's willingness to do so, certainly are examples of revelatory power as well as inspired preparations for creating a new civilization in a far-off land. However, they also can be seen as ways of celebrating Sukkot. Sukkot after all, traditionally emphasizes the value of family and friends, another

---

23. Robinson, *Essential Judaism*, 101.

example of God's bounteous blessings. Therefore it is customary for observant Jews to invite friends and family into their *sukkot* to share meals and to enjoy time together. As Rabbi Robinson writes, "The rules of hospitality are nowhere more apparent than in the custom of inviting *ushpizin/honored guests* to partake of the shelter of the *sukkah*."[24] In fact, according to Rabbi Greenberg, guests are considered "stand-ins" for the biblical patriarchs and, in recent years, matriarchs as well. These guests are often "those who are needy or who need a sukkah in which to eat."[25] Such an impulse, compounded with the emphasis on gathering "together all manner of seeds of every kind" (1 Ne. 8:1), another Sukkot activity, metaphorically come together in Lehi's instructions to sons to "return unto the land of Jerusalem, and bring down Ishmael and his family into the wilderness" so "that his sons should take daughters to wife, that they might raise up *seed* unto the Lord in the land of promise" (7:1). This sense of community as well as continuity seems to be on his mind as Lehi dwells in a tent and is very much consistent with the traditional celebration of Sukkot.

Simchat Torah

Sukkot also, as it is traditionally observed, is a time for appreciating and giving thanks for the Scriptures, especially the Torah, and this impulse also resonates with what happens during this time in the Book of Mormon. Immediately after Sukkot comes Simchat Torah, or "Rejoicing of the Torah"—a holiday that follows so close upon Sukkot that it is often considered part of it. Today Simchat Torah is celebrated as "the conclusion and the new beginning of the yearly Torah-reading cycle."[26] On this day, the last words of Deuteronomy are read as well as the first words of Genesis. According to Rabbi Dosick, Simchat Torah is a holiday "characterized by much joyous singing and dancing. It revels in the fact that Torah reading goes on endlessly and therefore provides ongoing instruction from God as well as "an unbroken continuity of the Jewish People and Jewish life."[27] Although there is no evidence that Simchat Torah was celebrated in pre-Exilic times, given the other Sukkot-like activities and attitudes in Lehi's family, it is easy for modern readers familiar with Simchat Torah to

---

24. Robinson, 104
25. Irving Greenberg, *The Jewish Way: Living the Holidays*, 112.
26. Dosick, *Living Judaism*, 149.
27. Dosick, 149.

connect it to what happens at this point in the Book of Mormon and to find in it appreciation for the ongoing relevance of this Jewish tradition.

In fact, while Lehi is dwelling in his tent, he gives Nephi and his brothers an assignment that, though involved, seems tailor-made for Simchat Torah. Citing a dream from the Lord, Lehi sends his sons back to Jerusalem to obtain "plates of brass," an early version of the Hebrew Scriptures, from Laban, a local Jewish leader. Laman and Lemuel balk at this "hard thing" their father has required of them, but Nephi famously asserts that the Lord "shall prepare a way for them that they may accomplish the thing which he commandeth them," and they agree to go (1 Ne. 3:3–7). Perhaps placing too much stock in Nephi's assertion, Laman first attempts to procure the plates simply by asking Laban to hand them over. Laban, however, becomes "angry, and thrust him out from his presence; and he would not that [Laman] should have the records" (v. 13). Discouraged, the brothers are about to return to their father empty-handed. However, Nephi urges them to try again and explains that the plates are essential for preserving "unto [their] children the language of [their] fathers" as well as for retaining for their descendants "the words which have been spoken by the mouth of all the holy prophets" (vv. 19–20). He then suggests that they retrieve the gold and silver that their father left behind and exchange these "precious things" for the plates (vv. 22–23). These reasons appeal to Nephi's brothers, and they return again to Jerusalem, convinced that the plates are worth such a trade.

Laban, however, is not, and instead of agreeing to exchange the plates for the brothers' valuables, he decides to keep their treasure for himself. He consequently chases the brothers out of his house and commands his servants to kill them. Nephi and his brothers, however, flee into the wilderness and elude these servants by hiding in a cave. There, the two older brothers take out their frustration on Nephi and begin to beat him with a rod. Nonetheless, so important are the plates that an angel intervenes, saves Nephi, and encourages the brothers to try to obtain them one more time, promising them that "the Lord will deliver Laban into [their] hands" (1 Ne. 3:29). What this promise means is not entirely clear at this point. Nonetheless, Nephi, despite the danger to his life, obeys the angel and sneaks back into Jerusalem at night. Once inside the city, he comes upon a drunken Laban passed out on the street, and the Spirit of the Lord "constrains" him to kill Laban. Nephi recoils at the idea. "Never at any time have I shed the blood of man," he says (4:10). Undaunted, however, the Spirit continues to press Nephi, reminding him of the angel's promise as well as the crimes that Laban has committed against his family. The Spirit again commands Nephi to kill Laban, explaining that "it is better that one man should perish than that a nation should dwindle and perish in unbelief" (4:13). This idea intrigues Nephi, and, as he mulls it over, he realizes (1) that his family's future prosperity—indeed their very existence—is dependent upon keeping the commandments of God; (2) that they cannot keep "the commandments of the Lord according to the law of Moses, save they should have the law," and (3) that they cannot have the law unless he obtains the brass plates, upon which it is written (vv. 14–17). In other words, Nephi feels he is faced with a crucial life and death decision—either he kills Laban, obtains the plates, and his descendants live; or he spares Laban, returns to his father empty-handed, and his descendants die, spiritually if not otherwise. In this way, the Book of Mormon shows that having the scriptures generally available to a large population is worth enduring hardship, being publicly humiliated, giving up all the gold and silver and precious things that one possesses, and even putting one's life on the line. But are they worth taking someone's life if one is commanded by the Lord to do so? Nephi decides that they are and subsequently kills Laban with his own sword, disguises himself using Laban's clothing and armor, and retrieves the plates from Laban's treasury (vv. 17–24).

All in all, this story, like Simchat Torah, clearly shows the absolute necessity of the scriptures as well as the purposes they serve. It also shows the happiness that the scriptures bring. When Nephi and his brothers return again to the "tent of their father" with the plates, Lehi is filled with joy, and not just for the safe return of his sons. Immediately after they appear, he takes the

> records which were engraven upon the plates of brass, and he did search them from the beginning. And he beheld that they did contain the five books of Moses, which gave an account of the creation of the world, and also of Adam and Eve, who were our first parents;
>
> And also a record of the Jews from the beginning, even down to the commencement of the reign of Zedekiah, king of Judah; And also the prophecies of the holy prophets, from the beginning, even down to the commencement of the reign of Zedekiah; and also many prophecies which have been spoken by the mouth of Jeremiah. (1 Ne. 5:10–13)

Lehi is then "filled with the Spirit" and begins to prophesy, saying that these plates of brass, as the Hebrew scriptures, should "go forth unto all nations, kindreds, tongues, and people" and "should never perish; neither should they be dimmed any more by time" (1 Ne. 5:17–19). Nephi consequently records that his people "searched" these plates and "found that they were desirable; yea, even of great worth" since they "could preserve the commandments of the Lord unto our children" (v. 21).

Just as Sukkot for many modern Jews is not complete without Simchat Torah, so the journey of these ancient Jews to the Promised Land could not be conducted without the scriptures. They point the way. They give the lives of these people direction, purpose, and joy. As Nephi concludes: "Wherefore, it was wisdom in the Lord that we should carry [these plates] with us, as we journeyed in the wilderness towards the land of promise" (1 Ne. 5:22). In this way, the Book of Mormon honors the three main ideas behind Simchat Torah: the irreplaceable need for the scriptures, their ongoing relevance to real life, as well as the happiness they bring to those who cherish them, study them, and follow their commandments. This incident then, like others in first few chapters in the Book of Mormon, shows in real, practical terms the relevance and spiritual utility of Mosaic festivals. Again, unlike the Gospels where such festivals are too often presented as hollow or otherwise devoid of meaning, the Book of Mormon portrays them as brimming with spiritual and practical significance consistent with a sincere worship of God.

Passover

After Lehi and his family leave the valley of Lemuel, the Book of Mormon's connection to Mosaic festivals becomes more intermittent as the story becomes more elliptical, skipping not just many months but many years as it focuses on incidents and events leading up to the coming of Jesus. However, despite the Book of Mormon's lack of linkages to the month by month progression of the Jewish calendar, it still connects to Passover in a way that shows the ongoing vitality and vibrancy of this festival. Again, as with Rosh Hashanah and Sukkot, the words *Passover* and *Pesach* (Passover in Hebrew) do not occur in the Book of Mormon. However, the themes and some of the practices that are at the core of this holy day are plainly evident. For instance, in the speech previously mentioned, Nephi not only evokes the Passover theme of deliverance from Egypt but specifically dwells on how "our fathers came . . . out of captivity" (1 Ne. 4:2), a point he returns to again and again. When he and his brothers return with the plates of brass, he notes that these plates contain the account of the Israelites being "led out of captivity and out of the land of Egypt" (5:15), and later on, when he is attempting to silence his brothers' murmuring, he recites the entire story of the Exodus, beginning with the account of the Israelites' being "led out of bondage" (17:23–25). Indeed, the Passover story is so important to Nephi that he describes God as "the God of our fathers, who were led out of Egypt, out of bondage" (19:10). This emphasis on the oppressed state of the children of Israel and on their liberation is central to Passover. It is the festival that more than any other Mosaic activity fulfills the commandment to remember the day "in which ye came out from Egypt, out of the house of bondage" (Ex. 13:3). Even the food associated with Passover reinforces this theme. Bitter herbs remind participants of the bitterness of slavery, *charoset* the difficult labor necessary to make bricks, salt the tears of the Israelites shed during their captivity, and *matzot*, the "bread of affliction" (Deut. 16:3), the difficulties Israel suffered at that time.

Remembering Israel's miraculous deliverance from bondage is similarly emphasized by other figures in the Book of Mormon. Abinadi, for instance, begins his recitation of the Ten Commandments by quoting their introduction. Here, he suggests that bringing Israel "out of the land of Egypt, out of the house of bondage" (Mosiah 12:34) demonstrates both how God is qualified to institute these commandments and why he would do so. Captain Moroni chastises Pahoran, the chief judge in his land, by asking him explicitly, "Have ye forgotten the captivity of our fathers?" (Alma 60:20). And Alma too takes pride in the fact that he remembers this captivity, exclaiming that "I surely do know that the Lord did deliver them out of bondage" (29:11). Alma, in fact, so values this memory that he advises his oldest son Helaman to "do as I have done" and remember "the captivity of our fathers, for they were in bondage, and none could deliver them except it was the God of Abraham, and the God of Isaac, and the God of Jacob; and he surely did deliver them in their afflictions" (36:2). In addition, as if to prove his point, Alma goes on to describe for Helaman his own experience with divine deliverance and concludes by saying:

> And I know that he will raise me up at the last day, to dwell with him in glory; yea, and I will praise him forever, for he has brought our fathers out of Egypt, and he has swallowed up the Egyptians in the Red Sea; and he led them by his power into the promised land; yea, and he has delivered them out of bondage and captivity from time to time.
>
> Yea, and he has also brought our fathers out of the land of Jerusalem; and he has also, by his everlasting power, delivered them out of bondage and captivity, from time to time even down to the present day; and I have always retained in remembrance their captivity; yea, and ye also ought to retain in remembrance, as I have done, their captivity. (Alma 36:28–29)

For Alma remembering the captivity of Israel in Egypt shows the place of humanity in relation to God and highlights His power as its deliverer. In these ways, the Book of Mormon shows Passover to be both helpful in the past as well as relevant on a continuing basis.

However, not only are Alma's words consistent with the general point of Passover, but they also seem to occur within an actual Passover Seder. Scripturally and traditionally, it is not enough for one to merely recite the Passover service, one must *tell* it, sitting down with others, going over it with them in detail, analyzing and explaining their meaning, especially "in the ears of thy son, and of thy son's son" (Ex. 10:2). According to Rabbi Robinson, to truly observe Passover participants must "retell the story of the Exodus as if [they], too, had been liberated from slavery in Egypt" and they must do so for their children.[28] In this way, Passover both passes on the story to the next generations as well as extends to them the personal promise of divine deliverance. The main function of the Passover Seder, therefore, is to serve as a catalyst for discussion. It provides the time as well as the "conversation prompts" to enable parents to pass down to their children their feelings, thoughts, and experiences with God. As Robinson continues,

> A seder is a joyous occasion, a gathering of family and friends that should include not only the recitation of the *Haggadah* [the Passover story], but a spiritual discussion with many questions and debate of the meaning of the holiday.[29]

Consequently Alma's sitting down with his children and telling them of his personal experience regarding his own divinely directed deliverance sounds very much like what happens during a Passover Seder. In addition to bookending his comments with references to the "captivity of our fathers" (Alma 36:2, 28), he uses imagery consistent with that experience. For instance, after realizing that he had rebelled against God, Alma describes himself as being "racked with eternal torment," "tormented with the pains of hell," "harrowed up to the greatest degree," and "encircled about by the everlasting chains of death" (vv. 12–14, 16–18)—all images of slave-like oppression and imprisonment. Similarly when his prayer is heard and he is released from his torment, Alma says that he was delivered "from prison, and from bonds, and from death" (v. 27). In addition, Passover, at its heart, is a meal served in symbolism. Consequently, it is consistent with a Seder that Alma employs food imagery to convey his

---

28. Robinson, *Essential Judaism*, 123.
29. Robinson, 122

message. Here Alma, possibly pointing to bitter herbs, explains that "there could be nothing so exquisite and so bitter as were my pains." He then, perhaps turning his attention to the Passover wine, a symbol of joy, says "on the other hand, there can be nothing so exquisite and sweet as was my joy" (v. 21). Reinforcing this possible culinary connection, Alma goes on to explain his desire to free others from their own spiritual prisons by saying that he wanted to "bring them to *taste* of the exceeding joy of which I did taste." Similarly, he claims that he found "exceedingly great joy in the *fruit* of my labors" (vv. 24–25). In fact, Alma seems to refer to the multi-sensory quality of the Passover meal when he rejoices in the result of his experience, saying that because of his deliverance many have "tasted as I have tasted, and have seen eye to eye as I have seen; therefore they do know of these things of which I have spoken" (v. 26).

Furthermore, as John W. Welch and Gordon C. Thomasson discovered, there are "several stunning similarities between [Alma's discussions with his sons] and the traditional Israelite observance of Passover." As Welch explains, the proper observance of Passover involves the spelling out of "the sequence of sin, suffering, repentance, and redemption." However, these concepts must be explained in a way that is adjusted to the "knowledge and understanding of the child."[30] To aid in this adjustment, the traditional *Haggadah* presents a parable of four different types of children—the wise child, the uninformed child, the wicked child, and the child who cannot ask a question—and explains how to reach and teach each of them appropriately. These approaches are based on several different questions concerning Passover that appear in the Hebrew scriptures and are well-known to modern Jews. Such an educationally accommodating approach is clearly evident as Alma tailors his sentiments to his three very different sons. For Helaman, Alma's faithful firstborn, Alma, answers the question of "wise" child: "What mean the testimonies, and the statutes, and the judgments, which the Lord our God hath commanded you?" (Deut. 6:20). In Alma 37, Alma uses the words *wisdom* or *wise* nine times and, consistent with the reinforcing way one might speak to a wise child, "explains the *meaning* of the laws and testimonies of God as he explains the meaning of the plates of Nephi (preserved for a 'wise purpose'), the twenty-four gold plates, and the Liahona."[31] Alma's tone is respectful, appreciative, almost collegial as he relates his own experiences with divine deliverance and tells Helaman of the future implications of his work, even

---

30. John W. Welch, ed., *Reexploring the Book of Mormon*, 196.
31. Welch, 197.

venturing into allegorical interpretation of one of them. It is clear that Alma trusts wise Helaman with his deepest thoughts and feelings.

Corianton, on the other hand, is a somewhat wayward son. He cannot be trusted. He forsook his ministry, went after the harlot Isabel, and seems confused about such basic doctrines such as the resurrection of the dead (Alma 40:1) and the justice of God (41:1–2). In many ways, Corianton corresponds to the Seder's "wicked" child, the one who asks the question, "What mean *ye* by this service?" (Ex. 12:26). According to Welch, "this son is depicted in Jewish literature as one guilty of social crimes, who had excluded himself from the community, and believed in false doctrines." The question therefore is almost a taunt, a challenge from the outside to make sense of something seemingly nonsensical. As Welch elaborates, the answer to this question should be such that will "set his teeth on edge"—meaning, a rebuke, a statement that if he had been in Egypt, "he would not have been redeemed."[32] Therefore, Alma's lengthy call to Corianton to repent is entirely consistent with this type of child. Corianton still has much to do to earn his father's trust.

Finally Shiblon, Alma's loyal but seemingly lackluster middle son, typifies the "uninformed" child of Passover. Alma's words to him answer the basic "What is this?" question of Exodus 13:14. Shiblon is like the child who needs to be taught the law and given "preventative instruction to keep him well away from any risk of breaking the law." As Welch points out, Alma simply teaches him to be diligent and gives him a "high code of conduct"[33] without laying out specific behaviors to avoid or doctrines to beware of. Shiblon is not a wicked child, rebellious and subject to stray. He just needs more information. Alma therefore commends him for his faithfulness, diligence, patience, and long-suffering and points out that he has already experienced many of the lessons of Passover, saying to him,

> For I know that thou wast in bonds; yea, and I also know that thou wast stoned for the word's sake; and thou didst bear all these things with patience because the Lord was with thee; and now thou knowest that the Lord did deliver thee. (Alma 38:4)

However, unlike Helaman, who is taught principles and their meaning, Shiblon is basically given rules to live by and follow as they are presented and not general principles he can interpret on his own:

---

32. Welch, 197.
33. Welch, 197.

See that ye are not lifted up unto pride; yea, see that ye do not boast in your own wisdom, nor of your much strength. Use boldness, but not overbearance; and also see that ye bridle all your passions, that ye may be filled with love; see that ye refrain from idleness.

Do not pray as the Zoramites do, for ye have seen that they pray to be heard of men, and to be praised for their wisdom. Do not say: O God, I thank thee that we are better than our brethren; but rather say: O Lord, forgive my unworthiness, and remember my brethren in mercy–yea, acknowledge your unworthiness before God at all times. (Alma 38:11–14)

Summary

The connection between the four sons in the *Haggadah* and the three sons of Helaman is not perfect, obviously. Nonetheless, as with the High Holy Days as well as with Sukkot and even Simchat Torah, there are intriguing echoes of this later practice that help support its use and reinforce the spiritual vitality of traditional Passover customs. In this way, the Book of Mormon reverses the approach used in the New Testament Gospels and revises how their readers view the Law of Moses in general. No longer are the Mosaic commandments nonsensical rules promoted by self-serving hypocrites. They have practical value and are observed by sincere, admirable people. The Mosaic festivals too are not simply empty names, without ancient or contemporary significance. By presenting them as rituals, consistent with ancient practice but with hints of modern additions to that practice, the Book of Mormon confirms their ongoing utility both for itself as well as for the entire Christian canon. And, again, it does so without changing the text of the New Testament or otherwise undermining its scriptural authority or reliability. Since Rosh Hashanah, Sukkot, and Passover are presented so vibrantly in the Book of Mormon, the fact that the New Testament does not follow suit simply suggests that its description of these festivals is incomplete—that is was abbreviated for some reason, perhaps only because time or papyrus was limited. The New Testament is therefore not wrong, per sé. There is just more to these festivals than it describes, and consequently any argument requiring their replacement based solely on the New Testament is severely undermined.

Chapter Five

Think Not That I Am Come to Destroy the Law

Think not that I am come to destroy the law or the prophets. I am not come to destroy but to fulfil; For verily I say unto you, one jot nor one tittle hath not passed away from the law, but in me it hath all been fulfilled. And behold, I have given you the law and the commandments of my Father, that ye shall believe in me, and that ye shall repent of your sins, and come unto me with a broken heart and a contrite spirit. Behold, ye have the commandments before you, and the law is fulfilled. (3 Ne. 12:17–19)

The positive portrayals of Rosh Hashanah, Sukkot, and Passover present in the Book of Mormon go far in countering many of the New Testament's most pervasive and persuasive anti-Mosaic suggestions. However, portrayals are not the only way the New Testament promotes such ideas. Setting is also important. Where, to whom, when, and under what circumstances Jesus's teachings are taught greatly influence how those teachings are understood. Consequently, it is significant that the Book of Mormon recasts three of the most powerful anti-Mosaic events in the New Testament in more pro-Mosaic settings.

The Presentation of the Sermon on the Mount

The Sermon on the Mount, as presented in the Gospel of Matthew, contains several compelling anti-Mosaic suggestions—mostly because of its setting. As several scholars point out, Jesus's initial "Ye have heard that it was said by them of old time. . . . But I say unto you" pronouncements (Matt. 5:21–22, 27–28, 33–34), although often called "antitheses," do *not* actually contradict the Ten Commandments or portray the Law of Moses as a worn out set of rules that requires replacing. For example, Bart Ehrman writes,

[Jesus] does not say, "You have heard it said 'You shall not commit murder,' but I say unto you that you should." Instead Jesus urges his followers to adhere to the Law, but to do it more rigorously than even the religious leaders of Israel.[1]

Philip L. Shuler similarly sees these statements as an effort "to offer a more radical form of Torah obedience," targeting not so much Mosaic practices themselves as "the manner in which these practices are often observed."[2] To Jacob Neusner not only are these "antitheses" clearly theses—positive points—but they are consistent with the long-standing rabbinic effort to "make a fence around the Torah." According to Neusner, Jesus, like the Talmudic rabbis, is simply admonishing his listeners to "conduct yourself in such a way that you will avoid even the things that cause you to sin, not only the sin itself."[3] These examples, therefore, do *not* represent efforts to dismantle the Law of Moses but instead "teach, explain, extend, amplify, enrich" and reinforce it.[4]

New Testament Setting

Nevertheless, despite the pro-Mosaic qualities present in the Sermon on the Mount, the fact that Jesus delivers it on an unnamed Galilean hill—far from Jerusalem, its temple, and the people who maintain that temple—gives his words a certain anti-Mosaic feel. There, the Beatitudes, in addition to appearing as alternatives to the more material blessings promised in Deuteronomy 28, seem to challenge the religiously powerful of Jesus's time. "Blessed are the poor in spirit: for theirs is the kingdom of heaven," for instance, appears to contest any monopoly wealthy priests might claim concerning the keys to that kingdom. "Blessed are the meek: for they shall inherit the earth" suggests that any control Jerusalem's privileged elite has over Jewish land is also tenuous, as does "Blessed are they which are persecuted for righteousness' sake: for theirs is the kingdom of heaven" regarding those who contest that control (Matt. 5:3–5, 10). In other words, although Jesus may not wear camel hair garments or eat locusts, here, on this lonely "mount," he looks and sounds very much like a rebel John the Baptist. He is a countercultural "voice of one crying in the wilderness" sent to straighten out the conventional "way of the Lord" (3:3).

---

1. Bart D. Ehrman, *The New Testament: A Historical Introduction to the Early Christian Writings*, 102.
2. Philip L. Shuler, "Response to Amy-Jill Levine," 43.
3. Jacob Neusner. *A Rabbi Talks with Jesus: An Intermillenial Interfaith Exchange*, 24.
4. Neusner, 26.

And, the people whom Jesus addresses in this sermon further reinforce its anti-establishment, anti-Mosaic aura. They are generally not "insider" Jews from Jerusalem—cultured people of power and prestige who are well-versed in temple sacrifices and other aspects of the Law of Moses; they include instead many "outsider" Jews who follow Jesus from Galilee, from Decapolis, and "from beyond Jordan" (Matt. 4:25)—people whose connections to the temple and its sacrifices are tenuous and rare.[5] Jesus's closest disciples for example, those who sit around him as he delivers this sermon, are not economically situated to make regular trips to Jerusalem or to master the intricacies of the Mosaic laws. They are "uneducated peasants," according to Ehrman, common folk who can neither read nor write.[6] Undoubtedly, they attend local synagogues and therefore are acquainted, through public readings and sermons, with the laws contained in the Torah. However, as the Gospel of Matthew goes on to show, these disciples are somewhat loose in their interpretation of those laws—plucking grains of wheat as they walk across fields on the Sabbath (12:1) as well as failing to wash their hands ritually before meals (15:2), behaviors which the Gospel of Mark states were unlike anything done by "all the Jews" (7:3). Furthermore, Jesus's disciples seem unfamiliar, or at least uncomfortable, with parables, a literary device commonly employed in both biblical and rabbinic literature (Matt. 13:10).[7] On the whole, the disciples appear to be poor, working class Jews whom, just one chapter previous, Jesus had snatched from their still-wet nets so that they could follow him and become "fishers of men" (3:18–22).

Given such an audience, Jesus's antagonistic "them of old time" (Matt. 5:21) can hardly refer to anyone but those Jerusalem Jews who have the time and the means to learn and promote the traditional approach to the Law of Moses. They are the metropolitan hypocrites who "sound a trumpet" before them when they do alms before large crowds, the status-conscious socialites who "love to pray standing in the synagogues and in the corners of the streets" (6:2, 5), the educationally privileged who "think that they

---

5. The Jerusalem Talmud supports this characterization of the Jews in Galilee. It records Yohanan ben Zakkai, one of the great first-century rabbinic teachers, as claiming that he had been asked only two questions in the eighteen years he spent in Galilee, causing him to despair for lack of devotion to the Torah in this region and cry, "O Galilee, O Galilee, in the end you shall be filled with wrongdoers." Jerusalem Talmud, 16:7, 15d.

6. Ehrman, *The New Testament*, 54, 59

7. Aaron M. Gale, note for Matt. 13:1–53, in Amy-Jill Levine and Marc Zvi Brettler, eds., *The Jewish Annotated New Testament*, 24–25

shall be heard for their much speaking," the moneyed classes who futilely attempt to "serve God and mammon" (vv. 7, 24). In contrast with Jesus's more rustic hillside hearers, these urbanites are unable to "behold the fowls of the air" or "consider the lilies of the field" (vv. 26, 28). They are religious city slickers, sophisticated "false prophets" who come to plain-speaking country Jews "in sheep's clothing, but inwardly they are ravening wolves" (7:15). These ancient establishmentarians may claim to support the Mosaic laws, but their efforts (as repeatedly documented in all of the Gospels) to take Jesus's life, twist his words, and spread lies about him strongly suggests that this approach is utterly ineffectual and profoundly hypocritical.

As a result, it is almost impossible for the casual Christian reader to *not* see Jesus's religious criticisms in this sermon as extending to the Law of Moses itself. Here, in this setting, his commands to "agree with thine adversary quickly," to "pluck out" lustful desires, and to "swear not at all" (Matt. 5:25, 29, 34), although conceptually consistent with the Law of Moses, nonetheless appear radical and even revolutionary. Given the emphasis Jesus gives these commands as well as the fact that they follow hard upon his intensification of individual Mosaic commandments, they feel like new directives designed not simply to reform how these commandments are obeyed but to replace them entirely. In other words, standing upon this "mount," in the wilderness of Galilee, Jesus looks very much like a new, alternative Moses.[8] He may have said that he has come not "to destroy the law" (v. 17), but here, in this setting, that is precisely what he appears to be doing—picking off its rules one by one, undermining their rationale, criticizing their observance, and minimizing their overall effect—all in order to abolish the entire Mosaic system and establish another in its place.

Little wonder then that when Jesus, according to the Gospel of Matthew, finally leaves Galilee and goes up to Jerusalem, the center of Mosaic worship, opposition against him intensifies as does his rhetoric against those who promote such worship. There, he disperses "all them that sold and bought in the temple" (21:12). There, he denounces those who "sit in Moses' seat" (23:2). And there he damns those who "make broad their phylacteries" (v. 5), who "enlarge the borders of their garments," and who

---

8. The Gospel of Matthew reinforces this impression by describing Herod ordering the killing of infants near the time of Jesus's birth just as Pharaoh ordered the killing of Israelite infants when Moses was born, as well as showing the young Jesus seeking refuge in Egypt just as the young Moses was rescued by a princess in Egypt when his life was similarly threatened. Some scholars have even think that the five major sermons in this Gospel are set up to recall the Five Books of Moses.

"love the uppermost rooms at feasts, and the chief seats in the synagogues," (v. 6). While such condemnations may not apply to Jews everywhere, the Gospel of Matthew offers no examples of people practicing Mosaic laws positively in order to offset it. Consequently, all Jews who attempt to obey the Law of Moses appear to be overly meticulous hypocrites, despicable people who "pay tithe of mint and anise and cumin" but omit "weightier matters" (vv. 15–16, 23). Indeed, Jesus concludes his sermon by condemning all of Jerusalem's inhabitants (v. 37) and even cursing the temple itself. As he says to his disciples when he departs from the temple, "See ye not all these things? verily I say unto you, There shall not be left here one stone upon another, that shall not be thrown down." (24:1–2).

Book of Mormon Setting

Nonetheless, as compelling as this anti-Mosaic interpretation of the Sermon on the Mount is, the Book of Mormon effectively dispels it, again not by altering the words of this sermon but by changing the literary qualities that promote such a reading—in this case, its setting. Several weeks after his death and resurrection, Jesus appears to the Nephites in the New World and there recites a version of the Sermon on the Mount that is nearly identical to the one he offered in the Old. However, the location and audience of this sermon are so different that it comes across not as a renunciation of the Law of Moses but rather as a reaffirmation of its ongoing utility and worth. Simply the fact that the Book of Mormon shows Jesus delivering this sermon at a temple in a city rather than on a mountain in the wilderness alters its religious feel dramatically. Here, Jesus looks more like a respectful participant in standard Mosaic worship than a rebel amassing supporters against it. Dressed like a Mosaic priest in a white robe (Lev. 8:7), Jesus descends from a point high above a group of worshipers and extends to them his hands in the traditional priestly sign of blessing (3 Ne. 9:22; Num. 6:22–27). He does not drive money changers from this temple (Matt. 21:13) or prophesy its destruction (24:2). Instead, he honors it as a sacred place where the voice of God can be heard, divine messengers can be received (3 Ne. 11:7–10), and the Law of God can be taught openly and respectfully.

Furthermore, the people Jesus speaks to at this temple also present a more positive view of those who follow the Law of Moses than is suggested in the New Testament. Here, Jesus addresses his listeners directly as he does in the Gospel of Matthew, using plural "you" forms, as in "blessed are *ye* when men shall revile *you*" (3 Ne. 12:11). However, this "you" is made up of people at the very center of Mosaic worship, not at its periphery. In the Book of Mormon, the Nephites and Lamanites who listen to Jesus are "more righteous" Mosaically than their brethren (9:13): they support their Mosaic government, they obey its Mosaic laws (6:4–5), and they offer Mosaic "sacrifices and . . . burnt offerings" to God—a fact that is apparent not only because they are gathered at a Mosaic temple but because Jesus commands them to cease offering up "the shedding of blood" (9:19), a demand that makes sense only if these people had been faithfully making such offerings.

In addition, the people Jesus speaks about similarly support a more pro-Mosaic interpretation. They are the "them" in the Sermon on the Mount—as in "Ye have heard that it hath been said by *them* of old time" (3 Ne. 12:21)—and are very different in the Book of Mormon than in the New Testament. In the New Testament, the "them" seems to refer to the Law-of-Moses-*loving* priests and scribes based primarily in Jerusalem (Matt. 15:2–3, 6). However, in the Book of Mormon, the "them" appears to refer instead to a group of Law-of-Moses-*hating* Nephites—those who lived in the cities that were destroyed just before Jesus's appearance. After all, it was these people who for generations had fought against the Mosaic laws of the land and persecuted the righteous Nephites (Hel. 5:2). They were the hypocritical city-dwellers who "did not sin ignorantly" but did "willfully rebel against God" (3 Ne. 6:18). They were the politically powerful who formed secret combinations (v. 28) in order "to gain power, and to murder, and to plunder, and to lie," in direct contradiction to the Mosaic commandments (Ether 8:16). This subgroup of wicked Nephites were worse than the "generation of vipers" condemned in the Gospel of Matthew (Matt. 3:7) since, for decades, they did "trample under their feet the commandments of God . . . and did build up unto themselves idols of their gold and their silver" (Hel. 6:31).

In short, the usual roles ascribed to the primary groups of people connected to the Sermon on the Mount are reversed in the Book of Mormon. Here, it is the Mosaically *observant*—those closely connected to the Mosaic temple, its laws, and sacrifices—who best resemble the blessed ones of Jesus's beatitudes. They are the people who mourn for their dead neighbors (3 Ne. 10:8), who are meek enough to inherit this part of the earth (v. 12), and who have hearts pure enough to see Jesus when he comes to them as a resurrected being (11:8–12). And it is the Mosaically *disobedient*—those disconnected from the Mosaic temple and its laws—who seem to have lost their salvific savor, persecuting the obedient (6:23), reviling the dutiful, and saying all manner of evil against the faithful falsely (12:10–11). It is these people then who are the corrupt tree, who have brought forth evil fruit, and who have been "hewn down, and cast into the fire," just as Jesus predicted; while it is the Mosaic Law-abiding people who have brought forth good fruit and have been preserved (14:17–19). In this way, by changing the location and audience of the Sermon on the Mount, the Book of Mormon, instead of undermining the Law of Moses, is actually reinforcing, even intensifying its commandments.

Shavuot

This point is further fortified by clues suggesting that the Book of Mormon's Sermon on the Mount was delivered on Shavuot. Once again, as with Rosh Hashanah, Sukkot, and Passover, Shavuot is not mentioned by name here or anywhere else in the Book of Mormon, and neither are the seven weeks that separates it from Passover definitively presented. Nevertheless, the timing of this Mosaic festival is consistent with Jesus's appearance according to both New Testament chronology as well as that of the Book of Mormon. John W. Welch writes,

> We do not know how the Nephite ritual calendar in Bountiful related to the Israelite calendar in Jerusalem, for there had been no contact between the two for over six hundred years. . . . If one can assume, however, that the two ritual calendars had not grown too far apart, the feast of Shavuot would have been celebrated in Bountiful a few months after the Passover crucifixion and shortly after the best-known ascension of Jesus from Jerusalem reported in Acts 1:9–11. Such a scenario would thus make good sense of the reference in 3 Nephi 10:18 to Christ's appearing in Bountiful "soon after" his ascension.[9]

What happens during this festival also dovetails neatly with many of the events surrounding Jesus's appearance in the Book of Mormon. During Shavuot, all Israel is commanded to come before the Lord and offer up thanks for the blessings they have received, regardless of the size or number of those blessings (Ex. 23:14–17). It is significant therefore that not only had a great multitude gathered together around about the temple but that they were "marveling and wondering one with another . . . showing one to another the great and marvelous change which had taken place" (3 Ne. 11:1). Such an upbeat reaction in the face of terrible storms, earthquakes, tidal waves, and volcanic eruptions suggests two things: first, that enough

---

9. John W. Welch, *Illuminating the Sermon at the Temple & the Sermon on the Mount*, 39.

time had passed for the Nephites to begin to repair some of the damage caused by these events and, second, that there was some religious reason for their reaction—perhaps a special occasion or holy day, which challenged their perspective and encouraged them to put this disaster into a more positive context. It is also significant that when Jesus descends "out of heaven" (v. 8), he does not deliver a speech consoling the Nephites or congratulating them on their restorative efforts; instead, he offers Shavuot-appropriate instructions that emphasize the necessity of obeying God's commandments with increased devotion as an example to the world.

One of the main purposes of Shavuot, according to the Talmudic rabbis, is to commemorate the giving of the Law to Moses on Sinai (Shabbat 86b; Exodus Rabbah 31) and to recreate, as much as possible, the time when all Israel committed themselves to obey it. As Rabbi Greenberg writes, on Shavuot "only one reading could satisfy the liturgy of reenactment, namely the account of Sinai and the text of the Ten Commandments."[10] As he explains, on that day in Jewish places of worship,

> the account of the encampment at Sinai is read. Again, Israel stands as one before its Maker. Again, the people are told, "If you will harken to My voice and observe My covenant, you shall be My treasured people among the nations. You shall be a kingdom of priests and a holy people to me." And again, the People answer together: "All that the Lord said we shall do" (Ex. 19:5–8). Again, the mountain shakes and the world is riven by eternal revelation. The Ten Commandments are chanted . . . [and when they are read] the entire congregation rises to stand in awe as if it were once again hearing the Voice at Sinai.[11]

Jesus's insistence that the Nephites avoid all thoughts and impulses that could lead to their breaking the Ten Commandments is consistent with Shavuot—as is his call for them to become the salvific "salt of the earth," the "light of this people," and even "perfect even as I, or your Father who is in heaven is perfect" (3 Ne. 12:48). Rather than replacing the Torah, Jesus seems to be recreating how it was given and intensifying how it is followed, all so that these New World Israelites may have another Sinai experience and pledge themselves to God once more. No wonder Jesus's Nephite and Lamanite hearers cried "Hosanna" when he appeared to them and blessed "the name of the Most High God" (11:17). Blood sacrifice may have ended, and burnt offerings may have been replaced (9:20), but, as this setting suggests, Mosaic festivals remain capable of supplying new insights, supporting fresh perspectives, and generally

---

10. Irving Greenberg, *The Jewish Way: Living the Holidays*, 83.
11. Greenberg, 84.

enhancing the religious experience of those who observe them in an ever-expanding, ongoing way.

The Institution of Christian Communion

Connecting Jesus's visit to the Nephites with post-biblical Jewish practices may seem inappropriate to some. After all, the idea that Shavuot commemorates the giving of the Law at Sinai was put forth by medieval rabbis, not by Moses or the pre-exilic prophets. It is entirely possible, therefore, even probable, that these Nephites would not have noted any "legal" connection between this festival and the Sermon on the Mount. However, once again, the Book of Mormon was not written for the Nephites, and the anti-Mosaicism it addresses was not their problem. Antinomianism, as this idea is also called, is instead a more modern difficulty, developed over time and incorporated into traditional Christian theology and practice. It is significant, therefore, that the Book of Mormon addresses one of the most anti-Mosaic of those practices, Christian Communion, and it does it at its source, the New Testament.

New Testament Setting

As previously noted, few events in the New Testament promote the idea that the Law of Moses has been replaced by the Gospel of Jesus as forcefully or as frequently as the institution of Christian Communion as it is presented in the synoptic Gospels. Reenacted as it is in churches throughout the world as a regular part of their worship services, this scene *shows* in concrete terms just how supersessionism works, and it does so chiefly because of its Passover setting. There, before a table, much as Jesus did in the synoptic Gospels (Matt 26:26; Mark 14:22; Luke 22:19), Christian ministers bless, break, and give bread to their congregants, and in so doing they transform this simple food item from a remembrance of the Exodus into a memorial of Jesus's death and resurrection. The whippings, the beatings, and the cruel deaths inflicted on the children of Israel by their Egyptian taskmasters are never mentioned nor is the power of their divine deliverance. Instead worshippers—frequently sitting in pews below crucifixes, crosses, and other reminders of Jesus's trials—concentrate on *his* whippings and *his* beatings as they remember *his* cruel death and contemplate *his* miraculous emergence from the grave. The same is true of the wine. Here, in this context, the wine is no longer the blessed fruit of the vine, the paschal representation of all the earthly blessings that God has provided for his children; it has been changed, converted into the blood of Jesus, into a "new wine" that effectively shatters the old Mosaic "bottle" and symbolizes instead the happiness that awaits Jesus's followers in heaven (Matt. 26:27–29; Mark 14:23–25; Luke 22:20–21).

Book of Mormon Setting

The Book of Mormon, like the Gospels of Matthew, Mark and Luke, also shows Jesus instituting Christian Communion among his followers. However, in the New World, he does so not during Passover but later, after he has observed Shavuot with his followers. In this way, through a change of setting, the bread and wine of Communion are disconnected from Passover, just as Communion itself is detached from any supersessionist implications derived from such a connection. Although one of the primary purposes of Shavuot is to commemorate God's giving of his Law to Israel at Sinai, it also serves as a harvest festival, when, according to Leviticus, the first fruits of the newly gathered in wheat harvest are offered to the Lord in the form of two special loaves of bread. Burnt offerings, sin offerings, peace offerings, as well as drink offerings are also brought forth (Lev. 23:17–19). These drink offerings are then consumed with the bread at the temple by those celebrating this festival. Like Sukkot, Shavuot is an upbeat thanksgiving festival, a feast where the gifts of God are celebrated and enjoyed gratefully, regardless of their quality or abundance. It is therefore telling that the bread and wine Jesus asks for in 3 Nephi 18 are apparently close at hand, and that after these food items are brought forth, blessed, and shared with all those in or around the temple, the Book of Mormon reports that the people "were filled" (3 Ne. 18:4, 9)—language identical to that used in the non-sacramental feedings of the 5,000 and the 4,000 in the Gospel of Matthew (14:20; 15:37).

Certainly, to many New Testament-influenced readers, this meal may seem closely linked to the institution of Christian Communion as it is presented in the synoptic Gospels. After all, here in the New World Jesus appears to act much as he did in the Old, even explaining that the bread is eaten in remembrance of his body and that the wine is drunk in commemoration of his blood. However, this connection is not as close as it may seem. A careful reading of 3 Nephi 18 shows that Jesus is not starting a new ritual at this time. He is instead using the established rituals of Shavuot to show what he *will* do later on. Here, Jesus employs the future tense instead of the present when he describes Communion. After his followers have eaten the bread, he tells them, "this *shall* ye do in remembrance of my body, which I have shown unto you" (v. 7); after they had partaken of the wine, he explains "this *shall* ye always do to those who repent and are baptized in my name; and ye *shall* do it in remembrance of my blood, which I have shed for you." Concerning the overall effect of these actions, he then adds "And if ye do always remember me ye *shall* have my Spirit to be with you" (v. 11). Rather than replacing or redefining the Jewish holiday with a new law, Jesus is celebrating Shavuot in accordance with the old Mosaic Law. However, during the course of this celebration he is using the elements of this festival to prepare his followers for a new non-Mosaic ritual he will institute later on. And this makes sense. After all, the Nephites have not yet been baptized (a requirement for participation in Communion (v. 3)), nor have his disciples been authorized to administer baptism. Therefore, it is significant that here in this chapter when both his disciples as well as the multitude had partaken of the bread and wine, they are "filled" but not yet with the Holy Spirit. Christian Communion with its spiritual blessings has at this point not been given and has instead only been introduced conceptually in the context of Shavuot, a festival that emphasizes remembrance, gratitude, and joy.

Jesus does *not* institute the sacrament of Christian communion among the Nephites until the next day—after Jesus's disciples have "ministered unto the people," after Nephi has been authorized to baptize "all those whom Jesus had chosen," and after the Holy Ghost has fallen upon the Nephites (19:1, 7, 12–13). It was on this day then, after all these things had occurred, that Jesus "came and stood in the midst and did minister unto them" (vv. 14–15). He commands the multitude to pray and as they do so he prays for them, three times—pleading with the Father to give his followers the Holy Ghost (v. 21), asking that they may be purified in him (v. 28), and speaking words so great and marvelous "that they cannot be written, neither can they be uttered by man" (v. 34). Obviously, this is a moving experience. Jesus seems to be preparing his listeners for something truly marvelous. He praises them for their faith, commands them to cease praying out loud, and orders them to "arise and stand up upon their feet" (20:2). And it is then, after all these preparations have been made, that he miraculously produces bread and wine, blesses them, and gives them first to his disciples and then to the multitude. As he does so, he declares in the present tense, "He that *eateth* this bread *eateth* of my body to his soul;

and he that *drinketh* of this wine *drinketh* of my blood to his soul" (20:8). The multitude is then "filled *with the Spirit*," just as Jesus promised (v. 9).

Given the high drama of this event as well as the grammatical tense Jesus uses at that time, it seems clear that in the Book of Mormon this Christian ordinance was not instituted on Passover or on Shavuot. It was instituted later, by itself, without any connection to these Mosaic festivals. This is significant, as it means that the spiritual utility and viability of Passover and Shavuot remain intact. The bread and wine used to institute Communion was produced, not from a Seder table nor from a first-fruits offering but from Jesus himself, seemingly out of the air, from nothing. They were new creations, much like Communion itself. Consequently, Communion and the Mosaic festivals exist symbolically as well as practically side by side, as separate religious rituals, sharing helpful and enlightening connections but without any sense of competition or contention. Each can then be celebrated individually by itself, effectively and reverentially, just as Jesus did in the New World without one superseding or replacing the other.

Passover

Once again, such a resetting of the institution of Communion in no way undermines the authority or the reliability of the New Testament. In fact, the Book of Mormon not only supports the New Testament by affirming that Jesus's death occurred during Nisan—"in the first month" (8:5), the same month when Passover is traditionally celebrated (Ex. 12:18)—but it upholds the ongoing relevance of Passover by reenacting the original event it commemorates in a new and original way. By the time of Jesus's death, most Nephites had become not so much an oppressed people as an oppressive people. Like the Egyptians of Exodus, they had built many new cities and repaired old ones (3 Ne. 6:7; Ex. 1:11); they were exceedingly rich and consequently were "lifted up unto pride and boastings . . . even unto great persecutions" of the people of God (3 Ne. 6:10; Ex. 1:14); they had even entered "into a covenant to destroy [the people of God] . . . and to establish a king over the land, that the land should no more be at liberty" (3 Ne. 6:29–30; Ex. 1:10–14). A prophet consequently came among these Nephites—Nephi, a man named after the original Nephi—who, like Moses, ministered "many things unto [his people] . . . with power and with great authority." However, like Pharaoh and his courtiers, many of the Nephites were "angry with Nephi because of his power." They did not believe the signs he spoke about and did harden their hearts against the Lord (3 Ne. 7:16–18, 20; Ex. 7:10–22). As a result, "there were but few righteous men among [the Nephites]" (3 Ne. 7:7), and consequently the majority of Nephites were afflicted, like the Egyptians, with divinely created lightning and thunder, "thick darkness" (8:19–20), and other calamities that caused them to be burned in their cities (v. 8), "carried away in the whirlwind" (v. 16) and "sink into the depths of the sea" (v. 9)—much like Pharaoh's army (Ex. 14:26–28).

In other words, many of God's plagues recalled during a Passover Seder are reenacted in the Book of Mormon, but so are his blessings. Here many of these faithful New World Israelites are "passed over" just like their Old World ancestors; they are not "buried up in the earth," "drowned in the depths of the sea," "burned by fire," "crushed to death," or otherwise obliterated like their oppressors. They are instead delivered miraculously, Mosaically, precisely because they, like the children of Israel, "received the prophets," (3 Ne. 10:12–15) and avoided the "wickedness and abominations" described in the Book of Exodus (9:7–13). In this way, the Book of Mormon verifies the New Testamental timing of Passover as well as the divine use and purpose of this Mosaic festival.

The Appearance of the Resurrected Jesus

Another powerful anti-Mosaic scene in the New Testament occurs around Passover, this time in the Gospel of John. In this Gospel, Jesus appears to his disciples soon after his resurrection, much as he does in the Gospels of Matthew, Mark, and Luke. However, because of what precedes and succeeds it, this scene suggests that the purposes of the Law of Moses have been accomplished and that it is of no further use.

The New Testament Setting

As in the synoptic Gospels, in the Gospel of John a special meal precedes Jesus's arrest, death, and resurrection. However, this meal is not the paschal "Last Supper" described in the Gospels of Matthew, Mark, and Luke. Instead, this meal occurs *before* Passover (John 13:1) and involves not the ceremonial consumption of unleavened bread and wine but the washing of feet (vv. 4–10), the giving of new commandments (vv. 34–35), the delivering of several important discourses (15:10–27; 16:7–15), as well as the offering of the great intercessory prayer (17:1–26). Similarly, Jesus's death in the Gospel of John also takes place before Passover. Unlike the

Gospels of Matthew, Mark, and Luke, in John it is on the day of "preparation of the Passover" that Jesus is brought before Pilate, crucified, and placed in Joseph of Arimathea's sepulcher (19:14, 31, 40–42)—one day earlier than it does in the Synoptics. This is significant, because contrary to the way he is portrayed in the other Gospels, in this Gospel Jesus does not *partake* of the Passover offering; he *is* the Passover offering—killed "about the sixth hour" (v. 14), precisely when the lambs "without blemish" (Ex. 12:5) were beginning to be ritually slaughtered.[12] In this setting then, Jesus is shown to be exactly what John the Baptist claimed he was: the paschal "Lamb of God who taketh away the sin of the world" (John 1:29).

And, in the Gospel of John, being sacrificed for sins on Passover is just about all that Jesus was ordained to do. After being nailed to a cross, he watches as his Roman executioners divide his clothing between them, he assigns the disciple "whom he loved" to take care of his mother (19:23–27), and then, "knowing that *all things* were now accomplished," he asks for a drink, receives some vinegar, and dies, immediately, quietly, and voluntarily (vv. 28–30). In the Gospel of John, no one takes Jesus's life; instead he lays it down of himself (10:18), and he does so only after he has made certain "the works which the Father hath given [him]" have all been accomplished. (5:36). Indeed, after Jesus pronounces his sacrificial task "finished" (19:30), there is little left for him to do. Roman soldiers leave his legs unbroken and pierce his side in accordance with prophecy and with Mosaic sacrificial requirements (John 19:32–37; Ex. 12:46; 34:25; Lev. 3:1–3, 8, 17). However, Jesus, being dead, does nothing. Even later, after he has been resurrected and has the ability to do something new or dramatic, he does not do so. Instead, Jesus simply appears to his closest disciples behind closed doors, offers them his hands and side, and then, after breathing on them to give them the Holy Ghost, sends them forth to "remit sins" (John 20:19–23). It is his disciples who, at this point, do all the "doing." *They* witness that he is yet alive; *they* behold his resurrected body; *they* verify that his sacrifice for sin has been accepted; and *they* go off to share the benefits of that sacrifice with others. Even when Jesus appears to his disciples again, later on in Galilee, his appearance serves mainly as a reminder that sinners need no longer "surely die" (Gen. 2:17), that they can live again, and that they can have eternal life if they believe in Jesus (John 3:15). Small wonder then when Peter begins his ministry on Pentecost, he does not speak of Jesus's Second Coming or any additional

---

12. Ehrman, *The New Testament*, 57.

work Jesus has yet to do. Instead he concentrates on what Jesus has already done and how his hearers can benefit from his accomplishments (Acts 2:38; 3:19; 5:31; 10:43; 13:38; 22:16; 26:18).

To many Christian readers, the way Jesus is portrayed at the end of the Gospel of John may not seem very anti-Mosaic. After all, the Law of Moses provides for the remission of some sins through sacrifice, and there is no overt disparagement here of the Law or any of its components. Nevertheless, by focusing solely on the sacrificial side of Passover and by setting up Jesus's sacrifice as the completion of his messianic mission, this Gospel seems to suggest that the purpose of Passover has also been realized and that it, as well as the Law of Moses itself, is no longer necessary or useful—a point that at least two New Testament writers stress. Paul, for instance, calls Jesus "our passover" and tells his Corinthian converts that because of his sacrifice there is no longer any need for them to celebrate this or any other Mosaic festival, as these festivals have been traditionally observed (1 Cor. 5:6–8). Similarly, the author of the Epistle to the Hebrews asserts that Jesus, having served both as sacrificer as well as sacrifice, "entered in once into the holy place" and there "by his own blood . . . obtained eternal redemption" for his people (Heb. 9:12). As this author continues, Jesus by this singular sacrifice brought a new covenant into being, even "a better covenant," which was "not according to the covenant that [God] made with [Israel] in the day when [He] took them by the hand to lead them out of the land of Egypt" (8:6–9). As a result, the old Mosaic covenant "decayeth and waxeth old [and] is ready to vanish away" (v. 13)—all of it, not just the laws pertaining to sacrifices but the kosher laws, the purity laws, the sabbatical laws, the governmental laws, as well as the laws pertaining to Passover, Shavuot, and the other festivals.

And this obsolescence of the Law of Moses is a good thing, according to both of these writers. In Galatians, Paul calls the Law "our schoolmaster," a set of overly strict rules designed expressly "to bring us unto Christ." However, now that Jesus has come he claims that that task has been accomplished, that "we are no longer under a schoolmaster," that we are now free of its tutelage (3:19, 24–25; 4:31). The author of the Letter to the Hebrews similarly sees the Law of Moses as a preparatory stage, a set of outward observances consisting of "meats and drinks, and divers washings, and carnal ordinances" (Heb. 9:10) that were imposed on Israel as "a shadow of good things to come." Certainly, they have some virtue in pointing to Jesus's sacrifice, but they themselves are "not the very image of the things" and therefore have little value otherwise. They may be "offered year by year"; however, they can never "make the comers thereunto perfect" (10:1). For, as this author explains, "it is not possible that the blood of bulls and of goats should take away sins" (vv. 3–4). Nonetheless, Jesus by his "one sacrifice for sins . . . hath perfected for ever them that are sanctified" and in so doing, brought his followers "a new and living way" that replaces the old Law of Moses (vv. 14, 20). In this way, the appearance of Jesus as a resurrected being in the Gospel of John is *extremely* anti-Mosaic. Because of its setting, the fact that Jesus at this point does little else besides sending his followers forth seems to confirm not only that his sacrifice completed his purpose but that it completed the purpose of the Law of Moses as well—and rendered it obsolete.

The Book of Mormon Setting

In the Book of Mormon, Jesus also appears to his closest followers much as he does in the New Testament, and he too does so expressly so that they may know that he has "been slain for the sins of the world" (3 Ne. 11:14). Nevertheless, despite this and other statements emphasizing the importance of Jesus's sacrificial mission (1 Ne. 11:33; 2 Ne. 31:4; Mosiah 26:23; Alma 5:48; 7:14; 34:8; 36:17; 39:15; 42:15), the Book of Mormon does not concentrate solely on his sacrificial mission or portray it as the totality of Jesus's messianic assignment. Jacob, for instance, states that "the Messiah," after he has died and been resurrected, shall "set himself again the second time to recover" the ancestors of those Jews who were forcibly removed from Jerusalem and will "manifest himself unto them in power and great glory" (2 Ne. 6:14). Nephi too speaks of a time when "the prophet of whom Moses spake" will miraculously gather all of his Israelite "children from the four quarters of the earth" and will do so in such a way that they will dwell with him in righteousness and peace (1 Ne. 22:21, 25–26). In other words, in the Book of Mormon Jesus still has a much to do, even after his death and resurrection, and the setting of his appearance to the Nephites emphasizes this point.

So while the Book of Mormon does not challenge the idea that Jesus died around the time of Passover, it does change what occurs after his death, and it does so mainly by filling a void in the New Testament narrative. As discussed previously, the Gospel of John promotes the idea that Jesus's "it is finished" referred to the totality of his mission by ending his story there, on the cross, without having Jesus do anything particularly new or dramatic afterwards. The Book of Mormon, however, refutes this idea by continuing Jesus story, by showing him doing significant work long after his death and resurrection. In this way, the Book of Mormon does not challenge Jesus's statement that his mission was "finished"; it instead confines that statement to his sacrificial mission and does so by adding more information to the Christian Canon. For instance, in addition to reciting for the Nephites the entire Sermon on the Mount and instituting among them Christian Communion, Jesus, as a resurrected being, heals their sick, blesses their children, and prays for them. He also tells these Nephites that although the sacrificial aspects of the Law of Moses have been fulfilled, the covenant which he has made with Israel has not been fulfilled and neither have his efforts on their behalf (3 Ne. 15:3–8). As he explains, the "other sheep" he referred to during his mortal ministry people who must still hear his voice (John 10:16), are not the Gentiles, or the "New Israel." They are instead the scattered tribes of "Old Israel," people "whom the Father hath led away out of the land" of Jerusalem (3 Ne. 15:15–24). Consequently, Jesus states that he will visit these Israelites, just as he did the Nephites, so that they be brought into his fold and numbered among his sheep (16:3).

However, this is not all. After Jesus lays out what he will do for Israel in the near future, he describes at length what he will do for them hundreds of years later—after *all* Israel has been scattered, cast out, and "trodden" under the feet of the Gentiles (3 Ne. 16:8). This will obviously be a difficult time for these Israelites, and many will be tempted to think that God has abandoned them. However, Jesus pledges to remember the covenant which he has made unto Israel (vv. 11–12) and promises to fulfill it personally, dramatically, miraculously (20:22). Likening himself to Moses (v. 23), he prophesies that the "powers of heaven" will be in their midst; indeed, that *he* will be in their midst (vv. 21–23), that he will make them strong and powerful, that he will enable them to resist the Gentiles (v. 19), and that he will at last gather them in "from their long dispersion" and "establish again among them [his] Zion" (21:1).

Zion

The word "Zion" seems to hang in the air like a guiding star. By it, Jesus does not simply mean Jerusalem, the physical city located in the north of Judea to which he will return the Jews. He also means the ideal society situated in the hearts and minds of Israel's prophets, the political/spiritual/psychological/religious state in which he will ennoble everyone, not just Israel but "all the kindreds of the earth" (3 Ne. 20:25). As Jesus says, quoting Isaiah, Zion represents an idyllic place where all of Israel will sing as one, where "they shall see eye to eye," and where they will reside as equals in "the land of their inheritance" (vv. 32–33). There the scattered remnants of Israel will come together in righteousness, "break forth into joy," and be comforted directly by the Lord (v. 34). There Israel will put on its strength, don its beautiful garments, shake itself from the dust, and awake in captivity no more (vv. 36–37). There those who have sold themselves "for naught" shall "be redeemed without money"; there they shall know the Lord's name, there they shall become familiar with His voice (vv. 38–39), there peace shall be published for them, and there their God will reign (v. 40). In other words, as important as Jesus's sacrifice is, it does not represent the totality of his messianic mission. He must still realize the grand vision given to Isaiah where the Messiah will "judge among the nations," will "rebuke many people"; and will usher in an era of such profound peace, prosperity, justice, and equality that all the world shall "walk in the light of the Lord." (Isa. 2:4; 2 Ne. 12:4). This realization the Book of Mormon not only confirms with words but with a real-life sample of what it is Jesus must yet do.

After Jesus departs, all the people—both Nephites and Lamanites—became converted to the Lord (4 Ne. 1:1). They then prosper "exceedingly" (v. 7), rebuild their cities, wax strong, and "multiply exceedingly fast" (v. 10). Nevertheless, they do all this according to Jesus's teachings and are consequently blessed according to the blessings Jesus described in the Beatitudes. As *peacemakers*, they tolerated "no contentions and disputations" among themselves and were indeed called the children of God (v. 39). *Merciful*, they "had all things common among them"; therefore they did obtain mercy, in that "there were not rich and poor, bond and free" among them but "were all made free" from judgment and societal condemnation (v. 3). *Meek*, they experienced no envyings "neither strifes, nor tumults, nor whoredoms, nor lyings, nor murders, nor any manner of lasciviousness," and therefore they inherited an earth where there were no robbers, "nor murderers, neither were there Lamanites, nor any manner of –ites" (vv. 15–17). As a result, these people who had previously been reviled and persecuted by their fellow Israelites received a glorious reward. In fact their society was so peaceful, prosperous, just, equal, and righteous that Mormon exclaims that "surely there could not be a happier people among all the people who had been created by the hand of God," so great was "the love of God which did dwell in the hearts of the people" (vv. 15–16). In this way, the Book of Mormon both proclaims that Jesus's messianic work is far from finished and shows what the culmination of that work will look like when the will of God will truly be "done in earth as it is in heaven" (3 Ne. 13:10; Matt. 6:10).

Sabbaths

Now, once again, some Christian readers may wonder what this preview of the Messianic Era has to do with the Law of Moses, and the answer is everything. Clearly, such a time is Isaiah's ultimate goal, but it is Moses's as well—and it is precisely what Shavuot, Passover, and the other Mosaic festivals were designed to produce. As Rabbi Irving Greenberg explains, as early as the first chapter of Genesis the Torah presents Jews with a powerful dream: "a vision of the world in its perfect state, an Eden of order and beauty in which life emerges from the divine ground of existence." This dream, however, does not simply show that this world originally "meant to be a paradise," but, according to Rabbi Greenberg, it tasks Jews with restoring that paradise and charges them with making this world again a place of peace, equality, prosperity, justice, and righteousness. As a result, Jewish existence without this dream is "almost inconceivable." It is how they fulfill the Abrahamic mission to bless the families of the earth (Gen. 12:3); it is how they achieve the Mosaic goal of becoming "a peculiar treasure" unto the Lord, "a kingdom of priests, and an holy nation" (Ex. 19:5–6); and it is how they fulfill the Isaianic task of preparing the way of the Lord (Isa. 40:3). However, as Rabbi Greenberg notes, this dream is not without significant challenges and difficulties. He therefore asks, "From where can these people draw the strength to renew their dream again and again?" His answer, coming from Jewish tradition: "Give people just a foretaste of the fulfillment, and they will never give it up. The Shabbat [or Sabbath, in English] is that taste."[13] It offers Jews regular, real-life experiences with the kind of lifestyle that will prevail during the Messianic era, and in so doing spurs Jews on to prepare the world, and themselves, for that time.

Nevertheless, the sabbaths Rabbi Greenberg speaks of are not just the twenty-four-hour periods observed at the end of each week. As Leviticus 23 makes clear, Passover, Shavuot, Rosh Hashanah, Yom Kippur, and Sukkot are also sabbaths, "holy convocations," periods of time in which their observers are to "do no work therein" (Lev. 23:2–8, 20–21, 24–28, 34–37). Shavuot is particularly Sabbath-like. In addition to being observed as a sabbath itself, it is described in sabbatical terms:

---

13. Greenberg, *The Jewish Way,* 127–28.

> And ye shall count unto you from the morrow after the sabbath, from the day that ye brought the sheaf of the wave offering [on Passover]; seven sabbaths shall be complete: Even unto the morrow after the seventh sabbath shall ye number fifty days; and ye shall offer a new meat offering unto the Lord. (Lev. 23:15–16).

Consequently, Shavuot is not simply a festival of "weeks," as its name implies; it is a *sabbath* of weeks, the culmination of a seven-week period of preparation, beginning at Passover, designed to deepen Israel's understanding of the Sabbath and reinforce its function as a foretaste of the messianic era by lengthening time period involved.

The sabbatical year serves a similar purpose. It too is a sabbath, not a "sabbath of days" or a "sabbath of weeks" but a "sabbath of years." Leviticus 25 explains:

> The seventh year shall be a sabbath of rest unto the land, a sabbath for the LORD: thou shalt neither sow thy field, nor prune thy vineyard. That which groweth of its own accord of thy harvest thou shalt not reap, neither gather the grapes of thy vine undressed: [for] it is a year of rest unto the land. And the sabbath of the land shall be meat for you; for thee, and for thy servant, and for thy maid, and for thy hired servant, and for thy stranger that sojourneth with thee, And for thy cattle, and for the beast that [are] in thy land, shall all the increase thereof be meat. (vv. 4–7)

In this way, "the dynamic of liberation and equality that [the Sabbath day] proclaims is extended in the sabbatical year"; human beings are liberated "from working the land for an entire year, not just one day a week"; and they experience what Rabbi Greenberg calls "the messianic fantasy" or dream for a longer period of time.[14]

This Sabbath-lengthening process seemingly culminates every fifty years with Jubilee. According to Rabbi Greenberg, "The climax of liberation from poverty and bondage is reached in the jubilee year (the fiftieth year), which is directly connected to the sabbatical year and, therefore, to the Sabbath."[15] For forty-nine years, Israel prepares for this "Sabbath of sabbatical years," a year when not only everyone and everything rests, but slaves are set free, the land reverts to its original owners, and all debts are forgiven (Lev. 25:8–17). At its start, a trumpet is sounded, liberty is proclaimed "throughout all the land," and the world appears to be on the brink of welcoming the Messiah. During this year, a profound peace prevails, righteous reigns supreme, and the earth brings forth its bounty abundantly,

---

14. Greenberg, 152–53.
15. Greenberg, 153.

naturally, spontaneously, just as it did in the Garden of Eden, without requiring humanity to eat of its bread in sorrow or by the sweat of its face (Isa. 2:2, 4; Gen. 3:19). Thus, Jubilee, more than any other Mosaic day or season, "prefigures a messianic era when all humans will be free and equal. Each individual and each family will sit under 'his vine and his own fig-tree' (Micah 4:4). That era will be 'a day [eon] which is entirely Shabbat.'"[16]

Jubilee then is the last step provided in the Law of Moses in a step-by-step progression towards the messianic era, and it would appear to be the ultimate "foretaste" of what that blessed era will be like. However the Book of Mormon offers one more. Consistent with the increasingly lengthened sabbaths proscribed by the Law of Moses, the Book of Mormon adds a "sabbath of centuries," a hundred-year-plus-long period of peace and prosperity that in addition to following the sabbatical pattern—occurring approximately "six hundred years from the time that Lehi left Jerusalem" (3 Ne. 1:1)—expands upon many of the messianic ideals promoted by the sabbatical year. For instance, although there was certainly some work being done at this time, there is no mention of farming and other agricultural labors. Indeed, the Nephites are described as "partakers of the heavenly gift," as though the land brought forth its abundance spontaneously, effortlessly, without human aid or assistance (v. 3). Furthermore, during this time there were no slaves or poor (v. 3), two of the most distinguishing characteristics of a sabbatical year (Deut. 15:1–4).

Summary

In this way then, by providing a longer sampling of the Messianic era, the Book of Mormon reinforces the idea that Jesus's work is far from finished. However, it also shows that the Law of Moses still has much to do as well. Jesus may indeed, as the Gospel of John suggests, have been the ultimate Passover sacrifice, the offering that allowed sins to be forgiven and did away with such sacrifices forever, but there is more to this festival than sacrifice and there is more to the Law of Moses than blood offerings. The Book of Mormon builds upon its positive portrayals of Passover and the other Mosaic festivals by offering a compelling glimpse of the goal of these festivals, a goal that is supported by the Sermon on the Mount, left intact by Christian Communion, and emphasized by Jesus himself.

---

16. Greenberg, 153.

Chapter Six

That the Last May Be First and the First May Be Last

And because that I have preserved the natural branches and the roots thereof, and that I have grafted in the natural branches again into their mother tree, and have preserved the roots of their mother tree, that, perhaps, the trees of my vineyard may bring forth again good fruit and that I may have joy again in the fruit of my vineyard, and, perhaps, that I may rejoice exceedingly that I have preserved the roots and the branches of the first fruit—Wherefore, go to, and call servants, that we may labor diligently with our might in the vineyard, that we may prepare the way, that I may bring forth again the natural fruit, which natural fruit is good and the most precious above all other fruit.

Wherefore, let us go to and labor with our might this last time, for behold the end draweth nigh, and this is for the last time that I shall prune my vineyard.

Graft in the branches; begin at the last that they may be first, and that the first may be last, and dig about the trees, both old and young, the first and the last; and the last and the first, that all may be nourished once again for the last time. (Jacob 5:60–63)

Viewed by themselves the New Testament settings of the Sermon on the Mount, the institution of Christian Communion, and the appearance of Jesus as a resurrected being may seem only slightly anti-Mosaic and not enough to make much of a difference in how readers view Jews or Judaism. However, because of Acts none of the various anti-Semitic elements in the New Testament can be approached in isolation. Working from its position between the Gospels and the Pauline letters, Acts unites these different elements structurally, bringing them together in such a way as to create a narrative so thoroughly supersessionist that only a scripture such as the Book of Mormon can alter it.

How Acts Structures the New Testament

If read by themselves, the Pauline Epistles seem almost "a-Semitic." Unlike the Mishnah, their Jewish near-contemporary, these letters never discuss when to recite blessings, how to observe Mosaic holy days, or what to bring to the temple when one offers a sacrifice—all matters of great interest to Mosaic Law-abiding Jews. Written in Greek for Greeks, these Epistles instead focus on Gentile issues: why God values Gentiles just as much as he values Jews (Rom. 3:29–30), why Gentile converts do not need to be circumcised (Gal. 5:1–12), why these converts should now, as followers of Jesus, refrain from eating meat offered to idols (1 Cor. 8:4–13), and why they should avoid marrying people outside of their new faith (2 Cor. 6:14–16). And the Epistles respond to these issues in very Gentile ways as well. For example, the Epistle to the Hebrews, a work once ascribed to Paul, assumes both a knowledge of and a sympathy for Greek philosophy. Echoing Plato's famous allegory of the cave, where shadows of unseen ideals cast upon a wall are mistaken for reality, much of Hebrews' criticism of Mosaic sacrifices is built on the idea that the physical "blood of bulls and of goats" (Heb. 10:4), unlike Jesus's more spiritual sacrifice, is "not the very image of the things" (10:10). These offerings are instead merely a "shadow of heavenly things" (8:5), even "a shadow of good things to come" (v. 1).

By Preceding the Epistles

Nonetheless, the Pauline Epistles *cannot* be read by themselves. The fact that the Acts of the Apostles precedes these letters and does so with an account that shows Paul going "unto the Gentiles" (Acts 18:6) in dramatic rejection of the "blaspheming Jews" profoundly alters how these letters are understood. Since, according to Acts, the Jews have assented to the murder of James (12:2–3), taken "counsel" to kill Paul (9:23), and have become so filled with "envy" that they have even taken an oath to "neither eat nor drink" until they have killed him (23:12), there is seemingly little doubt as to why Paul writes exclusively to Gentile congregations. As Stephen testifies, the Jews have not only persecuted and slain the prophets for centuries, but they continue to do so now, even murdering the greatest prophet of all, Jesus. Consequently, the Jews have been cast off by God just as they have been left behind by Paul (7:52). As Hebrews puts it, because the Jews "continued not in [God's] covenant," God no longer "regards" them, and their covenant with Him consequently "decayeth and waxeth old [and] is ready to vanish away" (Heb. 8:9, 13). In other words, according to the narrative flow in Acts, the Jews have been cut off from God, and the fact that the Pauline letters focus exclusively on Gentiles and Gentile issues seems to provide proof that this severance has indeed occurred.

By Succeeding the Gospels

Powerful as this supersessionist "proof" may be all by itself, Acts reinforces it by connecting to the Gospels literarily. Just as it serves as a kind of rejectionist *foreword* to the Epistles, so it similarly functions as a triumphalist *afterword* to the Gospels. Following the Gospels chronologically (as well as physically in bound versions of the Christian canon), Acts repeats many of the most damaging innuendos that the Gospels make against the Jews and amplifies them into outright condemnations. The Gospel of Matthew, for instance, may suggest that all Jews are responsible for Jesus's crucifixion, but Acts openly proclaims it—several times, in fact—with great clarity and rhetorical force (2:36; 3:15; 4:10). Acts also confirms the Gospels' portrayal of the Jews as murderous plotters by showing them openly attempting to kill Jesus's followers (5:33; 7:59; 9:29; 23:12, 27), and it affirms their critique of the Law of Moses by similarly presenting one of its most notable laws, kashrut, as meaningless and empty (11:5–10).

In this way, the book of Acts works retroactively to weave its supersessionist ideas back into the warp and woof of all three synoptic Gospels. It then reinforces this interweaving by elevating its ideas into a pattern, a theme, even a main point of these Gospels as it joins with them structurally. Moving stage-by-stage away from Jerusalem, through Judea and Samaria, to the Gentile world at Jesus's express command (1:8), Acts reverses the narrative movement present in the Gospel of Luke, its "scriptural sibling,"[1] and in so doing transforms its stories of Jesus's ministry into the first half of a chiastic expression of supersessionist theology.

Starting off the apostles' ministry in Jerusalem and Judea, where Jesus in the synoptic Gospels left off, Acts confirms that the Jews living in these places were indeed Christ-killers by having Peter say so—three times— and by showing them unambiguously killing Stephen, one of Jesus's most

---

1. The general scholarly consensus is that the Acts of the Apostles was written by the same author as the Gospel of Luke.

Figure 1. Narrative movement in Luke and in Acts with respect to place

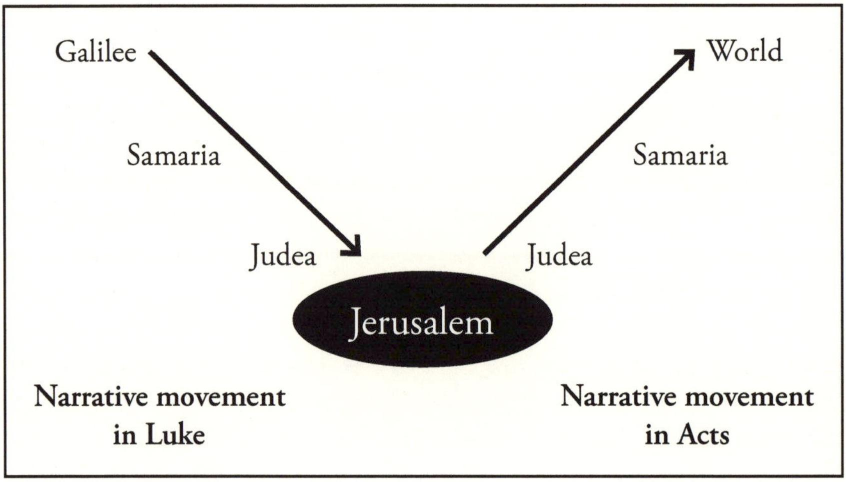

```
Galilee                              World
        ↘                          ↗
   Samaria                      Samaria
            ↘                ↗
        Judea              Judea
             ⬊ Jerusalem ⬈

  Narrative movement        Narrative movement
       in Luke                   in Acts
```

Christ-like witnesses (7:57–59). Moving into Samaria, Acts further condemns the Jews of Jerusalem and Judea by presenting the Samaritans, a Gentile people with connections to Jews, as receiving Phillip with "great joy," so much so that they are quickly baptized, "both men and women" (8:8, 12, 17). Furthermore, at this point a eunuch from Ethiopia (a man with no clear Jewish ties whatsoever) is presented as being eager to hear the apostles' message. As Acts introduces him, he is sitting in his chariot, reading Isaiah, and becoming frustrated at his inability to understand its fifty-third chapter. He bewails the fact that he has no guide and requests Phillip to explain this chapter to him. Not one to miss such an easy opportunity, Philip promptly does so and in the process preaches "unto him Jesus" (vv. 27–35). The eunuch is consequently so impressed that he demands baptism, despite his Gentile background, and Philip is only too willing to oblige him (vv. 36–38).

After Samaria, Acts continues on its trajectory away from Jerusalem, as it describes Paul moving north through Galilee into Syria, Asia Minor, Macedonia, and beyond, and there, in these decidedly Gentile lands, any significant distinction among Jerusalem Jews, Diaspora Jews, and quasi-Jews disappears. Now it is "the Jews" who become "filled with envy," "the Jews" who stir up the non-Jewish populace against the apostles, and "the Jews" who "use them despitefully" and stone them" (Acts 13:45, 50; 14:19). Gentiles, on the other hand, often react positively to the apostles' message, and they do so in ways that recall pro-Gentile characterizations and statements in the synoptic Gospels. For instance, Cornelius, a Roman centurion who "feared God, ... gave much alms to the people, and prayed to God always," seeks out Peter in order to be baptized (Acts: 10:1–48)—much as another centurion, a man whose faith Jesus said was so great that its equal could not be found in all of Israel, seeks out Jesus so that his daughter can be healed (Luke 7:9). Similarly, Peter's statement that his Pentecostal experience was a fulfillment of God's promise to Joel to pour out His Spirit "upon *all* flesh" (Acts 2:17) echoes Simeon's prophecy that Jesus as the Messiah will bring salvation to "*all* people" and will, in particular, "lighten the Gentiles" (Luke 2:30–32).

In addition, Jewish resistance to the apostles' message in Acts also resonates with Jesus's statement that "no prophet is accepted in his own country" (Luke 4:24), as does the general Gentile welcoming of that message calls to mind Jesus's claim that the "men of Nineve shall rise up in the judgment with this generation, and shall condemn it' (Luke 11:32). Indeed, the receptivity of Gentiles to the apostles' message in Acts seems to transform Jesus's curse upon Chorazin and Bethsaida into a prophecy. Here, the "mighty works" Jesus spoke of in connection with Tyre and Sidon are in fact performed in Gentile cities, and Gentiles do indeed seem to repent easily and quickly (Luke 10:13). Capernaum too is thrust "down to hell" during the first war with Rome in 66–73 CE, just as Jerusalem is "trodden down of the Gentiles" (Luke 10:14–15; 21:24). And those Jews who were not with Jesus in the Gospel of Luke are presented as being against him in the book of Acts—and are consequently scattered, again just as Jesus appears to predict (Luke 11:23).

By Suggesting a Reason for the Destruction of Jerusalem

Little wonder then that Hippolytus as well as other early Christian leaders saw the Roman destruction of Jerusalem and the resultant dispersal of its inhabitants as natural consequences of their alleged murder of Jesus.[2] By connecting to the Gospels chiastically, Acts transforms Jesus's death into the center not only of the New Testament but of Jewish-Christian religious history as well. Because of it, the Passion of the Christ becomes a kind of theological "Big Bang," a point in time where supreme good and "anti-good" come together so dramatically and so violently that Judaism

---

2. Rosemary Ruether, *Faith and Fratricide: The Theological Roots of Anti-Semitism*, 128

Figure 2. Narrative movement in Luke and in Acts with respect to people

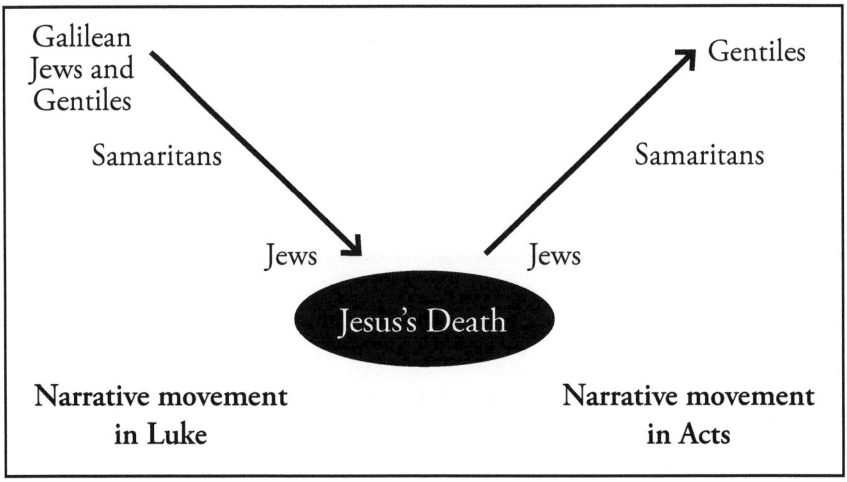

```
Galilean                              Gentiles
Jews and
Gentiles
      Samaritans            Samaritans

              Jews      Jews
                 Jesus's Death

Narrative movement      Narrative movement
     in Luke                 in Acts
```

essentially explodes, igniting a blast that sends God's favor hurtling away from the Jews and toward the Gentiles at the speed of light.

This chiastic connection between Acts and Luke turns the Gospels' world upside-down. The "last"—meaning Jesus's non-Jewish followers, those who later on enter in "at the strait gate"—are now the priority; and the "first"—meaning the Jews, those who had "eaten and drunk" with Jesus and had been taught by him in their homes and in their streets—have been left behind (Luke 13:24, 26, 30). It also flips the Pauline Epistles, transforming their neutrality towards Jews into evidence that they have been rejected by God.

In this way, the literary structure of Acts shows what one of its major figures proclaims. As Stephen states in Acts 7, the Jews had many chances to come unto God, but they proved themselves time and time again to be unalterably "stiffnecked and uncircumcised in heart and ears." They, like their fathers, "do always resist the Holy Ghost" and have perpetually persecuted and slain the prophets. Their murder of Jesus, as Stephen sees it, is simply the last straw in a massive wheat field of Jewish offenses. According to Stephen, the Jews "received the law by the disposition of angels," but they never kept it. They are therefore cast off forever. Having consistently "stopped their ears" against God's voice, they are no longer worthy of ongoing communication with Him (7:51–53) and are consequently ready to be "destroyed from among the people" (3:23). As a result of Stephen's speech, it came as no surprise to Jesus's early followers that Jerusalem,

Figure 3. Supersessionist structure of the New Testament

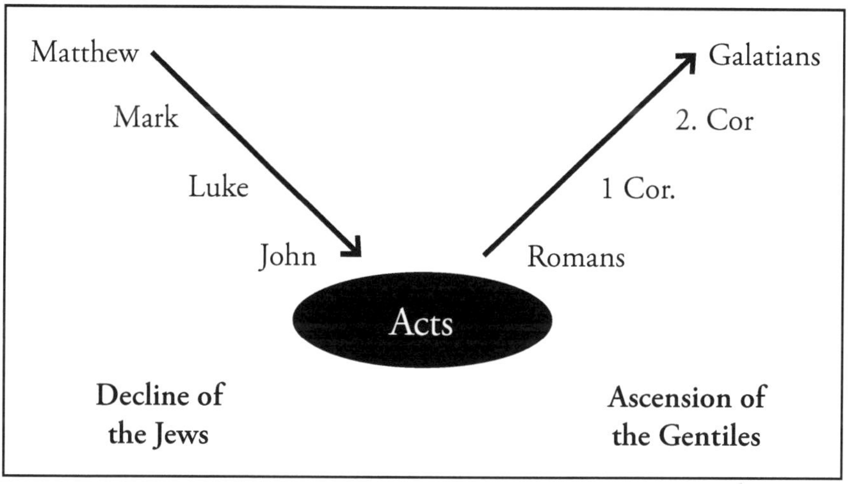

```
Matthew                                    Galatians
    Mark                                  2. Cor
       Luke                             1 Cor.
          John                       Romans
                    ╲   Acts   ╱
Decline of                              Ascension of
the Jews                                the Gentiles
```

the most prominent symbol of God's connection to the Jews, was leveled not long after Jesus's death or that the Jews living in that city were subsequently scattered and killed. Because of Acts, Christians came to see the entire New Testament, indeed the entire Christian Bible, as providing ample evidence that the Jews no longer have a place in God's heart or in His covenant.

How the Book of Mormon Restructures Acts' Structuring

None of this, however, is so in the Book of Mormon. In addition to refuting Acts' supersessionist suggestions by stating that God's covenant with the Jews is still very much intact, it also reinforces these statements using the same approach employed by the book of Acts. By situating itself literarily as well as historically between the Old and New Testaments of the Christian Bible, the Book of Mormon changes how the New Testament is understood by placing it in an older, larger, wider, and more Judaically positive context. In this way, the Book of Mormon effectively overwhelms Acts, restructuring the canonical structure it promotes and negating the supersessionist negativity it implies. Rather than removing the firstborn Jews from God's covenant and replacing them with the lastborn Gentiles (Luke 13:24–30), the Book of Mormon instead retains the Jews as God's chosen people and returns them to their place of prominence *after* the Gentiles' day in the sun. In other words, according to the Book of

Mormon, there is more to the story of God's dealings with the Jews than Acts lets on. As Zenos's allegory of the olive trees shows (discussed in detail in Chapter 3), many Jews will indeed be dispossessed of their land and dispersed. However, they remain in God's care and will eventually be gathered, nourished, strengthened, and taken back to Jerusalem. In this way, the Book of Mormon completes the chiasmus that Acts has created. It reverses Acts' reversal and does so so that once again the last "may be first, and that the first may be last" (Jacob 5:60–63).

By Countering Acts' Suggestions Regarding the Destruction of Jerusalem

One of the ways the Book of Mormon achieves this scriptural turnabout is by connecting with the book of Acts in such a way as to refute its supersessionist suggestions concerning Jerusalem and its destruction. Like Acts, the Book of Mormon shows a group of Jews traveling away from Jerusalem in three stages. These stages are very similar, in many ways, to the three stages in Acts. However, never, in any of these stages, is Jerusalem removed from God's favor or are its inhabitants cut off from the divine covenant that that city represents. Always there is the possibility—indeed the promise—of their eventual return. In this way, the Book of Mormon joins with the book of Acts literarily in order to undo the brooding sense of finality with which that book darkens the apostles' journey away from Jerusalem and to bring hope to an otherwise hopeless situation.

Jerusalem. Like the book of Acts, the Book of Mormon begins in and around a soon-to-be-destroyed Jerusalem. Lehi, like Peter, is "filled with the Spirit of the Lord" (1 Ne. 1:12; Acts 4:8) and testifies boldly concerning the wickedness of the Jerusalemites, the advent of Messiah, and "the redemption of the world." Like Peter, Lehi is mocked and rejected and eventually flees Jerusalem (1 Ne. 1:19; 2:1; Acts 4:1–3; 12:1–11). However, unlike Peter, Lehi does not leave these people or their city without a clear sense of their continued place within his and God's heart. Soon after he receives his vision concerning the destruction of Jerusalem, an experience so moving that it causes him to "quake and tremble exceedingly" on behalf of his people (1 Ne. 1:6), Lehi "returns to his own house at Jerusalem," and there he receives another, more forgiving vision. In fact, so compassionate is this vision that it prompts Lehi to declare God "merciful" and to praise him for not allowing "those who come unto [God] that they shall perish!" (vv. 7, 14). Lehi then goes out and addresses his fellow

That the Last May Be First and the First May Be Last 121

Figure 4. Narrative movement in Acts compared to the Book of Mormon

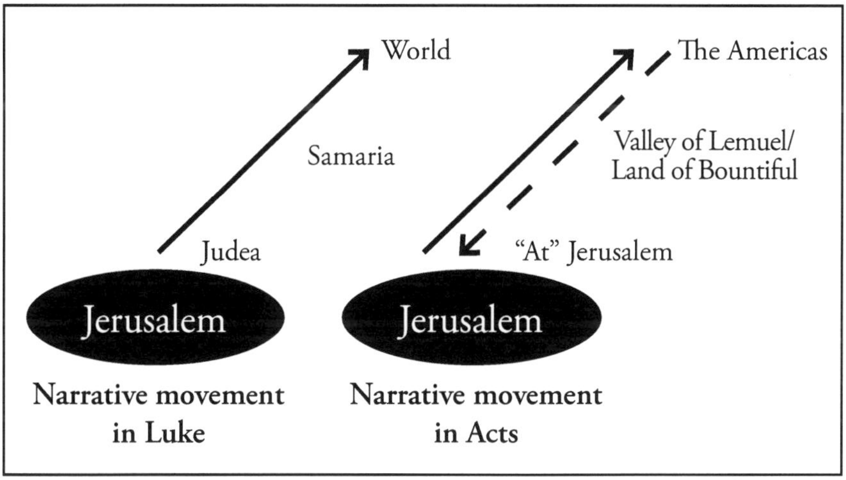

Narrative movement in Luke: Jerusalem → Judea → Samaria → World

Narrative movement in Acts: Jerusalem → "At" Jerusalem → Valley of Lemuel/Land of Bountiful → The Americas

Jerusalemites, those who live in and around his city, and relates to them "the things which he had both seen and heard," especially those things that pertain to "the redemption of the world" (v. 19). In other words, as wicked as these inhabitants of Jerusalem may be, there is still hope for them; they can repent; they can change; they can be redeemed. And even if their city is destroyed and many of them are "carried away captive into Babylon" (v. 13), these Jerusalemites can still return and rebuild. Despite the immanent destruction of Jerusalem, Lehi still cares deeply for Jerusalem and God remains intimately connected to its people.

Bountiful. The same is true during the next Acts-like stage of Lehi's trek. Even after some Jerusalemites "seek to take away [his] life" (1 Ne. 2:1), causing him to flee Jerusalem and take up residence outside the city, Lehi and his family continue to be tied emotionally to Jerusalem and to see God as covenantally linked to it and its people. There in the valley of Lemuel, Lehi, like Philip in Samaria, preaches Jesus to a much more receptive populace, and he does so, again like Philip, by interpreting Isaiah Christologically (Acts 8:5, 27–35). Soon after his sons have procured the plates of brass from Laban and brought them to his tent, Lehi gathers his family together and teaches them concerning a prophet that the Lord will raise up among the Jews, "even a Messiah, or, in other words, a Savior of the world" (1 Ne. 10:4). Lehi asserts that a number of prophets have testified concerning this Messiah, and as proof of this assertion he quotes Isaiah 40:3, explaining that the prophet mentioned in this verse will not only "prepare the way of the Lord" but will baptize "the Messiah with water" (vv. 8–9). Lehi's use of Isaiah here may seem like a small point. However, it has a significant impact on Nephi. Believing "all the words" of his father (11:5), much as the Ethiopian eunuch did Philip's (Acts 8:37), Nephi thoroughly embraces Lehi's messianic approach to Scripture and later reads "many things" to his family from those same Scriptures, explicitly in order to "more fully persuade them to believe in the Lord their Redeemer" (1 Ne. 19:23). Jacob similarly recites to his people three chapters of Isaiah (50 through 52) for much the same reason and rejoices that the Lord God shall "suffereth himself to become subject unto man in the flesh, and die for all men (2 Ne. 9:3, 5).

This positive reaction of Nephi and Jacob to their father's preaching differs distinctly from that of Lehi's Jerusalemite neighbors. Nonetheless, the Book of Mormon does not present the negative response of these neighbors in final or eternal terms. The homicidal plans of these Jews may have forced Lehi to flee Jerusalem and go into the wilderness, but the Book of Mormon, unlike the book of Acts (7:52), does not extend this murderous intent to all Jews everywhere; nor does it imply that their connection to God has been permanently severed. Almost as soon as Lehi sets up camp in the wilderness, he commands his sons again to return to Jerusalem not once but twice, each time bringing with them more Jerusalemites. In other words, some of the inhabitants of Jerusalem at that time may have been wicked enough to merit divine punishment but not all (1 Ne. 2:1). In fact, the Book of Mormon tells of another, much larger group of Jews who also came "out from Jerusalem" around the same time as Lehi. Led by Mulek, a surviving son of King Zedekiah, these Jews were apparently righteous enough to have been spared destruction and captivity and, like the Lehites, were "brought by the hand of the Lord across the great waters" to a promised land in the Americas (Omni 1:15).

Nonetheless, all of these "remnants of the house of Israel," as Lehi calls them, are to be "gathered together again" (1 Ne. 10:14), and, as if to emphasize this point, Nephi's first effort to teach his people from the book of Isaiah does not center on Jesus's mortal ministry, as his father's did, but rather on this universal Jewish return to Jerusalem. Nephi records, "I did rehearse unto them the words of Isaiah, who spake concerning the restoration of the Jews [and stated that] . . . after they were restored they should no more be confounded, neither should they be scattered again" (15:20). Indeed, when Nephi later turns to Isaiah, he reads aloud to his people two complete chapters from his book of Isaiah that reinforce these ideas:

- Isaiah 48 portrays pre-exilic Jews as an "obstinate" people with a neck made of "iron sinew" and a brow made of brass. Nevertheless, it also shows the Lord promising to "cut [them] not off" but to instead refine them "in the furnace of affliction" (1 Ne. 20:4, 9–10).
- Isaiah 49 similarly presents the "house of Israel" as having been driven out of their land "because of the wickedness of the pastors of [God's] people." Yet, it quotes God as calling them His servants and pledging to "raise up the tribes of Jacob," to "restore the preserved of Israel," and to help them "inherit the desolate heritages" (1 Ne. 21:1, 6, 8).

After reading these chapters, Nephi expounds upon them and offers an interpretation that rejects the idea that the destruction of Jerusalem and his father's departure from it imply that the God has cursed Jerusalem and cut the Jews off from His blessings. Instead, Nephi affirms that God will yet "bring them again out of captivity," that "they shall be gathered together to the lands of their inheritance," that "they shall be brought out of obscurity and out of darkness," and that "they shall know that the Lord is their Savior and their Redeemer, the Mighty One of Israel" (1 Ne. 22:12).

The Americas. This affirmation of the Jews' continued place in God's covenant is also evident in the Book of Mormons's third Acts-like stage, long after Lehi and his family finally cross the sea and arrive in the Americas. There, four of Lehi's descendants—Ammon, Aaron, Omner, and Himni—much like Paul, become "a great hindrement to the prosperity of the church of God" (Acts 8:3; Mosiah 27:9). These sons of the Nephite king Mosiah, along with Alma (the son of his namesake father and Nephite high priest), diligently work to steal "away the hearts of the people" and callously cause "much dissension" within the Nephite church (Mosiah 27:9–10). However, like Paul, they experience a visitation from an angel who speaks to them "with a voice of thunder," causes them to fall to the earth, and asks Alma, sounding just like Jesus challenging Paul, "why persecutest thou the church of God?" (Mosiah 27:11–13; Acts 9:4). Like Paul, they consequently repent, turn to Jesus, and attempt to serve him as best they can as ministers for the rest of their days. The four brothers even eventually leave their people, as Paul did, in order to "impart the word of God" (Mosiah 28:1) to a people not their own. (See Chapter 3.) However, the sons of Mosiah, unlike Paul, do not do so because their people rejected them. As the Book of Mormon makes clear, immediately after their conversion the brothers traveled "round about" throughout the land of the Nephites, "publishing to all the people the things which they had heard and seen." While they experience some persecution from "unbelievers"—possibly those they associated with before their conversions—and are occasionally "smitten by many of them," as "instruments in the hands of God" they still manage to bring "many [of their fellow Nephites] to the knowledge of the truth" and, in the end, are highly respected (27:32–36).

In this way, the Book of Mormon limits the apparent universality of Paul's rejection of the Jews, as portrayed in Acts. Certainly, Paul had conflicts with the Jews of Thessalonica (Acts 17:1–5, 13). Undoubtedly, many of the Jews of Athens did not believe him. And surely at least some of the Jews of Corinth "opposed" and "blasphemed" him. But does that mean that when Paul shook his raiment at these Jews and told them that their sinful blood was upon their own heads that all Jews everywhere were similarly cursed and removed from God's covenant (18:5–6)? The experience of the sons of Mosiah would seem to suggest not. Despite being persecuted by the Nephites and leaving them for the Lamanites, the sons of Mosiah retain a close connection with their people and come back to them after their mission among the Lamanites has been completed. On their way back to their homeland, they encounter Alma, now the high priest of the Nephites, and the meeting is so joyful that one of their number is overcome with emotion and falls to the earth (Alma 27:17). They then proceed with Alma to Zarahemla, the Nephite capital, and are there received by Nephihah, the chief judge of the Nephites, and asked to recount publicly all that has "happened unto them." Nephihah listens intently to their report and then sends "a proclamation throughout all the land," inquiring of his people what should be done with the sons of Mosiah and their Lamanite converts, and "the voice of the people" responds kindly, deeding to them land within their realm as an inheritance forever—a gift which Ammon, Alma, Omner, Himni and all of the people with them gladly accept (vv. 19–22). There is no rift, religious or otherwise, between the Nephites and the sons of Mosiah, nor is there any rupture in the Nephites' relationship with God. As Ammon affirms, God is still very much "mindful of *this people*," a term that includes Nephites as well as Lamanites; they remain "a branch of the tree of Israel"; and they continue to be covenantally connected to God despite their being lost from the main body of Israelites and roaming like "wanderers in a strange land" (26:36).

Figure 5. Chiastic relationship between periods in the Hebrew Scriptures and in the Book of Mormon

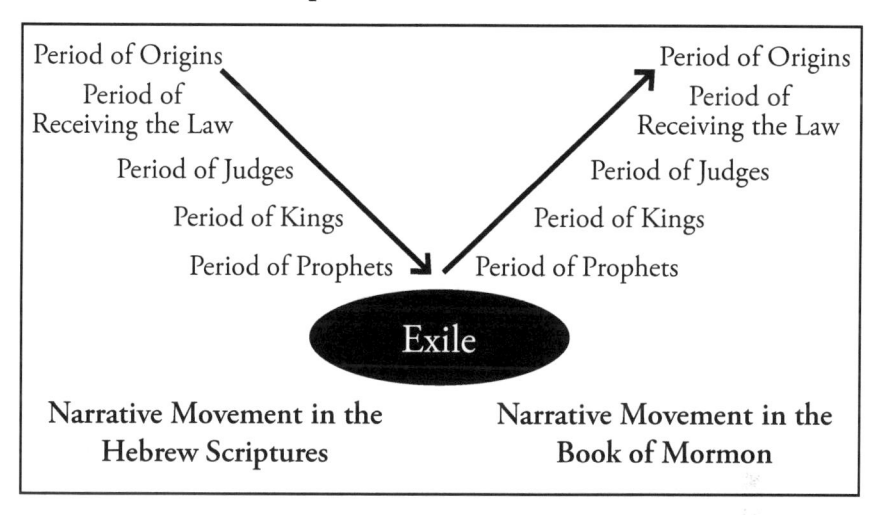

```
Period of Origins                        Period of Origins
   Period of                                 Period of
Receiving the Law                        Receiving the Law
   Period of Judges                      Period of Judges
      Period of Kings                 Period of Kings
         Period of Prophets       Period of Prophets
                          Exile

Narrative Movement in the        Narrative Movement in the
   Hebrew Scriptures                Book of Mormon
```

By Succeeding the Hebrew Scriptures

Further reinforcing this theme of reconciliation and return, the Book of Mormon provides a number of Judaically positive incidents in contrast with many of the most significant negative incidents in the Hebrew Scriptures, and it does so in such a way as to highlight that contrast and refute any possible anti-Semitic rejectionism that these negative incidents might imply. Much as Acts, coming chronologically after the synoptic Gospels, connects with them, moving stage by stage away from Jerusalem just as Matthew, Mark, and Luke inch towards it, so the Book of Mormon, coming chronologically after the pre-exilic books of the Hebrew Scriptures, joins with them, retracing their progression backwards, historical period by historical period, chiastically turning their downward flow of mistakes, miscues, and misery upward, to a more favorable view of Jews.

The pre-exilic books of the Hebrew Scriptures and those of the Book of Mormon can be grouped into five general historical/scriptural periods that correspond closely to each other in subject matter and treatment.[3]

---

3. This is further discussed in Bradley J. Kramer, *Beholding the Tree of Life: A Rabbinic Approach to the Book of Mormon*, 112–15.

Table 1. Historical Periods in Relation to the Books in the Hebrew Scriptures and those in the Book of Mormon

Period	Hebrew Books	Mormon Books
Period of Origins	Genesis	Mormon, Ether, Moroni
Period of Receiving the Law	Exodus, Leviticus, Numbers, Deuteronomy	3 Nephi, 4 Nephi
Period of Judges	Joshua, Judges	Alma, Helaman
Period of Kings	1 Samuel, 2 Samuel, 1 Kings, 2 Kings	Words of Mormon, Mosiah
Period of Prophets	Isaiah, Jeremiah, Ezekiel, Minor Prophets	1 Nephi, 2 Nephi, Jacob, Enos, Jarom, Omni

Period of Prophets. For instance, the Book of Mormon begins much as the Hebrew Scriptures end, with a "Period of Prophets," an era that includes prophetic visions, prophetic dreams, prophetic rebukes, as well as lengthy citations from biblical prophets and numerous allusions to their experiences.[4] During this period, Lehi, like Isaiah, sees God on His heavenly throne; like Ezekiel, he is given a book to read by an angel; and like Jeremiah, he is told to warn his people "that they must repent, or the great city Jerusalem must be destroyed" (1 Ne. 1:4, 19; Jer. 4:4–6). However, the way people react to these experiences is not always consonant with what occurs in the Hebrew Scriptures. Certainly, most of the inhabitants of Jerusalem at Lehi's time ignore him just as they did his prophetic contemporaries. However, Lehi's family and a few others flee Jerusalem and do so expressly because they believe in him and in his God-given message. Nephi, in particular, proclaims that the truth of his father's claims were manifested unto him "by [God's] Holy Spirit" and exclaims that he will therefore "go and do the things which the Lord hath commanded" (1 Ne. 2:17; 3:7). In this way, the Book of Mormon counters the way pre-Captivity Jews are generally portrayed in the Hebrew Scriptures and refutes two of Stephen's most potent charges against them. As Nephi and those like him demonstrate, Jews do not "*always* resist the Holy Ghost," nor do *all* of their fathers persecute the prophets (Acts 7:51–52). These Jews, at least, follow their prophets faithfully, go into the wilderness willingly, enter their Promised Land eagerly, and worship the Lord exclusively.

---

4. Kramer, 120–33.

Period of Kings. Similarly, the next period in the Book of Mormon, a "Period of Kings," challenges Stephen's third claim: that the Jews despite receiving the Law of Moses "by the disposition of angels" have never kept it (v. 52). Certainly, at least one of several kings who reign during this period is a self-serving despot who, like most of monarchs of Israel and Judah, leads his people into selfishness, wickedness, and captivity. However, others are more benevolent—and much more Mosaic.[5] King Benjamin, for instance, is described as a "holy man" who ruled over his people "in righteousness" (W of M 1:17). He credits the brass plates for keeping the commandments "always before our eyes" and commands his heir-apparent sons to search these plates diligently" as Deuteronomy requires Israelite kings to do, (Mosiah 1:5–7; Deut. 17:18–19). King Benjamin also offers "sacrifice and burnt offerings according to the law of Moses" before his great Sukkot sermon (see Chapter 4) and, in that sermon, describes how he, as king, obeys the Mosaic commandments to not "greatly multiply to himself silver and gold" (Deut. 17:17; Mosiah 2:12) or consider himself "above his brethren" (Deut. 17:20). As King Benjamin tells his people,

> I have not commanded you to come up hither that ye should fear me, or that ye should think that I of myself am more than a mortal man. I am like as yourselves, subject to all manner of infirmities in body and mind; yet I have been chosen by this people, and consecrated by my father, and was suffered by the hand of the Lord that I should be a ruler and a king over this people; and have been kept and preserved by his matchless power, to serve you with all the might, mind and strength which the Lord hath granted unto me. (Mosiah 2:10–11)

Period of Judges. King Benjamin's point that a king should serve his people with the same devotion demanded by God (Mosiah 1:11–14, 2:17; Deut. 6:4–5) is not lost on his son Mosiah. In fact he is so committed to such service that at the end of this reign he initiates the "Period of Judges" by doing away with the monarchy altogether and returning the Nephites to a system of nonhereditary judges not unlike the one described in the Hebrew Scriptures (Mosiah 29:25). In this way, King Mosiah shows that Israel's tragic choice when "the elders of Israel gathered themselves together" to demand that the prophet Samuel "make [them] a king to judge [them] like all the nations" is reversible, that they have not rejected God forever as their ultimate sovereign nor have they renounced their Mosaic role as a "peculiar" people, distinct from "all the nations that are upon the earth" (1 Sam. 8:5–7; Deut. 14:2). Certainly Stephen is, to some

---

5. Kramer, 136–43.

degree, correct. Israel has not always kept the Law of Moses, but that does not mean that they have never done so or that they cannot do so in the future. As the Book of Mormon demonstrates, there is always hope. Israel can repent, embrace their God-given role, recommit themselves to obey God's commandments, and understand, at last, that "it is better that a man should be judged of God than of man" (Mosiah 29:12).

And this counterpoint pattern continues through the balance of the Book of Mormon, as it works backwards through many of the most prominent sins committed by Jews in the Hebrew Scriptures. During the "Period of Judges," New World Jews, much like their Old World counterparts, frequently fall into a vicious cycle of sin. However, in the books of Alma and Helaman their heroes do not fight this tendency solely from the outside, superficially with swords and spears, as do those described in the book of Judges. Instead Alma, Amulek, Ammon, and even the military leader Captain Moroni rely more on words—preaching and prayers—to attack the internal causes of sin: pride, selfishness, status-seeking, envy, and greed.[6] Granted, these Book of Mormon heroes are not always successful in their attempts to arrest this cycle, but they are much more effective than Othniel, Ehud, Jephthah, and Samson—their biblical counterparts—are, and the peace they produce is much more deeply rooted and long lasting.

Period of Receiving the Law. This turn to peace is especially evident in the Book of Mormon's "Period of Receiving the Law," an era that corresponds to the time covered in Exodus, Leviticus, Numbers, and Deuteronomy.[7] Like the ancient Israelites, here the righteous escape a sentence of death (3 Ne. 1:9–13), and, like the ancient Egyptians, the wicked are plagued with darkness and drowned in the sea (8:9, 19–23). Like Moses too, Jesus also descends from above and recites the Law to them. However, in the Book of Mormon the Israelites he appears to do not "remove" themselves or stand "afar off" when their great lawgiver appears (20:18). Instead, they go up to Jesus, bless the "name of the Most High God," and so embrace him and the law he affirms that they form, for a time, a "holy nation" just as they were originally commanded (3 Ne. 11:15, 17; Ex. 19:6)—a realm ruled directly by God, where there are "no envyings, nor strifes, nor tumults, nor whoredoms, nor lyings, nor murders," nor any of the decidedly un-Mosaic lasciviousness that dogged the children of Israel as they wandered for forty years in the wilderness (4 Ne. 1:16).

---

6. Kramer, 146–65.
7. Kramer, 169–77.

Period of Origins. Nonetheless, despite the fact that during this period "there could not be a happier people among all the people who had been created by the hand of God" (4 Ne. 1:16), this ideal society eventually degenerates into self-destructive chaos. One person is left—Mormon's son Moroni—to finish his people's story. As part of this effort, Moroni includes a book with his writings that reaches back even further into the books of Moses, to a "Period of Origins," as he attempts to explain why his people turned in on themselves so quickly and with such ferocity. This book, the book of Ether, begins around the time of the Tower of Babel and recounts how one group, the Jaredites, is spared God's wrath and is led instead on a "reverse Genesis" journey—trekking into the valley of Nimrod, travelling through an area "where there never had man been," and traversing across a great sea in barges sealed "tight like unto the ark of Noah" to a "land which is choice above all the earth" (Ether 1:38; 2:4–5; 6:7). This favored land, however, like the antediluvian world, soon becomes "filled with violence," (Gen. 6:11; Ether 13:25). It is there that the ultimate cause of the Nephite destruction is revealed: vindictive oaths that "had been handed down even from Cain, who was a murderer from the beginning," that have been administered to people in order "to keep them in darkness," and that "help such as sought power to gain power, and to murder, and to plunder, and to lie, and to commit all manner of wickedness and whoredoms" (Ether 8:15–16). It is these oaths then, and the secret societies they spawned, that, according to Moroni, ultimately "caused the destruction of [the people described in the book of Ether], and also the destruction of the people of Nephi" (v. 21).

Nevertheless, as dark as this journey may seem, Moroni sees light in it. He explains,

> I am commanded to write these things that evil may be done away, that the time may come that Satan may have no power upon the hearts of the children of men, but that they may be persuaded to do good continually, that they may come unto the fountain of all righteousness and be saved. (Ether 8:26)

Moroni still has hope—if not for his people at least for his future readers—and this hope seems to be based mainly on the story of the brother of Jared. Reaching back even further into Genesis to Eden, Moroni portrays this "highly favored [man] of the Lord" as being presented with an Adam-and-Eve-like choice—not between obeying God by having children and obeying God by not partaking of the fruit of the tree of knowledge (2 Ne. 2:22–25), but between crossing the sea with light and crossing it in safety.

As the Lord tells the brother of Jared, "What will ye that I should do that ye may have light in your vessels? For behold, ye cannot have windows, for they will be dashed in pieces; neither shall ye take fire with you, for ye shall not go by the light of fire" (Ether 2:23). However, the brother of Jared, noting perhaps that the Lord's response is framed more as a question than as a statement, is not content with it and attempts to solve this dilemma—not by choosing one of the two options, according to his own, unaugmented, understanding as Adam and Eve did, but by coming up with a third option in close consultation with God. And so, the brother of Jared climbs a mountain and moltens out of rock sixteen transparent stones until they are "white and clear." He then pleads with the Lord to touch them with his finger so "that [His people] may have light while [they] shall cross the sea" without endangering themselves, their mission, or their barges (3:1–4). It is an ingenious solution, and the Lord is so impressed with it and the faith the brother of Jared demonstrated in presenting it to Him that He not only does as the brother of Jared asks but redeems him from the Fall, welcoming him back into His presence and revealing Himself unto him in glory (v. 13).

In other words, in the Book of Mormon even Adam's sin can be reversed. Just as it shows Jews faithfully following prophets, Israelite kings ruling in righteousness, and the children of Israel being blessed by effective judges as well as embracing the Law and becoming, for a time, a holy nation, the Book of Mormon depicts one pre-Israelite man effectively returning to the garden of Eden, talking freely with God, even walking with Him again figuratively in the cool of the day (Gen. 3:8; Ether 3:13). In this way, the Book of Mormon refutes the supersessionist insinuations of Stephen and does so just as the book of Acts reinforces them: by connecting with other books of scripture structurally, positively, and by altering the canonical context in which they are understood. Here the exile of the Jews from their homeland becomes not the endpoint of a long sin-filled journey toward divine rejection but a turning point, a nadir from which these same Jews can bounce back, ascending upwards through repentance to their previous place of blessedness. As Moroni asserts, there is hope for the Jewish people, as there is for all people. Evil can yet be done away with, people can still do good continually, and they can yet come again unto the fountain of all righteousness and be saved (Ether 8:26).

By Preceding the New Testament

However, just as the Book of Mormon alters how the apparent "fall" of the Jews is understood by succeeding the Hebrew Scriptures and by following them with more Judaically positive examples and events, so it similarly modifies how the "rise" of the Gentiles is seen by preceding the New Testament and by prefacing it with less supersessionist precedents and prophecies. Coming, as most of it does, before Jesus's life and the spread of his gospel, the Book of Mormon sets the stage for the New Testament and functions relative to it much as the book of Acts does in relation to the Pauline Epistles—not by laying out a kind of itinerary that this later material fits into but by preemptively altering the literary landscape in which its story unfolds. Obviously, the Book of Mormon does not deal with first-century Gentiles specifically, and therefore it cannot comment on them directly. Its pages contain no Corinthians, no Ephesians, no Philippians, and certainly no Romans. However, the Book of Mormon does describe a people who are Gentile-*like,* and, through them, by analogy, it counters any zero-sum suggestion, offered by the New Testament, that the ascension of the Gentiles necessitates a corresponding descent of the Jews.

As discussed previously, Ammon and his companions bear a remarkable resemblance to Paul and his companions. In addition, the similarities between the people these missionaries teach, though Israelites themselves, are also quite striking—and helpful in determining the covenantal relationship between Jews and Gentiles. Like the Gentiles Paul goes to, the Lamanites the sons of Mosiah encounter start off violent (Alma 17:14; Acts 14:2–5), idolatrous (Alma 17:15; Acts 17:16), and superstitious, even to the point of mistaking them for gods, just as the citizens of Lystra did Paul and Barnabas (Alma 18:2; Acts 14:8–11). However, after these Lamanites are taught by Ammon and his brothers, the Spirit of God is "poured out" upon them, and they, again like Paul's Gentiles, are soon baptized and quickly become a "righteous people" (Alma 19:14, 35; Acts 10:45–48). In fact, the faith of one group of Lamanites, like the converted Romans, easily deserves to be "spoken of throughout the whole world" (Rom. 1:8). After they convert, the Anti-Nephi-Lehites (discussed in Chapter 3) resolve to never again murder, "nor to plunder, nor to steal, nor to commit adultery, nor to commit any manner of wickedness" (Alma 23:3; Rom. 13:9).

Nonetheless, despite their great faith, which at one point eclipses that of the Nephites, these Anti-Nephi-Lehites never replace or displace the

Nephites as far as the God's covenant is concerned. Instead, they are welcomed by the Nephites into their territory, offered protection, given land, and basically absorbed into Nephite society. They are not simply "among the people of Nephi" physically but are instead "numbered among" the Nephites religiously and as such become a "beloved people" to them (Alma 27:27, 30). In this way, by analogy, the Book of Mormon demonstrates how Mosaically lawless people can join in on God's blessings without superseding those who are already established within that covenant.

Just as the sons of Mosiah are sent out from Zarahemla to bring God's blessings to the Lamanites, so the Jews, according to the Book of Mormon, are dispatched from their homeland in order to extend those same blessings to the Gentiles. Certainly, some ancient Judahites were exiled from Jerusalem as punishment for their sins. However, many went willingly and did so under divine direction. Lehi and his family are the most obvious example of Israelites who leave Jerusalem in this manner. Not only do they go into the wilderness by express commandment of God, but they are also told to keep an account of their journey and their resultant history in order to aid future Gentiles (1 Ne. 13:34–36; 2 Ne. 30:3). Mulek and his people similarly are "brought by the hand of the Lord across the great waters" from their Judean homeland to the Americas and are part of this effort (Omni 1:16). Furthermore, the words the Book of Mormon uses to describe the general Jewish departure from Jerusalem, *scattering* and *dispersion*, are much less pointed than *exile* and seem to include Jews who left voluntarily to benefit others, including the Gentiles.

Along these lines, the Book of Mormon confirms on several occasions that the Abrahamic mission to bless "all the families of the earth" (Gen. 12:3) remains very much intact despite this dispersion, and it does so as part of an explanation as to why Abraham's progeny was scattered. Nephi, for instance, just before the First Temple is destroyed, explains that the Jewish diaspora enables the Lord to "show his power unto the Gentiles" and, consequently, allows "all the kindreds of the earth [to] be blessed" (1 Ne. 15:17–18). Similarly, when Nephi discovers that the First Temple has in fact been destroyed (2 Ne. 6:8), he again states that because of the Abrahamic mission the Lord will "proceed to do a marvelous work among the Gentiles" (1 Ne. 22:8–10). Jesus too, four decades before the Second Temple is destroyed, cites "the covenant which the Father made with . . . Abraham" (3 Ne. 20:25) as the reason why the Nephites, like the rest of Israel, will participate in the "pouring out of the Holy Ghost through [Jesus] upon the Gentiles" (vv. 25–27).

In this way, the Book of Mormon anticipates a general acceptance of God's law on the part of the Gentiles, the beginning of which Acts appears to document. However, never in this process are the Jews as a people cut off or superseded. They are instead to be blessed by the Gentiles in turn. Quoting Isaiah, Nephi writes:

> Thus saith the Lord God: Behold, I will lift up mine hand to the Gentiles, and set up my standard to the people; and they shall bring thy sons in their arms, and thy daughters shall be carried upon their shoulders.
> And kings shall be thy nursing fathers, and their queens thy nursing mothers; they shall bow down to thee with their face towards the earth, and lick up the dust of thy feet; and thou shalt know that I am the Lord; for they shall not be ashamed that wait for me. " (1 Ne. 21:22–23; Isa. 49:22–23)

So important is this blessing of the Jews that Nephi, as well as his brother Jacob, return to this subject later on, each time stressing how the Gentiles will nurse the Jews and figuratively carry them back to their lands and all that those lands represent (1 Ne. 22:6; 2 Ne. 6:6–7). As these prophets assert, Gentile kings, Gentile queens, and mighty Gentile nations will befriend the Jews, bring them out of "obscurity and out of darkness" (1 Ne. 22:7, 12), gather them "in from their long dispersion," and assemble them "from the four parts of the earth." In this way "the nations of the Gentiles shall be great in the eyes of [God]" and will transport Jews "forth to the lands of their inheritance" (2 Ne. 10:8–9).

There is, in other words, more to the "rise" of the Gentiles than the New Testament records. According to the Book of Mormon, there is another chapter to this story, perhaps even several chapters. After the Jews have helped the Gentiles—sending them Peter, Paul, and other missionaries of Jewish descent to teach them—and after the Gentiles have prospered spiritually and materially as a result of these teachings, they will then help the Jews—gathering them in, supporting them, respecting them, building them up, helping them fulfill their mission in their own land and on their own terms. Like the Anti-Nephi-Lehites and the Nephites, the Gentiles and the Jews will not be in conflict or in competition. Many Gentiles will be folded in with Jews and "numbered among the house of Israel" (1 Ne. 14:2).

Repentance, however, is the key to bringing these two groups together. Only *repentant* Gentiles are joined with Jews. Their place within God's good graces is therefore neither permanent nor unconditional. As the resurrected Jesus states in the Book of Mormon, "*if* the Gentiles will repent and return unto me, saith the Father, behold they shall be numbered among my people" (3 Ne. 16:13). However, if they will not, they will eventually be destroyed by "a remnant of the house of Jacob." Jesus explains, "The "sword of [God's] justice shall hang over [the Gentiles] at that day; and except they repent it shall fall upon them" (20:15–16, 20). Consistent with this explanation, the Book of Mormon is replete with prophetic pleas imploring the Gentiles to change their behavior so that they may come into the covenant. Mormon in particular calls upon them to turn from a long list of "wicked ways"—including lying, whoring, thieving, idolatry, murder, and priestcraft—all so that they may "be numbered with my people who are of the house of Israel" (30:2). As Mormon sees it, the Gentiles are in great peril. "Know ye not," he asks them, "that ye are in the hands of God? Know ye not that he hath all power, and at his great command the earth shall be rolled together as a scroll? Therefore, repent ye, and humble yourselves before him, lest he shall come out in justice against you" (Morm. 5:22–24).

Ironically then, according to the Book of Mormon, it is the Gentiles, not the Jews, who are in danger of being rejected by God. Similar to the way Ezekiel envisions Jewish priests committing "great abominations" within the First Temple just before it was destroyed (Ezek. 8:6), Nephi is shown a vision of a Gentile-dominated "great and abominable *church*," an organization not to be confused with any extent Christian denomination, that has corrupted the "fair jewels" God had given them (1 Ne. 16:17). This hypocritical group of fake religionists has an all-consuming lust for "gold, and silver, and silks, and scarlets, and fine-twined linen, and all manner of precious clothing." They are also obsessed with power, and it is with that power that they "slayeth the saints of God, yea, and tortureth them and bindeth them down, and yoketh them with a yoke of iron, and bringeth them down into captivity" (1 Ne. 13:6–7, 26; Ezek. 16:36–41). Explicitly founded by the devil, this "mother of abominations" sits "upon many waters" and has "dominion over all the earth" (1 Ne. 13:6; 14:10–11). It removes from "the gospel of the Lamb many parts which are plain and most precious" (13:26), and in so doing it causes "an exceedingly great many" Gentiles to "stumble, yea, insomuch that Satan hath great power over them" (v. 29). The Gentiles are therefore in an "awful state of blindness" (v. 32), and it is because of this blindness that they scatter and smite the remnant of the Book of Mormon peoples (v. 14) as well as curse and hate the Jews (2 Ne. 29:5). In fact, so great is its power that this "church" gathers "together multitudes upon the face of all the earth, among all the nations of the Gentiles," all to fight against God and His people (1 Ne. 14:13). Victory seems almost certain. However the power of God at some point descends upon both "the saints of the church of the Lamb, and upon the covenant people of the Lord" (v. 14), and, in the end, this "great and abominable church," like Ezekiel's corrupt temple, must fall (2 Ne. 28:18).

And what a fall it will be. As Nephi continues, in the end "that great and abominable church, the whore of all the earth, must tumble to the earth" (2 Ne. 28:18). Consequently, much like Jeremiah excoriating the Judahites of his time and Jesus chastising the Judeans of his, Nephi rebukes future Gentiles:

> O the wise, and the learned, and the rich, that are puffed up in the pride of their hearts, and all those who preach false doctrines, and all those who commit whoredoms, and pervert the right way of the Lord, wo, wo, wo be unto them, saith the Lord God Almighty, for they shall be thrust down to hell!
>
> Wo unto them that turn aside the just for a thing of naught and revile against that which is good, and say that it is of no worth! For the day shall come that the Lord God will speedily visit the inhabitants of the earth; and in that day that they are fully ripe in iniquity they shall perish. (2 Ne. 28:15–16)

The Gentiles' only hope is to repent, as Nephi makes clear, and discontinue their war against Israel (2 Ne. 6:12). Otherwise, they will be destroyed and removed from God's covenant. As Jesus himself in the Book of Mormon prophesies,

> At that day when the Gentiles shall sin against my gospel, and shall reject the fulness of my gospel, and shall be lifted up in the pride of their hearts above all nations, and above all the people of the whole earth, and shall be filled with all manner of lyings, and of deceits, and of mischiefs, and all manner of hypocrisy, and murders, and priestcrafts, and whoredoms, and of secret abominations; and if they shall do all those things, and shall reject the fulness of my gospel, behold, saith the Father, I will bring the fulness of my gospel from among them. (3 Ne. 16:10).

All in all, the Book of Mormon places the New Testament's emphasis on the ascension of the Gentiles in a larger context, much as it does the decline of the Jews in the Hebrew Scriptures. It again does not call into question the New Testament but sets it up as a portrayal of a specific people living at a specific time in a specific place and not as a generalized pattern with everlasting consequences. Paul's "going to" the Gentiles is therefore not a final rejection of the Jews nor is it an unalterable embrace of the Gentiles. It is simply the second step in a three-step process that brings both repentant Gentiles and Jews into the full embrace of God's blessings. The Jews retain their God-given mission to "bless the families of the earth," and the era of Gentile ascendance sets the stage for a Jewish resurgence and allows them to fulfill it. In this way, the Pauline Epistles may indeed reflect a time when "first shall be last; and the last shall be first (Matt. 19:30). However, according to the Book of Mormon that sequence will one day be reversed; the Jews will be restored to their place of prominence in such a way as to allow "the last that they may be first, and that the first may be last" (Jacob 5:63).

Chapter Seven

I Will Gather Them In

And I command you that ye shall write these sayings after I am gone . . . that these sayings which ye shall write shall be kept and shall be manifested unto the Gentiles, that through the fulness of the Gentiles, the remnant of their seed, who shall be scattered forth upon the face of the earth because of their unbelief, may be brought in, or may be brought to a knowledge of me, their Redeemer. And then will I gather them in from the four quarters of the earth; and then will I fulfil the covenant which the Father hath made unto all the people of the house of Israel. (3 Ne. 16:4–5)

In summary, the Book of Mormon attempts to bring Christians and Jews together by picking up where *Nostra Aetate* and other similar efforts leave off. Not only does it denounce the age-old Christian war against Judaism and renounce all belligerent behavior towards Jews, but it engages the scriptural source of this conflict, the New Testament, and does so on its own terms and on its own turf. By adding a formidable lineup of pro-Jewish statements, pro-Jewish portrayals, pro-Jewish settings, and pro-Jewish structuring elements to the Christian canon, the Book of Mormon effectively neutralizes the New Testament's potent array of similar anti-Semitic elements, *and* it does so respectfully, even reverentially, without altering the New Testament's text or undermining its spiritual authority or dependability. In this way, the Book of Mormon significantly advances Christianity's post-Holocaust quest to "de-anti-Semitize" itself and puts this effort on a much more firm and scripturally sustainable ground.

And yet, one has to wonder if this effort is not ultimately doomed to failure. After all, the Book of Mormon may soften the New Testament's supersessionism, but it seems to harden its already adamantine line on salvific exclusivity. In addition to affirming the New Testament's assertion that Jesus is the only name under which humanity can be saved (Acts 4:12; 2 Ne. 25:20; 31:21; Mosiah 3:17; 5:8; Alma 38:9), the Book of Mormon connects this assertion specifically with Jews, stating that "as many of the

Jews as will not repent" and believe in Jesus shall be "cast off" (2 Ne. 30:2). It would appear, therefore, that even with the canonical inclusion of the Book of Mormon, Christians remain locked in an uncompromising theological conflict with Jews. Jews themselves may no longer be the enemy, but their Judaism is, and consequently Christians continue to be scripturally poised to go on the attack—to launch anti-Judaic ad campaigns, to publish anti-Judaic pamphlets, and to create special anti-Judaic missions—all designed to pressure Jews into accepting Jesus at the expense of their heritage, their history, and their ancestral hope.

But, this is not so.

Yes, according to the Book of Mormon, Jews need Jesus. Very much. In addition to the statements previously quoted, the Book of Mormon states that there is no hope for the Jews "except they shall be reconciled unto Christ" (2 Ne. 33:8–9), asserts that Jesus is "the only sure foundation, upon which the Jews can build" (Jacob 4:11–16), and claims that the final restoration of the Jews is entirely dependent upon their acceptance of Jesus as "the Christ, the Son of the living God" (Morm. 5:14). However, despite the apparent intensity of this need, the Book of Mormon never commissions Christians to meet it. That privilege is reserved exclusively for Jesus. Consistent with the idea that he is the Redeemer Isaiah saw in vision (2 Ne. 11:2) and that "all the prophets" have prophesied of him (Mosiah 13:33; 3 Ne. 20:24), Jesus comes to the Nephites just as these prophets predicted—wiping out the wicked, rescuing the righteous, and ushering in an era of profound peace, justice, prosperity, and equality. However, never does Jesus claim that this appearance is proof that he is indeed the Jewish Messiah or that the account of this event should be presented to Jews as evidence that they "need not look forward any more for a Messiah to come" (2 Ne. 25:18). Instead Jesus speaks of a time when "the remnant of [the] seed" of his people in Jerusalem, now scattered, will be "brought to a knowledge of [him], their Redeemer" (3 Ne. 16:4), not by surrogates nor by servants, but by Jesus himself. As Jesus emphasizes to the Nephites:

> And then will *I* gather them in from the four quarters of the earth; and then will *I* fulfil the covenant which the Father hath made unto all the people of the house of Israel. . . . And then will *I* remember my covenant which *I* have made unto my people, O house of Israel, and *I* will bring my gospel unto them. (3 Ne. 16:5, 11)

I, I, I, I. There is no hint here of any special "Jewish" missionaries or ministers or evangelists. Instead, it is Jesus himself who comes to the Jews directly, personally, even individually. In fact, Jesus seems quite possessive of the Jews. As he states a few chapters later, "I shall gather in, from their long dispersion, *my* people, O house of Israel, and shall establish again among them *my* Zion" (3 Ne. 21:1). In the Book of Mormon, no one comes between Jesus and the Jews. Theirs is a private relationship, a treasured association that only Jesus can address properly and appropriately.

In other words, Jesus's appearance in the New World is no more the ultimate fulfillment of his messianic mission than was his mortal ministry in the Old. It is instead a prophecy, a foretaste, a kind of scaled-down "pre-enactment" of what Jesus, as the Promised Messiah, must yet do. As confirmed by both the Hebrew Scriptures and the Book of Mormon, he must "gather together the dispersed of Judah" (Isa. 11:12; 2 Ne. 21:12), establish the Lord's house in the top of the mountains," and "suddenly come to his temple" (Mal. 3:1; 3 Ne. 24:1). And it is there, at this temple that he will "rebuke many people: and they shall beat their swords into plowshares, and their spears into pruninghooks: nation shall not lift up sword against nation, neither shall they learn war any more" (Isa 2:3–4; 2 Ne. 2:3–4). As Jesus tells the Nephites:

> Verily, verily, I say unto you, *all these things* shall surely come, even as the Father hath commanded me. Then shall this covenant which the Father hath covenanted with His people be fulfilled; and then shall Jerusalem be inhabited again with my people, and it shall be the land of their inheritance. (3 Ne. 20:46)

Consequently, Christians, as faithful followers of Jesus, are duty-bound *not* to evangelize or missionize or otherwise press Jews to accept Jesus. They should instead have enough faith in their Master to put this complex issue on the shelf, as it were, to let it go, and to allow Jesus to do what he has covenanted to do, on his own terms and in his own way without any interference from them. As the Book of Mormon records Jesus telling his future followers:

> Ye need not any longer hiss, nor spurn, nor make game of the Jews, nor any of the remnant of the house of Israel; for behold, the Lord remembereth his covenant unto them, and he will do unto them according to that which he hath sworn. (3 Ne. 29:8)

But does this mean that Christians should avoid all contact with Jews? Certainly not. According to the Book of Mormon, Christians should welcome Jews into their families, much as they have been welcomed into the family of Israel. Echoing Isaiah, Jacob prophesies that future Gentile leaders will be adoptive "nursing fathers" and "nursing mothers" to Israel, and he predicts that individual Gentiles will carry Jewish sons and daughters, like their own children, in their arms and upon their shoulders (Isa. 29:22–23; 2 Ne. 6:6–7, 14). Christians should therefore embrace Jews. They should work with Jews, socialize with Jews, play games and party and dance and laugh and sing and joke and eat with Jews, freely, openly, respectfully, joyfully. They should also not shy away from talking meaningfully with Jews and discussing with them their deepest thoughts and feelings—including their thoughts and feelings about Jesus. Again, Jacob makes it clear that Christians should have faith that Jesus will someday personally "manifest himself unto [the Jews] in power and great glory" (2 Ne. 6:14), but this does not mean that they should avoid talking about Jesus altogether. For true friends, no topic is off limits. Everything is open to discussion, even religion. However, as true friends, Christians should share their thoughts and feelings with Jews in the context of a close relationship and not as part of a membership drive, a national program, or a church-sponsored initiative. Such discussions should instead be spontaneous, not planned, and they should be honest and thoughtful, sincere interactions where doubts and fears are expressed as well as hopes and beliefs. Christians should also ask questions of their Jewish friends, real questions about matters they do not fully understand. They should not be pre-fabricated prompts, manipulative "hooks" designed to pull Jews in and snag them into "conversion dialogues." Furthermore, Christians should genuinely listen, attentively and respectfully, as their Jewish friends respond. Never should these discussions become one-way conversations where Christians speak down to Jews from a supposedly superior religious vantage point. Always, these discussions should be exchanges between equals, where each party is learning from the other and becoming better for the interaction. As Nephi reminds his readers, Jews have much to teach Christians:

> I know that the Jews do understand the things of the prophets, and there is none other people that understand the things which were spoken unto the Jews like unto them, save it be that they are taught after the manner of the things of the Jews. (2 Ne. 25:5)

Christians should therefore seek to understand this peculiarly Jewish manner and relate to Jews as religious partners, fellow students even, not only of the Scriptures but of life, the universe, everything. As Nephi later advises, Christians should in all things "respect the words of the Jews" (2 Ne. 33:14).

Some Jews, of course, may choose to join with Jesus on their own, because of a direct, unmediated connection with him. Christians should obviously support these Jews, but they should do so again with respect.

Never should a Jew's acceptance of Jesus be portrayed as a renunciation of Judaism. Recall that no one in the Book of Mormon ever speaks about "converting" the Jews. Nephi and Mormon talk about how Jews may be "persuaded to believe in Christ" (2 Ne. 25:16; Morm. 3:22), and Moroni claims that one of the main purposes of the Book of Mormon is "the convincing of the Jew and Gentile that Jesus is the Christ" (title page). However, these prophets never require Jews to disavow their heritage or give up their tradition. On the contrary, the Book of Mormon very much values the contributions Jews have made to the creation, preservation, and comprehension of the Bible as well as to other important matters, and it reprimands latter-day Gentiles for not appreciating "the travails, and the labors, and the pains of the Jews" (2 Ne. 29:4). Just as Jesus honored Jewish customs and traditions, so should Christians. Everything Jews have learned and experienced is valuable and should be preserved.

And yet, is there nothing that Christians can do to help bring Jews and Christians together? Yes. Most definitely. They can look to themselves. They can examine their actions. And they can repent of their sins and weaknesses, especially sins and weaknesses they have historically ascribed to Jews. As Mormon writes in the last chapter of 3 Nephi, seemingly as the main message his future Christian readers should "take-away" from Jesus's pre-messianic visit:

> Hearken, O ye Gentiles, and hear the words of Jesus Christ, the Son of the living God, which he hath commanded me that I should speak concerning you, for, behold he commandeth me that I should write, saying:
>
> Turn, all ye Gentiles, from your wicked ways; and repent of your evil doings, of your lyings and deceivings, and of your whoredoms, and of your secret abominations, and your idolatries, and of your murders, and your priestcrafts, and your envyings, and your strifes, and from all your wickedness and abominations, and come unto me, and be baptized in my name, that ye may receive a remission of your sins, and be filled with the Holy Ghost, *that ye may be numbered with my people who are of the house of Israel.* (3 Ne. 30:1–2)

Only in this way, by having faith in Jesus *as* the Messiah *to be* the Messiah, by repenting of their sins, and by treating Jews respectfully as brothers and sisters of equal worth, importance, and value can Christians hope to end their age-old conflict with the Jews and, at last, be gathered with them together in one.

Bibliography

Beck, Norman A. *Mature Christianity in the 21st Century: The Recognition and Repudiation of the Anti-Jewish Polemic in the New Testament.* New York: The Crossroad Publishing Company, 1994.
Brown, Michael L. *Answering Jewish Objections to Jesus, Volume One: General and Historical Objections.* Grand Rapid, MI: BakerBooks, 2000.
Brown, Raymond E. *An Introduction to the New Testament.* New Haven, CT: Yale University Press, 1997.
Childs, Brevard S. *The New Testament as Canon: An Introduction.* London, SCM Press, 1984.
Cohen, Jeremy. *Christ Killers: The Jews and the Passion from the Bible to the Big Screen.* New York: Oxford University Press, 2007.
Evangelical Lutheran Church in America. "Declaration of ELCA to Jewish Community." Evangelical Lutheran Church in America. accessed April 16, 2018, http://download.elca.org/ELCA%20Resource%20Repository/Declaration_Of_The_ELCA_To_The_Jewish_Community.pdf.
Cook, Michael J. *Modern Jews Engage the New Testament: Enhancing Jewish Well-Being in a Christian Environment.* Woodstock, VT: Jewish Lights Publishing, 2008.
Crossan, John Dominic. *Who Killed Jesus?: Exposing the Roots of Anti-Semitism in the Gospel Story of the Death of Jesus.* New York: HarperCollins Publishers, 1995.
Donin, Hayim Halevy. *To Be a Jew: A Guide to Jewish Observance in Contemporary Life.* New York: BasicBooks, 1972.
———. *To Pray as a Jew: A Guide to the Prayer Book and the Synagogue Service.* New York: BasicBooks, 1980.
Dosick, Rabbi Wayne. *Living Judaism: the Complete Guide to Jewish Belief, Tradition, and Practice.* New York: HarperCollins Publishers, 1995.
Eckstein, Yechiel. *What You Should Know about Jews and Judaism.* Waco, TX: Word Books, 1994.
Ehrman, Bart D. *The New Testament: A Historical Introduction to the Early Christian Writings,* 3rd edition. New York: Oxford University Press, 2004.

Eisenbaum, Pamela. *Paul Was Not a Christian: The Original Message of a Misunderstood Apostle.* New York: HarperCollins Publishers, 2009.

Fisher, Eugene J. *Faith without Prejudice: Rebuilding Christian Attitudes toward Judaism.* New York: The Crossroad Publishing Company, 1993.

Fredriksen, Paula. *Augustine and the Jews: A Christian Defense of Jews and Judaism,* New York: Doubleday, 2008.

Freudmann, Lillian C. *Antisemitism in the New Testament.* New York: University Press of America, 1994.

Gager, John G. *The Origins of Anti-Semitism: Attitudes Toward Judaism in Pagan and Christian Antiquity.* New York: Oxford University Press, 1983.

———. *Reinventing Paul.* New York: Oxford University Press, 2000.

Greenberg, Irving. *For the Sake of Heaven and Earth: The New Encounter between Judaism and Christianity.* Philadelphia: The Jewish Publication Society, 2004.

———. *The Jewish Way: Living the Holidays.* New York: Simon & Schuster, 1988.

Johnson, Paul. *A History of the Jews.* New York: HarperCollins Publishers, 1987.

Hall, Sidney G., III. *Christian Anti-Semitism and Paul's Theology.* Minneapolis: Fortress Press, 1993.

HarperCollins Study Bible. Harold W. Attridge, General Editor, Revised Edition. San Francisco: HarperCollins Publishers, 2006.

Keefer, Kyle. *The New Testament as Literature: A Very Short Introduction.* New York: Oxford University Press, 2008.

Klinghoffer, David. *Why the Jews Rejected Jesus: The Turning Point in Western History.* New York: Doubleday, 2005.

Kramer, Bradley J. *Beholding the Tree of Life: A Rabbinic Approach to the Book of Mormon.* Salt Lake City: Greg Kofford Books, 2014.

Levine, Amy-Jill. *The Misunderstood Jew: The Church and the Scandal of the Jewish Jesus.* New York: HarperCollins Publishers, 2006.

Levine, Amy-Jill and Marc Zvi Brettler, eds. *The Jewish Annotated New Testament.* New York: Oxford University Press, 2011.

McKnight, Scot. "A Loyal Critic: Matthew's Polemic with Judaism in Theological Perspective." In *Anti-Semitism and Early Christianity: Issues of Polemic and Faith,* edited by Craig A. Evans and Donald A Hagner, 55–79. Minneapolis: Fortress Press, 1993.

Nibley, Hugh. *Lehi in the Desert; The World of the Jaredites; There Were Jaredites.* Salt Lake City: Deseret Book Co., 1988.

Neusner, Jacob. *A Rabbi Talks with Jesus: An Intermillenial Interfaith Exchange.* New York: Doubleday, 1993.

Nicholls, William. *Christian Antisemitism: A History of Hate.* Northvale, NJ: Jason Aronson Inc., 1995.

Ruether, Rosemary. *Faith and Fratricide: The Theological Roots of Anti-Semitism.* Eugene, OR: WIPF and Stock Publishers, 1997.

Bibliography

Robinson, George. *Essential Judaism: A Complete Guide to Beliefs, Customs, and Rituals.* New York: Pocket Books, 2000.

Rust, Richard Dilworth. *Feasting on the Word: The Literary Testimony of the Book of Mormon.* Salt Lake City: Deseret Book and FARMS, 1997.

Sabbath and Festival Prayer Book. The Rabbinical Assembly of America and the United Synagogue of America, 1973.

Salmon, Marilyn J. *Preaching without Contempt: Overcoming Unintended Anti-Judaism.* Minneapolis, MN, Fortress Press, 2006.

Sandmel, Rabbi Samuel. *A Jewish Understanding of the New Testament.* Woodstock, VT: Jewish Lights Publishing, 2005, reprint from 1956.

———. *Anti-Semitism in the New Testament?* Philadelphia: Fortress Press, 1978.

Schiffman, Lawrence H. *From Text to Tradition: A History of the Second Temple & Rabbinic Judaism.* Hoboken, NJ: Ktav Publishing House, Inc., 1991.

Shuler, Philip L. "Response to Amy-Jill Levine." In *Anti-Judaism in the Gospels*, edited by William R. Farmer, 37–46. Harrisburg, PA: Trinity Press International, 1999.

Smiga, George M. *Pain and Polemic: Anti-Judaism in the Gospels.* New York: Paulist Press, 1992.

Sorenson, John L. *An Ancient American Setting for the Book of Mormon.* Salt Lake City: Deseret Book Company and FARMS, 1985.

Southern Baptist Convention. "Resolution On Anti-Semitism." Southern Baptist Convention. Accessed April 16, 2018, http://www.sbc.net/resolutions/653/resolution-on-antisemitism.

Spivey Robert A., D. Moody Smith, Jr., and C. Clifton Black. *Anatomy of the New Testament.* 6th edition. Minneapolis, MN: Fortress Press, 2010.

Spong, John Shelby. *Liberating the Gospels: Reading the Bible with Jewish Eyes.* New York: HarperCollins Publishers, 1996.

Stendahl, Krister. *Paul among Jews and Gentiles.* Philadelphia: Fortress Press, 1976.

Tanner, Norman, ed. *Vatican II: The Essential Texts.* New York: Image Books, 2012.

Thompson, John S. "Isaiah 50–51, the Israelite Autumn Festivals, and the Covenant Speech of Jacob in 2 Nephi 6–10." In *Isaiah in the Book of Mormon*, edited by Donald W. Parry and John W. Welch, 124–127. Provo, UT: FARMS, 1998.

Weiss-Rosmarin, Trude. *Judaism and Christianity: The Differences.* Middle Village, NY: Jonathan David Publishers, Inc., 1997.

Welch, John W. *Illuminating the Sermon at the Temple & the Sermon on the Mount.* Provo, UT: Foundation for Ancient Research and Mormon Studies, 1999.

———, ed. *Reexploring the Book of Mormon.* Salt Lake City, UT: Deseret Book Company and FARMS, 1992.

Wilson, Marvin R. *Our Father Abraham: Jewish Roots of the Christian Faith.* Grand Rapids,: Wm. B. Eerdmans Publishing Company: 1989.

World Council of Churches. "Ecumenical Considerations on Jewish-Christian Dialogue." World Council of Churches. Accessed April 16, 2018, http://www.oikoumene.org/en/resources/documents/wcc-programmes/inter-religious-dialogue-and-cooperation/interreligious-trust-and-respect/ecumenical-considerations-on-jewish-christian-dialogue.

———. "What is the World Council of Churches?" World Council of Churches. Accessed April, 16 2018, http://www.oikoumene.org/en/who-are-we.html.

The Writings of Irenaeus, trans. Alexander Roberts and W. H. Rambaut Vol. 1. Edinburgh: T. & T. Clark, 1868.

Scripture Index

Hebrew Scriptures

Genesis
Gen. 2:17 — 104
Gen. 3:8 — 130
Gen. 3:16–17 — 44
Gen. 3:19 — 111
Gen. 4:14 — 26
Gen. 6:11 — 129
Gen. 12:3 — 109, 132

Exodus
Ex. 1:10–14 — 102
Ex. 2:6–12 — 79
Ex. 2:15 — 68
Ex. 3:6 — 68
Ex. 3:18 — 79
Ex. 4:1–12 — 79
Ex. 5:1–2 — 79
Ex. 5:3 — 79
Ex. 5:20–23 — 68
Ex. 5:21 — 79
Ex. 6:3 — 79
Ex. 7:6 — 46
Ex. 7:10 — 46
Ex. 7:10–22 — 103
Ex. 7:20 — 46
Ex. 8:27 — 79
Ex. 9:7–13 — 103
Ex. 10:2 — 87
Ex. 11:4–6 — 79
Ex. 12:5 — 104
Ex. 12:18 — 102
Ex. 12:25–27 — 72
Ex. 12:26 — 89
Ex. 12:46 — 104
Ex. 13:3 — 86
Ex. 13:17–20 — 69
Ex. 13:21–22 — 79
Ex. 14:11 — 79
Ex. 14:26–28 — 103
Ex. 15:1–19 — 79
Ex. 16:2–3 — 69
Ex. 16:7–8 — 79
Ex. 17:15 — 79
Ex. 19:5–6 — 109
Ex. 19:5–8 — 98
Ex. 19:6 — 128
Ex. 23:14–17 — 97
Ex. 23:14–19 — 30
Ex. 32:9 — 79
Ex. 34:22 — 30
Ex. 34:25 — 104

Leviticus
Lev. 3:1–3 — 104
Lev. 3:8 — 104
Lev. 3:17 — 104
Lev. 8:7 — 95
Lev. 19:18 — 7
Lev. 23:15–19 — 110
Lev. 23:2–8 — 109
Lev. 23:20–21 — 109
Lev. 23:24–28 — 109
Lev. 23:33–37 — 81
Lev. 23:34–37 — 109
Lev. 23:36–38 — 81
Lev. 23:40 — 72
Lev. 23:42 — 72
Lev. 23:42–43 — 78
Lev. 25:4–17 — 110

Numbers
Num. 6:22–27 — 95
Num. 14:3 — 79
Num. 21:7 — 68
Num. 28:26 — 30

Deuteronomy
Deut. 6:4–5 — 127
Deut. 6:20 — 88
Deut. 11:1–5 — 79
Deut. 12:5–14 — 68
Deut. 14:2 — 127
Deut. 15:1–4 — 111
Deut. 16:3 — 86
Deut. 16:13–14 — 71
Deut. 17:17–20 — 127
Deut. 27:1–7 — 68
Deut. 28:15 — 44
Deut. 28:25 — 44
Deut. 28:29 — 44
Deut. 28:37 — 44
Deut. 33:1–25 — 79

1 Samuel
1 Sam. 8:5–7 — 127

2 Kings
2 Kgs 22–23 — 69

Isaiah
Isa. 2:2 — 111
Isa. 2:3–4 — 5–6, 139
Isa. 2:4 — 108, 111
Isa. 11:12 — 139
Isa. 29:22–23 — 140
Isa. 40:3 — 109
Isa. 49:6 — 58
Isa. 49:22–23 — 133
Isa. 51:5 — 55

Jeremiah
Jer. 2:5 — 42
Jer. 2:31 — 43
Jer. 3:10 — 42
Jer. 4:4–6 — 126
Jer. 4:22 — 42
Jer. 5:7 — 42
Jer. 5:21 — 43
Jer. 6:13 — 43
Jer. 7:6 — 43
Jer. 23:3 — 44
Jer. 31:8 — 44
Jer. 31:31 — 44
Jer. 31:33 — 44
Jer. 32:37 — 44
Jer. 43 — 42

Ezekiel
Ezek. 8:6 — 134
Ezek. 16:36–41 — 134

Micah
Micah 4:4 — 111

Malachi
Mal. 3:1 — 139

New Testament

Matthew
Matt. 2:1 — 33
Matt. 3:3 — 92
Matt. 3:7 — 96
Matt. 3:18–22 — 93
Matt. 4:25 — 93
Matt. 5:3–5 — 92
Matt. 5:10 — 92
Matt. 5:17 — 94
Matt. 5:21 — 93
Matt. 5:21–22 — 91
Matt. 5:25 — 94
Matt. 5:27–28 — 91
Matt. 5:29 — 94
Matt. 5:33–34 — 91
Matt. 5:34 — 94
Matt. 5:44 — 7
Matt. 6:2 — 93
Matt. 6:5 — 93
Matt. 6:7 — 51, 94
Matt. 6:10 — 109
Matt. 6:24 — 94
Matt. 6:26 — 94
Matt. 6:28 — 94
Matt. 7:3 — 93
Matt. 7:15 — 94
Matt. 7:23 — 49
Matt. 8:10 — 33
Matt. 8:27 — 33
Matt. 8:29 — 33
Matt. 9:4 — 49
Matt. 9:11 — 13
Matt. 10:6 — 33
Matt. 11:21 — 33
Matt. 12:1 — 93
Matt. 12:2 — 13
Matt. 12:10 — 67
Matt. 12:14 — 13
Matt. 12:24 — 13
Matt. 12:33 — 13
Matt. 12:38 — 13
Matt. 12:41 — 33
Matt. 13:10 — 93
Matt. 14:20 — 100
Matt. 15:1 — 13
Matt. 15:2 — 16, 49, 67
Matt. 15:2–3 — 96
Matt. 15:3 — 72
Matt. 15:6 — 96
Matt. 15:12 — 13
Matt. 15:14 — 13
Matt. 15:24–28 — 33
Matt. 15:37 — 100
Matt. 16:3 — 13
Matt. 16:6 — 13
Matt. 16:21 — 45
Matt. 19:8 — 14
Matt. 19:30 — 136
Matt. 21:12 — 94
Matt. 21:13 — 95
Matt. 21:33 — 57
Matt. 21:38 — 58
Matt. 21:41 — 58
Matt. 21:43 — 58
Matt. 21:45–46 — 58
Matt. 22:1–15 — 37
Matt. 22:15 — 13
Matt. 22:23 — 45
Matt. 22:39 — 7
Matt. 23:13 — 51
Matt. 23:13–16 — 68
Matt. 23:15–16 — 95
Matt. 23:23 — 95
Matt. 23:36–38 — 68
Matt. 23:2 — 94
Matt. 23:4 — 68
Matt. 23:5 — 67, 94
Matt. 23:6 — 95
Matt. 23:23 — 13
Matt. 23:28–38 — 49
Matt. 23:33–39 — 56
Matt. 23:34–35 — 14
Matt. 23:37 — 95
Matt. 24:1–2 — 95
Matt. 26:14–15 — 51
Matt. 26:26 — 99
Matt. 26:27–29 — 100
Matt. 26:45 — 9
Matt. 26:47 — 9, 45
Matt. 26:55 — 9
Matt. 26:57 — 9
Matt. 27:12 — 56

Scripture Index

Matt. 27:15 — 8
Matt. 27:19 — 11
Matt. 27:20 — 8, 31, 45
Matt. 27:22–23 — 8
Matt. 27:23–25 — 9
Matt. 27:24 — 8, 11
Matt. 27:25 — 8, 14, 53
Matt. 27:26 — 11
Matt. 27:39 — 40 — 14
Matt. 27:46–49 — 14
Matt. 27:52–54 — 14
Matt. 28:15 — 14
Matt. 28:19 — 34

Mark
Mark 2:23–24 — 21
Mark 3:2–3 — 21
Mark 3:6 — 21
Mark 7:2–4 — 21
Mark 7:6–7 — 21
Mark 11:15–17 — 21
Mark 12:31 — 7, 18
Mark 12:33 — 7
Mark 14:1 — 22
Mark 14:22 — 99
Mark 14:23–25 — 100
Mark 14:24–25 — 22
Mark 15:13 — 21
Mark 15:15 — 11

Luke
Luke 2:21–22 — 21
Luke 2:25–32 — 21
Luke 2:28–32 — 33n71
Luke 2:30–32 — 117
Luke 4:24 — 117
Luke 4:24–28 — 33n71
Luke 6:1–2 — 21
Luke 6:6–11 — 21
Luke 6:17 — 33n71
Luke 6:27 — 7
Luke 6:35 — 7
Luke 7:9 — 117
Luke 10:13–15 — 117
Luke 10:27 — 18
Luke 10:29–37 — 7
Luke 11:23 — 117
Luke 11:32 — 117
Luke 11:44 — 21
Luke 11:48–49 — 32
Luke 13:24 — 118
Luke 13:24–30 — 119
Luke 13:26 — 118
Luke 13:30 — 118
Luke 19:45–47 — 21
Luke 20:20 — 51
Luke 21:24 — 117
Luke 22:1, 7, 15–20 — 22
Luke 22:7 — 22
Luke 22:12 — 30
Luke 22:15–20 — 22
Luke 22:19 — 99
Luke 22:20 — 22
Luke 22:20–21 — 100
Luke 23:21 — 21

John
John 1:9 — 41
John 1:11–13 — 42
John 1:29 — 104
John 1:39 — 41
John 1:46 — 41
John 2:6 — 20
John 2:13 — 72
John 2:13–16 — 20
John 2:18 — 19
John 3:9–12 — 19
John 3:10 — 41
John 3:15 — 104
John 3:19 — 19
John 5:8–10 — 19
John 5:16–18 — 18–19
John 5:36 — 104
John 6:4 — 20
John 6:4–11 — 20
John 6:35 — 20
John 6:41 — 20
John 6:60–61 — 20
John 7:1 — 19, 72
John 7:2 — 20, 72
John 7:13 — 19
John 7:19 — 19
John 7:37 — 70
John 7:37–38 — 20
John 7:44 — 20
John 8:12 — 20
John 8:16 — 41
John 8:17 — 20
John 8:23 — 19
John 8:40 — 19
John 8:44 — 41
John 8:59 — 20
John 9:16 — 20
John 9:39–40 — 19
John 9:39–41 — 41
John 10:16 — 107
John 10:18 — 104
John 10:31 — 19–20
John 10:34 — 20
John 11:55 — 20, 72
John 12:46 — 19, 41
John 13:1 — 103
John 13:4–10 — 103
John 13:14–16 — 41
John 13:34–35 — 103
John 15:10–27 — 103
John 15:12 — 18
John 15:25 — 20
John 16:7–15 — 103
John 17:1–26 — 103
John 18:31 — 20
John 19:7 — 21
John 19:14 — 104
John 19:15–16 — 19
John 19:23–31 — 104
John 19:38 — 19
John 19:40–42 — 104
John 19:42 — 20
John 20:19 — 19
John 20:19–23 — 104

Acts
Acts 1:8 — 34, 115
Acts 1:18 — 29
Acts 2:2–6 — 31
Acts 2:9–11 — 31
Acts 2:10 — 30
Acts 2:17 — 117
Acts 2:22–23 — 31
Acts 2:36 — 31, 115
Acts 2:38 — 105
Acts 3:12–15 — 31
Acts 3:15 — 115
Acts 3:19 — 105
Acts 3:23 — 118
Acts 4:1–3 — 120
Acts 4:8 — 120
Acts 4:10 — 31, 115
Acts 4:12 — 137
Acts 5:31 — 105
Acts 5:33 — 115
Acts 7:51 — 32
Acts 7:51 — 49
Acts 7:51–52 — 126
Acts 7:51–53 — 118
Acts 7:52 — 32, 114, 122
Acts 7:54 — 32
Acts 7:57–59 — 32, 116
Acts 7:59 — 115
Acts 8:3 — 123
Acts 8:5 — 33, 121
Acts 8:6 — 33
Acts 8:8 — 116
Acts 8:9 — 33
Acts 8:12 — 33, 116
Acts 8:13 — 33
Acts 8:17 — 116
Acts 8:27–35 — 121
Acts 8:27–38 — 116
Acts 8:37 — 122
Acts 9:4 — 123
Acts 9:15 — 34
Acts 9:20 — 34
Acts 9:23 — 34, 114
Acts 9:29 — 115
Acts 10:1–48 — 117
Acts 10:43 — 105
Acts 10:45–48 — 131
Acts 11:5–10 — 115
Acts 12:1–11 — 120
Acts 12:2–3 — 114
Acts 13:38 — 105
Acts 13:45 — 34, 116
Acts 13:50 — 116
Acts 14:2 — 34
Acts 14:2–5 — 131
Acts 14:8–11 — 131
Acts 14:19 — 116
Acts 14:21–27 — 33
Acts 15:2–3 — 33
Acts 16:12–15 — 33
Acts 16:30–34 — 33
Acts 17:1–4 — 33
Acts 17:1–5 — 124
Acts 17:12 — 33
Acts 17:13 — 34, 124
Acts 17:5 — 34
Acts 17:16 — 131
Acts 18:5–6 — 124
Acts 18:6 — 30, 34, 114
Acts 22:16 — 105
Acts 23:12 — 114–15
Acts 23:27 — 115
Acts 26:18 — 105

Romans
Rom. 1:8 — 131
Rom. 3:29–30 — 114
Rom. 5:6 — 25
Rom. 8:34 — 25
Rom. 11:1–2 — 27
Rom. 11:2 — 58
Rom. 11:11 — 58
Rom. 11:17 — 59
Rom. 11:17–18 — 27
Rom. 11:17–19 — 58
Rom. 11:20–23 — 59
Rom. 13:9 — 131

1 Corinthians
1 Cor. 5:6–8 — 105
1 Cor. 8:4–13 — 114
1 Cor. 8:11 — 25
1 Cor. 15:3 — 25

2 Corinthians
2 Cor. 5:15 — 25
2 Cor. 6:14–16 — 114

Galatians
Gal. 3:19 — 105
Gal. 3:24 — 68
Gal. 3:24–25 — 105
Gal. 4:31 — 105
Gal. 5:1–12 — 114

1 Thessalonians
1 Thess. 2:14–15 — 25

Philemon
Phil. 3:5–6 — 25

Hebrews
Heb. 8:1 — 114
Heb. 8:5 — 114
Heb. 8:6–9 — 105
Heb. 8:9 — 115
Heb. 8:13 — 105, 115
Heb. 9:10 — 105
Heb. 9:12 — 105
Heb. 10:1 — 105
Heb. 10:3–4 — 105
Heb. 10:4 — 114
Heb. 10:10 — 114
Heb. 10:14 — 106
Heb. 10:20 — 106

James
James 1:27 — 21

Book of Mormon

Title Page — 2, 141

1 Nephi
1 Ne. 1:2 — 46, 79

Scripture Index

1 Ne. 1:4 — 42, 74, 126
1 Ne. 1:5 — 68, 74, 76
1 Ne. 1:5–6 — 43
1 Ne. 1:6 — 68, 76, 79, 120
1 Ne. 1:7 — 14, 43
1 Ne. 1:8 — 43, 76
1 Ne. 1:11 — 76
1 Ne. 1:12 — 120
1 Ne. 1:13 — 43, 67, 76, 121
1 Ne. 1:14 — 77–78, 120
1 Ne. 1:19 — 79, 120–21
1 Ne. 1:19–20 — 68
1 Ne. 2:1 — 120–21
1 Ne. 2:1 — 122
1 Ne. 2:1–6 — 69
1 Ne. 2:2 — 43
1 Ne. 2:4 — 81
1 Ne. 2:6 — 78–79
1 Ne. 2:7 — 68, 79, 81
1 Ne. 2:9–10 — 48, 79
1 Ne. 2:11 — 47, 69, 79
1 Ne. 2:12 — 79
1 Ne. 2:13 — 47
1 Ne. 2:14 — 79
1 Ne. 2:15 — 78
1 Ne. 2:17 — 126
1 Ne. 2:18 — 79
1 Ne. 2:20 — 70
1 Ne. 3:1–4 — 78
1 Ne. 3:3–7 — 83
1 Ne. 3:5 — 79
1 Ne. 3:7 — 46, 126
1 Ne. 3:13 — 83
1 Ne. 3:19–20 — 83
1 Ne. 3:22–23 — 83
1 Ne. 3:29 — 48, 83
1 Ne. 4:2 — 85
1 Ne. 4:2–30 — 80
1 Ne. 4:10 — 83
1 Ne. 4:13–17 — 84
1 Ne. 4:15 — 46

1 Ne. 4:17–24 — 84
1 Ne. 4:38 — 78
1 Ne. 5:7 — 78
1 Ne. 5:9 — 68, 79, 81
1 Ne. 5:10–13 — 84
1 Ne. 5:11 — 46
1 Ne. 5:14 — 46
1 Ne. 5:15 — 79, 85
1 Ne. 5:17–19 — 84
1 Ne. 5:21–22 — 85
1 Ne. 7:1 — 82
1 Ne. 7:2 — 78
1 Ne. 7:5 — 68, 78
1 Ne. 7:7 — 47, 79
1 Ne. 7:16 — 47
1 Ne. 7:22 — 68, 81
1 Ne. 8:1 — 82
1 Ne. 10:4 — 121
1 Ne. 10:8–9 — 122
1 Ne. 10:14 — 122
1 Ne. 11:5 — 122
1 Ne. 11:33 — 53, 106
1 Ne. 12:23 — 47
1 Ne. 13:6 — 134
1 Ne. 13:6–7 — 134
1 Ne. 13:14 — 48, 134
1 Ne. 13:23 — 42
1 Ne. 13:24–26 — 7
1 Ne. 13:25–26 — 42
1 Ne. 13:26 — 134
1 Ne. 13:29 — 134
1 Ne. 13:30–31 — 48
1 Ne. 13:32 — 134
1 Ne. 13:33–34 — 46
1 Ne. 13:34–36 — 132
1 Ne. 13:39–40 — 39
1 Ne. 14:1–2 — 62
1 Ne. 14:2 — 133
1 Ne. 14:10–11 — 134
1 Ne. 14:13 — 134
1 Ne. 14:14 — 42, 135
1 Ne. 15:17–18 — 132
1 Ne. 15:20 — 122

1 Ne. 16:17 — 134
1 Ne. 16:36–37 — 47
1 Ne. 17:23–25 — 86
1 Ne. 17:48 — 47
1 Ne. 17:53 — 48
1 Ne. 19:7–10 — 54
1 Ne. 19:10 — 86
1 Ne. 19:13 — 54
1 Ne. 19:16 — 49
1 Ne. 19:23 — 122
1 Ne. 19:24 — 46
1 Ne. 20:4 — 123
1 Ne. 20:9–10 — 123
1 Ne. 21:1 — 123
1 Ne. 21:6 — 123
1 Ne. 21:8 — 123
1 Ne. 21:22–23 — 133
1 Ne. 22:6–7 — 133
1 Ne. 22:8–10 — 132
1 Ne. 22:12 — 123, 133
1 Ne. 22:21 — 106
1 Ne. 22:25–26 — 106
1 Ne. 29:5 — 40

2 Nephi
2 Ne. 1:4 — 69
2 Ne. 1:9 — 70
2 Ne. 1:20 — 70
2 Ne. 2:3–4 — 139
2 Ne. 2:22–25 — 129
2 Ne. 4:4 — 70
2 Ne. 5:10 — 47, 69
2 Ne. 5:10–11 — 67, 70
2 Ne. 5:16 — 69–70
2 Ne. 5:2 — 47
2 Ne. 5:7 — 47
2 Ne. 5:24 — 47, 69
2 Ne. 6:6–7 — 133, 140
2 Ne. 6:8 — 132
2 Ne. 6:12 — 135
2 Ne. 6:13 — 41
2 Ne. 6:14 — 106, 140
2 Ne. 6:17 — 42

152   *Gathered in One*

2 Ne. 9:3–5 — 122
2 Ne. 10:5 — 54
2 Ne. 10:8–9 — 133
2 Ne. 10:21–22 — 55
2 Ne. 11:2 — 138
2 Ne. 12:4 — 108
2 Ne. 19:16 — 44
2 Ne. 21:12 — 44, 139
2 Ne. 25:1 — 46
2 Ne. 25:2 — 43
2 Ne. 25:5 — 42, 140
2 Ne. 25:6 — 46
2 Ne. 25:10–13 — 54
2 Ne. 25:15–17 — 45
2 Ne. 25:16 — 141
2 Ne. 25:18 — 138
2 Ne. 25:20 — 137
2 Ne. 28:15–16 — 135
2 Ne. 28:18 — 135
2 Ne. 29:4 — 141
2 Ne. 29:4–5 — 42
2 Ne. 29:5 — 134
2 Ne. 29:13–14 — 1
2 Ne. 30:2 — 138
2 Ne. 30:3 — 132
2 Ne. 30:4 — 46
2 Ne. 31:4 — 106
2 Ne. 31:21 — 137
2 Ne. 33:8 — 41, 46
2 Ne. 33:8–9 — 138
2 Ne. 33:14 — 140

Jacob
Jacob 1:17 — 69
Jacob 4:11–16 — 138
Jacob 4:14 — 44
Jacob 5:3–4 — 59
Jacob 5:6 — 60
Jacob 5:7 — 61
Jacob 5:7–9 — 60
Jacob 5:13 — 61
Jacob 5:14 — 55
Jacob 5:20–23 — 55
Jacob 5:32 — 61
Jacob 5:37 — 60
Jacob 5:47 — 61
Jacob 5:52 — 60
Jacob 5:54 — 61
Jacob 5:57 — 60
Jacob 5:60 — 61
Jacob 5:60–63 — 113, 120
Jacob 5:63 — 136
Jacob 5:68 — 61
Jacob 5:71 — 61
Jacob 5:75 — 61
Jacob 6:4 — 65

Enos
Enos 1:20 — 47, 71

Jarom
Jarom 1:5 — 70
Jarom 1:5–6 — 47
Jarom 1:6 — 71
Jarom 1:7–9 — 70
Jarom 1:11 — 70

Omni
Omni 1:6 — 70
Omni 1:14 — 63
Omni 1:15 — 62, 122
Omni 1:16 — 132
Omni 1:17 — 63
Omni 1:19 — 63
Omni 1:21 — 63

Words of Mormon
W of M 1:17 — 127

Mosiah
Mosiah 1:5–7 — 127
Mosiah 1:7 — 70
Mosiah 1:11–14 — 127
Mosiah 1:18 — 69
Mosiah 2:10–12 — 127
Mosiah 2:17 — 127
Mosiah 2:22 — 70
Mosiah 2:31 — 70
Mosiah 3:17 — 137
Mosiah 5:8 — 137
Mosiah 7:9 — 56
Mosiah 9:12 — 71
Mosiah 10:11 — 71
Mosiah 11:1–8 — 56
Mosiah 12:25–37 — 65
Mosiah 12:34 — 86
Mosiah 13:33 — 138
Mosiah 13:33–34 — 56
Mosiah 15:7 — 53
Mosiah 15:7–9 — 56
Mosiah 17:16–18 — 56
Mosiah 19:4–24 — 65
Mosiah 19:20 — 57
Mosiah 21:5–15 — 57
Mosiah 25:2 — 63
Mosiah 25:13 — 63
Mosiah 26:23 — 106
Mosiah 27:9–13 — 123
Mosiah 27:32–36
Mosiah 28:1 — 123
Mosiah 28:7 — 49
Mosiah 29:12 — 128
Mosiah 29:25 — 127

Alma
Alma 1:1–15 — 65
Alma 5:48 — 106
Alma 7:14 — 106
Alma 9:1 — 50
Alma 9:13 — 70
Alma 10:13 — 50
Alma 10:17 — 50
Alma 10:31 — 50
Alma 11:22 — 51
Alma 11:46 — 51
Alma 12:1 — 51
Alma 14:1 — 50
Alma 14:7 — 51
Alma 14:17 — 50
Alma 14:23–27 — 50
Alma 15:3–12 — 51
Alma 17:14–15 — 131

Scripture Index

Alma 18:2 — 131
Alma 19:14 — 131
Alma 19:35 — 131
Alma 23:1–3 — 49
Alma 23:3 — 131
Alma 23:4–5 — 49
Alma 24:16 — 49
Alma 24:22–24 — 49
Alma 25:8–12 — 57
Alma 26:24 — 49
Alma 26:36 — 124
Alma 27:17 — 124
Alma 27:19–22 — 124
Alma 27:27 — 132
Alma 27:30 — 132
Alma 29:11 — 86
Alma 31:13 — 51
Alma 31:18 — 51
Alma 31:23–24 — 51
Alma 32:2 — 51
Alma 32:4 — 51
Alma 32:8 — 51
Alma 34:8 — 106
Alma 34:19–26 — 52
Alma 34:28 — 52
Alma 35:3 — 52
Alma 35:6 — 52
Alma 36:1 — 70
Alma 36:2 — 86–87
Alma 36:12–14 — 87
Alma 36:16–18 — 87
Alma 36:17 — 106
Alma 36:21 — 88
Alma 36:24–26 — 88
Alma 36:27–28 — 87
Alma 36:28–29 — 86
Alma 36:30 — 70
Alma 37:13 — 70
Alma 38:1 — 70
Alma 38:4 — 89
Alma 38:9 — 137
Alma 38:11–14 — 90
Alma 39:15 — 106

Alma 41:1–2 — 89
Alma 42:15 — 106
Alma 48:15 — 70
Alma 50:25–36 — 65
Alma 60:20 — 86

Helaman
Hel. 1:15–33 — 65
Hel. 5:2 — 96
Hel. 6:1 — 50
Hel. 6:10 — 63
Hel. 6:31 — 96
Hel. 13:1 — 50
Hel. 13:6 — 53
Hel. 13:10 — 71
Hel. 13:22–24 — 50
Hel. 15:5 — 71
Hel. 16:2 — 50

3 Nephi
3 Ne. 1:1 — 111
3 Ne. 1:3 — 111
3 Ne. 1:9–13 — 128
3 Ne. 6:4–5 — 96
3 Ne. 6:7 — 102
3 Ne. 6:10 — 102
3 Ne. 6:18 — 96
3 Ne. 6:23 — 96
3 Ne. 6:28 — 96
3 Ne. 6:29–30 — 102
3 Ne. 7:7 — 103
3 Ne. 7:16–18 — 103
3 Ne. 7:20 — 103
3 Ne. 8:5 — 102
3 Ne. 8:8–9 — 103
3 Ne. 8:9 — 128
3 Ne. 8:16 — 103
3 Ne. 8:19–20 — 103
3 Ne. 8:19–23 — 128
3 Ne. 9:13 — 96
3 Ne. 9:19 — 96
3 Ne. 9:20 — 98
3 Ne. 9:22 — 95
3 Ne. 10:8 — 96

3 Ne. 10:12 — 96
3 Ne. 10:12–15 — 103
3 Ne. 11:1 — 69, 97
3 Ne. 11:7–10 — 95
3 Ne. 11:8 — 98
3 Ne. 11:8–12 — 96
3 Ne. 11:14 — 53, 106, 128
3 Ne. 11:17 — 98, 128
3 Ne. 12:10–11 — 96
3 Ne. 12:17–19 — 91
3 Ne. 12:21 — 96
3 Ne. 12:48 — 98
3 Ne. 13:2 — 52
3 Ne. 13:5 — 52
3 Ne. 13:10 — 109
3 Ne. 14:17–19 — 97
3 Ne. 15:3–8 — 107
3 Ne. 15:15–24 — 107
3 Ne. 16:3 — 107
3 Ne. 16:4 — 138
3 Ne. 16:4–5 — 137
3 Ne. 16:5 — 138
3 Ne. 16:8 — 107
3 Ne. 16:10 — 135
3 Ne. 16:11 — 138
3 Ne. 16:11–12 — 107
3 Ne. 16:13 — 62, 133
3 Ne. 18:3 — 101
3 Ne. 18:4 — 100
3 Ne. 18:7 — 101
3 Ne. 18:9 — 100
3 Ne. 18:11 — 101
3 Ne. 19:1 — 101
3 Ne. 19:7 — 101
3 Ne. 19:12–15 — 101
3 Ne. 19:21 — 101
3 Ne. 19:28 — 101
3 Ne. 19:34 — 101
3 Ne. 20:2 — 101
3 Ne. 20:8–9 — 102
3 Ne. 20:15–16 — 134
3 Ne. 20:18 — 128

3 Ne. 20:19 — 107
3 Ne. 20:20 — 134
3 Ne. 20:21–23 — 107
3 Ne. 20:22–23 — 107
3 Ne. 20:24 — 138
3 Ne. 20:25 — 107, 132
3 Ne. 20:25–27 — 132
3 Ne. 20:32–34 — 108
3 Ne. 20:36–40 — 108
3 Ne. 20:46 — 139
3 Ne. 21:1 — 107, 138
3 Ne. 21:6 — 62
3 Ne. 21:22 — 62
3 Ne. 24:1 — 139
3 Ne. 29:8 — 40, 139
3 Ne. 30:1–2 — 141
3 Ne. 30:2 — 62–64, 134

4 Nephi
4 Ne. 1:1 — 108
4 Ne. 1:1–2 — 52
4 Ne. 1:3 — 108
4 Ne. 1:7 — 108
4 Ne. 1:10 — 108
4 Ne. 1:15–17 — 108
4 Ne. 1:16 — 128–29
4 Ne. 1:31 — 54
4 Ne. 1:36–38 — 63
4 Ne. 1:39 — 108

Mormon
Morm. 3:21 — 42
Morm. 3:22 — 141
Morm. 4:14 — 48
Morm. 4:21 — 48
Morm. 5:14 — 138
Morm. 5:22–24 — 134
Morm. 6:15 — 48
Morm. 8:15 — 42

Ether
Ether 1:38 — 129
Ether 2:4–5 — 129
Ether 2:23 — 130
Ether 3:1–4 — 130
Ether 3:13 — 130
Ether 6:7 — 129
Ether 8:15–16 — 129
Ether 8:16 — 96
Ether 8:21 — 129
Ether 8:26 — 129–30
Ether 13:25 — 129

Doctrine and Covenants
D&C 19:27 — 46

Subject Index

A

Aaron (brother of Ammon), 49, 123
Aaron (brother of Moses), 46
Abraham, 1, 27, 31–32, 64, 132
Abrahamic mission, 109, 132
Acts
    chiastic connection to Book of Mormon, 119–24
    chiastic connection to Luke, 115–19
Adam, 44, 84, 129–30
allegory of olive tree, 59–62, 65, 120
allegory of the cave, 114
Alma (the younger), 50–52, 65, 70, 86–89, 123–24, 126, 128
Ammon, 49, 123–24, 128, 131
Amulek, 50–51, 128
anti-Judaism, ix
anti-Mosaic
    elements in appearance of Jesus, 103–6
    elements in Communion, 99–100
    portrayals, 19–24
    Sermon on the Mount, 91–95
    settings, 19–24, 30–32, 71–73
Anti-Nephi-Lehies, 49–50, 131–33
anti-Semitism, ix, 2–5, 7, 10, 13, 15, 18, 22–25, 30–32, 35–38, 39–41, 114, 125, 138
    Catholic efforts against, 2
    countering, 2–3, 5, 35–40
anti-Semitism in New Testament
    elements, x, 4–5, 24, 30–31, 35, 113–14
    portrayals, 13–24, 31–32
    sentiments, 3
    statements, 4, 7–13
    structure of the New Testament, 28–34, 118–19
anti-supersessionism, 24–28, 65
Aseret Y'may T'Shuvah, 74
Augustine, 25–27

B

Barabbas, 8, 11–12
Barnabas, 131
Beatitudes, 51, 92, 96, 108
Benjamin (king), 70, 74, 127
blood curse, 8, 10–15, 22, 26, 31
Book of Mormon
    anti-supersessionism in, 57–65
    chiastic connection to Acts, 119–24
    chiastic connection to Hebrew Scriptures, 125–30
    Christ-killer charges, 53–57
    connection to New Testament, x–xi, 40
    institution of Communion, 100–102
    peer of New Testament, 4
    pro-Judaic statements in, 39–40
    relation to Hebrew Scriptures, 125–30, 135–36
    relation to John, 42–45
    relation to King James Version, xi
    relation to Synoptic Gospels, 45–52
    restructures Acts' structuring, 119–25
    uniqueness, 1–2
    views of Jews, 41

Bountiful, 53, 97, 121
Brass plates
  contain Books of Moses, 46, 84
  Hebrew Scriptures, 64, 83–85
  required, 46–47, 84
Brother of Jared, 129–30
Brown, Michael L., 35
Brown, Raymond E., 8, 10

C

Catholic Church, 2–3
chiastic structure
  of Acts and Book of Mormon, 119–24
  of Hebrew Scriptures and Book of Mormon, 125–30
  of Luke and Acts, 115–19
Childs, Brevard S., 28, 40
Christian-Jewish relations, 2, 15–16, 24, 139–41
Christians, conflict with Jews, 15–17, 24
Christ-killer accusation
  complicated, 11, 13
  effect of, 9
  origin, 9
  refuted by Book of Mormon, 41, 53–57
  renounced by Catholic Church, 3
  supported by NT, 14–15, 19, 22, 31, 41, 115, 117–19
Communion, 99–102
covenant
  dual, 27
  fulfilled, 105–16
  Gentiles added to, 27
  Gentiles do not replace Jews, 131–32
  Gentiles replace Jews, 26, 29, 32
  Jews remain in, 41–53, 57–65, 119–24
  Jews removed from, 42, 53, 114–15, 119
  new, 105
  not fulfilled, 107
  people, 40–41, 135
  remembered by Jesus, 107
Crossan John Dominic, 12–13

D–F

David, 64
Donin, Hayim Halevy, 75–76, 78–80
Dosick, Wayne, 75–77, 80, 82
Dunn, James D. G., 28
Eckstein, Yechiel, 3
Eden, 109, 111, 129–30
Ehrman, Bart D., 91–93
Enos, 71, 126
Ether, 64, 126
Evangelical Lutheran Church in America, 3
Eve, 44, 84, 129–30
Ezekiel, 43, 126, 134–35
Feast of Tabernacles. *See* Sukkot.
Feast of Weeks. *See* Shavuot.
Fisher, Eugene, 10–11, 15, 17–18, 24–25, 36–37
Freudmann, Lillian C., 4, 22

G

Gager, John G., 26, 34
Galilee, 29, 93–94, 104, 116
Gentiles
  chastisement of, 133–35, 141
  efforts to convert Jews, 139–41
  in Acts, 116–19
  Paul goes to, 114
  Pauline epistles written to, 114
  replace Jews, 26–27, 29, 32, 57–65, 117–18, 131–32
  rise of, 131–36
Gospels
  four-fold approach to, 18, 40
  historical approach to, 10–13, 15–18, 23–24
  influence of Acts on, 29, 113, 115
great and abominable church, 7, 134–35
Greenberg, Irving, 4, 10, 82, 98, 109–11

H–I

Hall, Sidney G. III, 25, 27–28
Hebrew Scriptures

Subject Index

brass plates, 64, 83–85
  chiastic connection to Book of Mormon, 125–30
  messianic prophecies in, 139
  relation to Book of Mormon, 125–30, 135–36
  structure of, 125–30
Herodians, 45, 56
Hillel, 16
Holocaust, 2, 26, 137
International Fellowship of Christians and Jews, 3
Isaiah, 17, 44, 48, 55–56, 58, 73, 107–09, 116, 121–23, 126, 133, 138–39

J

Jacob (son of Isaac), 46, 62, 123, 134
Jacob (son of Lehi), 41–43, 47, 54–55, 65, 73, 106, 122, 126, 133
Jaredites, 64, 129
Jeremiah, 17, 42–44, 84, 126, 135
Jerusalem
  calendar, 97
  conquered by Romans, 16
  corruption of, 92–94
  destruction of, 117–23
  dispersion from, 55–56, 62–63, 106–7, 111, 132
  goodness of, 78–83
  involvement in Jesus's death, 55–57
  Jesus resurrected in, 53
  Jesus's ascension in, 97
  and Lehi's family, 46–47, 79
  movement from in Acts, 115–17, 125
  movement to in Gospels, 115, 125
  percentage of Jews who lived in, 54
  progress from in Acts, 30–32
  progress to in Gospels, 29
  prophecies of destruction, 42–43, 48, 67, 75–78, 126
  return to, 107–9, 120, 138–39
  and Sermon on the Mount, 92
  temples outside of, 68–69
Jesus, 4, 7
  appearance of, 91–98, 100–102, 106–7, 128, 133, 138
  as Messiah, 2, 107–9, 111, 113, 122, 132, 138–41
  as Savior, 137–38
  death of, 3, 8–14, 25–26, 31–32, 37, 53–57, 102, 115, 117–19
  portrayals of, 15–19, 41–42, 72
  teachings of, 10, 51–52, 57–58, 62, 67, 69, 117, 121, 133–35
Jewish New Testament, 3
Jewish scholars, 4, 8, 9
Jewish-Christian relations, 2, 15–16, 24, 139–41
Jews
  in Acts, 115–16
  blindness of, 43, 45
  and Book of Mormon peoples, 46–47
  continue in covenant, 42, 59–62
  convincing of Jesus, 2
  cursed, 8–9, 12
  Diaspora, 54
  expelled from covenant, 57–59, 114–15
  gathered, 1
  in John, 18–21, 41–42
  in Luke, 21–23
  in Mark, 21–23
  in Matthew, 14–18
  minority in Palestine, 54
  modern, 3, 72, 74, 77, 82, 85, 88, 90, 139–41
  in New Testament, 8–9, 92–95
  on trial, 9
  in Pauline epistles, 25
  Pharisees, 15–17
  pre-Captivity, 42–44
  relations with Christians, 2, 15–16, 24, 139–41
  replaced by Gentiles, 28–29, 32–34, 57–65
  responsible for Jesus's death, 3, 9, 11–14, 31–32, 53–57

stereotypes, 4, 25
subgroups of, 47–52
traditional practices of, 71–90
violence against, 9
wickedness of, 29–32
Jubilee, 110–11
Judas, 36, 51
Judea, 29–30, 33–34, 53, 56, 107, 115–16, 121, 132, 135

K–L

Keefer, Kyle, 29
L'shanah tovah tikatevu, 77
Laban, 44, 80, 83–84, 121
Laman, 46–48, 79, 83
Lamanites, 46–50, 57, 69–71, 96, 98, 108, 124, 131–32
Law of Moses, 19
  in Acts, 30–32, 114–15
  and appearance of Jesus, 103–9
  blessings of, 70–71
  and Communion, 99–102
  festivals, 73–90
  flouted by Lamanites, 47–48, 69,–71
  in John, 19–21, 71
  in Mark and Luke, 21–22
  in Matthew, 67
  necessity of Brass Plates, 46–47
  observed by Lamanites, 50, 71
  observed by Lehi, 68–69
  observed by Nephites, 46–47, 69–70
  portrayal of, 19–23
  receiving, 127–28
  relation to Messianic Era, 109–11
  replaced by Gospel of Jesus, 31, 90, 92–94, 98–99, 102, 105–6
  sabbaths, 109–11
  sacrifices fulfilled, 107
  and Sermon on the Mount, 93–97
  vibrant, 71–72, 91–92
Lehi, 43, 46–48, 62, 67–70, 75–85, 111, 120–23, 126, 132
Levine, Amy-Jill, 3, 9, 35

M

McKnight, Scot, 8
Messianic Era
  example of, 108–11
  Jesus to bring, 107–8, 138–39
  vision of, 5, 109, 111
Mormon, 40, 49, 64, 71, 108, 126, 129, 134, 141
Moroni (general), 65, 86, 128
Moroni (prophet), 42, 126, 129–30, 141
Mosaic goal, 98, 109
Moses, 14, 44, 46, 64, 68–69, 79–80, 94, 99, 102, 106–7, 109, 128
Mulekites, 62–65, 122, 132

N–O

Nephi (descendant of Nephi), 102
Nephi (son of Lehi), 41–47, 53, 61–62, 70, 78–79, 83–85, 88, 101, 106, 122–23, 126, 132–35, 140–41
Nephites, 47–52, 56–57, 63–64, 69–71, 95–99, 101–3, 106–8, 111, 123–24, 127, 129, 132–33, 138–39
Neusner, Jacob, 92
New Testament
  anti-Semitic structure of, 28–34, 118–19
  date of composition, 10
  connection to Book of Mormon, 40
  institution of Communion, 99–100
  peer of Book of Mormon, 4
new-perspective scholarship, 26–28
Nibley, Hugh, 64
Noah (king), 56–57, 64–65
Noah (prophet), 129
Nostra Aetate, 2–3, 10, 39, 137
Old Testament. *See* Hebrew Scriptures.

P–R

Passover, 8, 11, 20–22, 30–31, 72, 74, 85–91, 97, 99–100, 102–6, 109–11
Paul, 25, 27–30, 33–34, 58–61, 63, 65, 68, 105, 114, 116, 123–24, 131, 133

Subject Index

Pauline Epistles
  influence of Acts on, 29–30, 113–19
  portrayal of Jews, 25
  and supersessionism, 25–28, 34—35
Pentecost, 30–31, 74, 104, 117
Period of Judges, 127–28
Period of Kings, 127
Period of Origins, 129–30
Period of Prophets, 126–27
Period of Receiving the Law, 128
Pesach. *See* Passover.
Peter, 30–32, 104, 115, 117, 120, 133
Pharisees, 13–17, 19, 21–22, 25, 37–38, 45, 48–52, 58, 69, 72
  ancestors of rabbinic Jews, 13
Philip, 33, 116, 121–22
Pilate, 8–12, 20, 23, 31, 104
Plato, 114
pro-Judaism
  incidents, 125–30
  portrayals, 41–52
  statements, 4, 40–42
  use of word, ix
pro-Mosaic
  portrayals, 73–90
  settings, 91–109
rejectionism, 57–59, 65, 114–17, 125
Robinson, George, 74–75, 80–82, 87
Rosh Hashanah, 74–75
Ruether, Rosemary, 30, 117

S

sabbaths, 19–21, 47, 67, 70, 75, 81, 93, 109–11
sabbatical year, 110–11
Sacrament. *See* Communion.
Sadducees, 14, 16, 22, 45
Salmon, Marilyn, 11–12, 35, 37
Samaria, 29–30, 33, 115–16, 121
Samaritans, 12, 33, 116, 118
Samuel the Lamanite, 50
Sanders, E.P., 28
Sandmel, Samuel, 8, 9, 14, 16, 34, 54

scribes, 9, 14, 22, 45, 51, 96
Sermon on the Mount
  in Bountiful, 52, 95–97, 99, 107
  in Galilee, 17, 35, 51, 91–95, 111, 113
Shavuot, 73, 97–102, 105, 109–10
Shuler, Philip L., 92
Simchat Torah, 82–85, 90
Sinai, 30–31, 98–100
Smiga, George M., 8
Southern Baptist Convention, 3
Spong, John Shelby, 12, 35–36
Stendahl, Krister, 25, 28
Stephen, 32–33, 114–15, 118, 126–27, 130
Sukkot, 20, 71–73, 78–82, 85, 90–91, 97, 100, 109, 127
supersessionism, 5, 26–27, 34, 42, 45–46, 57, 59–60, 65, 73, 99–100, 113, 115, 119–20, 130–31, 137
Szink, Terrence L., 74

T–W

Ten Days of Repentance, 74–77
Tower of Babel, 64, 129
war against the Jews
  Christian, 2, 9, 18–19, 39–40, 135–41
  Roman, 12, 16, 23, 25, 117
Weiss-Rosmarin, Trude, 3, 7
Welch, John W., 74, 89, 97
Wilson, Marvin R., 16
World Council of Churches, 3
Wright, N. T., 28

Y–Z

Yom Kippur, 74, 76–78, 109
Zarahemla, 57, 63, 124, 132
Zealots, 45
Zeezrom, 50–51
Zeniffites, 56–57
Zenos, 44, 55, 59–61
Zion, 107–8, 139
Zoramites, 51–52

Also available from
GREG KOFFORD BOOKS

Beholding the Tree of Life: A Rabbinic Approach to the Book of Mormon

Bradley J. Kramer

Paperback, ISBN: 978-1-58958-701-4
Hardcover, ISBN: 978-1-58958-702-1

Too often readers approach the Book of Mormon simply as a collection of quotations, an inspired anthology to be scanned quickly and routinely recited. In Beholding the Tree of Life Bradley J. Kramer encourages his readers to slow down, to step back, and to contemplate the literary qualities of the Book of Mormon using interpretive techniques developed by Talmudic and post-Talmudic rabbis. Specifically, Kramer shows how to read the Book of Mormon closely, in levels, paying attention to the details of its expression as well as to its overall connection to the Hebrew Scriptures—all in order to better appreciate the beauty of the Book of Mormon and its limitless capacity to convey divine meaning.

Praise for *Authoring the Old Testament*:

"Latter-day Saints have claimed the Book of Mormon as the keystone of their religion, but it presents itself first and foremost as a Jewish narrative. *Beholding the Tree of Life* is the first book I have seen that attempts to situate the Book of Mormon by paying serious attention to its Jewish literary precedents and ways of reading scripture. It breaks fresh ground in numerous ways that enrich an LDS understanding of the scriptures and that builds bridges to a potential Jewish readership." — Terryl L. Givens, author of *By the Hand of Mormon: The American Scripture that Launched a New World Religion*

"Bradley Kramer has done what someone ought to have done long ago, used the methods of Jewish scripture interpretation to look closely at the Book of Mormon. Kramer has taken the time and put in the effort required to learn those methods from Jewish teachers. He explains what he has learned clearly and carefully. And then he shows us the fruit of that learning by applying it to the Book of Mormon. The results are not only interesting, they are inspiring. This is one of those books that, on reading it, I thought 'I wish I'd written that!'" — James E. Faulconer, author of *The Book of Mormon Made Harder* and *Faith, Philosophy, Scripture*

Authoring the Old Testament: Genesis–Deuteronomy

David Bokovoy

Paperback, ISBN: 978-1-58958-588-1
Hardcover, ISBN: 978-1-58958-675-8

For the last two centuries, biblical scholars have made discoveries and insights about the Old Testament that have greatly changed the way in which the authorship of these ancient scriptures has been understood. In the first of three volumes spanning the entire Hebrew Bible, David Bokovoy dives into the Pentateuch, showing how and why textual criticism has led biblical scholars today to understand the first five books of the Bible as an amalgamation of multiple texts into a single, though often complicated narrative; and he discusses what implications those have for Latter-day Saint understandings of the Bible and modern scripture.

Praise for *Authoring the Old Testament*:

"*Authoring the Old Testament* is a welcome introduction, from a faithful Latter-day Saint perspective, to the academic world of Higher Criticism of the Hebrew Bible.... [R]eaders will be positively served and firmly impressed by the many strengths of this book, coupled with Bokovoy's genuine dedication to learning by study and also by faith." — John W. Welch, editor, *BYU Studies Quarterly*

"Bokovoy provides a lucid, insightful lens through which disciple-students can study intelligently LDS scripture. This is first rate scholarship made accessible to a broad audience—nourishing to the heart and mind alike." — Fiona Givens, co-author, *The God Who Weeps: How Mormonism Makes Sense of Life*

"I repeat: this is one of the most important books on Mormon scripture to be published recently.... [*Authoring the Old Testament*] has the potential to radically expand understanding and appreciation for not only the Old Testament, but scripture in general. It's really that good. Read it. Share it with your friends. Discuss it." — David Tayman, The Improvement Era: A Mormon Blog

Traditions of the Fathers: The Book of Mormon as History

Brant A. Gardner

ISBN: 978-1-58958-665-9

**2015 Best Religious Non-fiction Award
by the Association for Mormon Letters**

"In the study of historical texts, context is king. Traditions of the Fathers masterfully contextualizes the diverse peoples of the Book of Mormon as they move, merge, and multiply across the Mesoamerican landscape. More than a simple lens, Gardner's multidisciplinary approach provides readers with illuminating, prismatic views of the Book of Mormon." — Mark Alan Wright, Assistant Professor of Ancient Scripture at Brigham Young University and Associate Editor of the *Journal of Book of Mormon Studies*

"The work he has done is rich, thorough, provocative. Like all Kofford books, this one is attractively produced, easy to hold in the hands and easy on the eyes. But best of all, it's informative, cogent, and altogether worth reading. I recommend it." — Julie J. Nichols, Association for Mormon Letters

As Iron Sharpens Iron: Listening to the Various Voices of Scripture

Julie M. Smith

Paperback, ISBN: 978-1-58958-501-0

**2016 Best Religious Non-fiction Award,
Association for Mormon Letters**

Our scripture study and reading often assume that the prophetic figures within the texts are in complete agreement with each other. Because of this we can fail to recognize that those authors and personalities frequently have different—and sometimes competing—views on some of the most important doctrines of the Gospel, including the nature of God, the roles of scripture and prophecy, and the Atonement.

In this unique volume, fictionalized dialogues between the various voices of scripture illustrate how these differences and disagreements are not flaws of the texts but are rather essential features of the canon. These creative dialogues include Abraham and Job debating the utility of suffering and our submission to God, Alma and Abinidi disagreeing on the place of justice in the Atonement, and the authors Mark and Luke discussing the role of women in Jesus's ministry. It is by examining and embracing the different perspectives within the canon that readers are able to discover just how rich and invigorating the scriptures can be. The dialogues within this volume show how just as "iron sharpeneth iron," so can we sharpen our own thoughts and beliefs as we engage not just the various voices in the scriptures but also the various voices within our community (Proverbs 27:17).

Made in the USA
Columbia, SC
11 September 2019